PENGUIN BUSINESS LIBRARY

The Money Machine

After being educated at Sidney Sussex College, Cambridge, Philip Coggan became Assistant Editor of *Euromoney Currency Report* and *Euromoney Corporate Finance*. He has edited two books, *Currency Options* and *Foreign Exchange Management*, for Gee & Co. He is now a journalist for the *Financial Times*.

Philip Coggan

The Money Machine

How the City Works

Penguin Books

Penguin Books Ltd, Harmondsworth, Middlesex, England
Viking Penguin Inc., 40 West 23rd Street, New York, New York 10010, U.S.A.
Penguin Books Australia Ltd, Ringwood, Victoria, Australia
Penguin Books Canada Limited, 2801 John Street, Markham, Ontario, Canada L3R 1B4
Penguin Books (N.Z.) Ltd, 182–190 Wairau Road, Auckland 10, New Zealand

First published 1986

Made and printed in Great Britain by
Richard Clay Ltd, Bungay, Suffolk
Filmset in Monophoto Times

To Churchy

Contents

Acknowledgements

A book covering such a wide field could not be produced without the help and advice of many people. First and foremost, I would like to thank Nick Shepherd and Diane Pengelly for reading through all the chapters and pointing out the numerous grammatical errors and non-sensical statements. Many others read through individual chapters: my father, Ken Ferris, John Presland, David Bowen, Clifford German, Paul and Vanessa Gilbert, Lynton Jones, David Morrison and Nigel Falls, and I thank them for their helpful comments. All mistakes are, of course, mine and not theirs. A distinguished mention should be given to Mr Alan Michael Sugar for bringing out his Amstrad word-processor at just the right time and price to allow me to benefit. Last but not least, I thank Churchy for all the help in typing and for putting up with the sight of my back as I slaved away on the manuscript.

P.C.
March 1986

Introduction

Finance has always been presented as a very complex and rather boring subject, understood only by a few men in pinstripe suits. The City has traditionally been viewed with suspicion by the political left and with wide-eyed awe by the right. There is something about financiers that attracts either disgust or hero worship. Men like Jim Slater, the financial whizzkid of the early 1970s, have their every word treated as holy writ one year and face disgrace and opprobrium the next.

In fact, the world of finance is not as complex, nor the financiers as expert, as they like to pretend. As recently as 1984 the bank Johnson Matthey went bust. It was found that the bank had lent 115 per cent of its capital to two foreign businessmen, when the Bank of England recommendation was that no more than 10 per cent should be lent to any one borrower. It was a mistake forgivable perhaps in a schoolboy but incomprehensible in a major financial institution, and it led to allegations of fraud in the House of Commons. The incident was merely the latest in a long series of cases of financial fraud and mismanagement dating back to the South Sea Bubble in the eighteenth century.

Yet the myth of the infallibility of the man in the pinstripe suit lives on. It is a self-perpetuating myth because too few people attempt to understand the workings of the financial system. Although the details of individual financial deals can be very complex, there are basic principles in finance which everyone can understand and which apply as much to the finances of Mr Smith, the grocer, as to Barclays Bank. The more fully people understand these principles, the more they will be able and willing to criticize, and perhaps even participate in, the workings of the financial system. Like all areas of public life, it needs criticism to ensure its efficiency.

The City's efficiency is important to everyone because of the role which it plays in the economy. In 1984 nearly 2 million people were employed in the financial services sector, around 8 per cent of the total workforce. The City's income was £22 billion that year, about 7.5 per cent of national income, of which £6 billion came from overseas. It is hoped that the series of changes now taking place in the City, collectively known as the 'Big Bang' (see Chapter 2), will boost the City's income and job-creating ability. But if the 'Big Bang' fails to work and the City loses its place in the world financial system, the jobs and income currently provided by the City might disappear.

The City

First of all, what is the role of the UK financial system, and in particular of the City of London, which is at its heart?

Its primary function is to put people who want to lend (invest) in touch with people who want to borrow. A simple example of this role is that of the building societies. They collect the small savings of individuals and lend them to house buyers who want mortgages.

Why do the savers not just lend directly to borrowers, without the intervention of financial institutions? The main reason is that their needs are not compatible with those of the end borrowers. People with mortgages, for example, want to borrow for at least twenty-five years. Savers may want to withdraw their money next week. In addition, the amounts needed are dissimilar. Companies and governments need to borrow amounts far beyond the resources of most individuals. Only by bundling together all the savings of many individuals can the financial institutions provide funds on an appropriate scale.

Who are the borrowers? One prominent set is industrial companies. Companies will always need money to pay for raw materials, buildings, machinery and wages before they can generate their own revenues by selling their goods or services. To cover the period before the cash flows in, companies borrow, either from the banks or through The Stock Exchange in the form of shares. Without this borrowing it would be impossible for companies to invest and for the economy to expand.

The second major set of borrowers is governments. No matter what their claims to fiscal rectitude, few governments have ever managed to avoid spending more than they receive. The UK government and other nations' governments come to the City to cover the difference.

Who wants to lend? In general, the only part of the economy which is a net saver (i.e. its savings are greater than its borrowings) is the personal sector – individuals like you and me. Rarely do we lend directly to the government or industry or other individuals: instead we save, either through the medium of banks and building societies or, in a more planned way, through pension and life assurance schemes. Lending, saving and investing are thus different ways of looking at the same activity.

So financial institutions are there to channel the funds of those who want to lend into the hands of those who want to borrow. They take their cut as middle men. That cut can come in two forms: banks can charge a higher interest rate to the people to whom they lend than they pay to the people from whom they borrow, or they can simply charge a fee for bringing lender and borrower together.

There is no doubt that financial institutions perform an immensely valuable service: imagine life without cheque books, cashpoint cards, mortgages and hire-purchase agreements. Although by tradition a large percentage of Britons do not have a bank account, they would never be paid if the companies for which they work did not have one. Indeed, the companies might not have been founded without loans from banks.

It is important, when considering some of the practices discussed in this book, to remember that the business of financial institutions is the handling of money. Some of their more esoteric activities, like financial futures, can appear to the observer to be mere speculation. But speculation is an unavoidable part of the world of financial institutions. They must speculate, when they borrow at one rate, that they will be able to lend at a higher rate. They must speculate that the companies to whom they lend will not go bust. To criticize the mechanisms by which they do speculate is to ignore the basic facts of financial life.

Financial institutions are a vital part of the British economy. Whether the rewards they receive are in keeping with the importance of the part they play is another question, which we will examine in the final chapter.

The Institutions

The most prominent financial institutions are the banks, which can be divided roughly into two groups, commercial (retail) and merchant (investment) banks. The former rely on the deposits drawn from ordinary individuals, on which they pay little or no interest and which they re-lend at a profit. Commercial banks must ensure that they have enough money to repay their customers, so their investments tend to be short-term. The latter group relies more on fees earned from arranging complicated financing deals. Both groups are examined in Chapter 4.

The second group of financial institutions, known as the investment institutions, include the pension funds and life insurance companies. They bundle together the monthly savings of individuals and invest them in a range of assets, including British and overseas industry and commercial property. This is a vital function, since industry needs long-term funds to expand. Banks also lend to industry, but by tradition they have been less ready to lend for long periods. Pension funds can count on regular contributions and can normally calculate in advance when and how much they will have to pay out to claimants. Life insurance companies have the laws of actuarial probabilities to help them calculate their likely outgoings.

The third main group is the exchanges, which form a market for the trading of the various forms of debt issued by those who need to borrow. If debt can be traded, people and institutions are more willing to lend money because they can reclaim their funds if the need arises. The best-known exchange in the UK is The Stock Exchange.

Within and outside these groups is a host of institutions which perform specialized functions. The building societies have already been mentioned, but we will also need to look at the Bank of England, discount houses and brokers, to name but a few.

The Instruments

Chapter 3 examines in detail questions about the definition of money and the determination of interest rates. But for the moment the best way to understand the workings of the financial system is to stop thinking of money as a homogeneous commodity and instead to think of notes and coins as constituting one of a range of financial assets. It is the *liquidity* of those assets that distinguishes them from each other. The liquidity of an asset is judged by the speed with which it can be exchanged for goods without financial loss.

Notes and coins are easily the most liquid because they can be traded immediately for goods. At the opposite extreme is a long-term loan, which may not be repaid for twenty-five years. Between the two extremes are various financial assets which have grown up in response to the needs of the individuals and institutions that take part in the financial markets.

Essentially, financial instruments can be divided into three types: *loans*, *bonds* and *equities*.

Loans are the simplest to understand. One party agrees to lend another money in return for a payment called *interest*, normally quoted as an annual rate. It is possible, as in the case of most mortgages or hire-purchase agreements, for the principal sum (that is, the original amount borrowed) to be paid back in instalments with the interest. Alternatively, the principal sum can be paid back in one lump at the end of the agreed term.

Bonds are pieces of paper like IOUs, which borrowers issue in return for a loan and which are bought by investors, who can sell them to other parties as and when they choose. Bonds are normally medium- to long-term (between five and twenty-five years) in duration. The period for which a loan or bond lasts is normally known as its *maturity*, and the interest rate a bond pays is called the *coupon*. Shorter-term bonds (lasting three months or so) are generally known as *bills*.

Equities are issued only by companies and offer a share in the assets of the firm, which has led to their being given the more common name of *shares*. They differ from other financial instruments in that they confer ownership of something more than just a piece of paper. In the financial sense, shareholders *are* the company, whereas bondholders are merely outside creditors.

The initial capital invested in shares will rarely be repaid unless the company folds up. (But shares, like bonds, can be sold to other investors.) The company will generally announce a semi-annual dividend (a sum payable to each shareholder as a proportion of the profit), depending on the size of its profits. All ordinary shareholders will receive that dividend. However, if the company makes only a small profit or a loss, the company need not issue a dividend.

Because of this risk, investors normally demand a higher return than lenders or bondholders before investing in shares. That brings us to one of the most important principles in finance. *Greater risk demands greater reward.* If a lender is dubious about whether a borrower will be able to repay the loan, he or she will charge a higher rate on that loan. Why lend money at 10 per cent to a bad risk when you can lend money at 10 per cent to a good risk and be sure that your money will be returned with interest?

Alchemy

Financial institutions must perform a feat of alchemy. They must transform the cash savings of ordinary depositors, who may want to withdraw their money at any moment, into funds which industry can borrow for twenty-five years or more. This process involves risk – the risk that the funds will be withdrawn before the institutions' investments mature. They must therefore charge more for tying up their money for long periods, so that they can offset that risk. This brings us to a second important principle of finance. *Lesser liquidity demands greater reward.* The longer an investor must hold an asset before being sure of achieving a return, the larger he will expect that return to be. However, in Chapter 3 we shall see how, for a variety of reasons, long-term interest rates can often be below short-term rates.

The range of financial assets extends from cash to long-term loans. Cash, the most liquid of assets, gives no return at all. A building society account that can be withdrawn without notice might give a return of, say, 10 per cent. In the circumstances, why should lenders make a twenty-five-year loan at less than 10 per cent? They would be incurring an unnecessary risk for no reward. So lenders generally demand a greater return to compensate them for locking up their money for a long period. In the same way some banks and building societies offer higher-interest accounts to those who agree to give ninety days' notice before withdrawal. The borrowers (in this case, the banks and building societies) are willing to pay more for the certainty of retaining the funds.

Bonds and shares are usually liquid in the sense that they can be sold, but the seller has no guarantee of the price that he or she will receive for them. This differentiates them from savings accounts, which guarantee the return of the capital invested. Thus bond- and shareholders will generally demand a higher return. For both, that extra return may come through an increase in the price of the investment rather than through a high interest rate or dividend. This applies especially to shares. As a consequence, the dividends paid on shares are often, in percentage terms, well below the dividends paid on bonds such as gilts (highly reliable investments because they are issued by the UK government).

There is another group of financial instruments, which confers the right to buy or sell another instrument. In this category are options, futures and warrants. They allow two important activities, *hedging* and *leverage*.

Hedging is the process whereby an institution buys or sells a financial instrument in order to offset the risk that the price of another financial instrument or commodity may rise or fall. For example, coffee importers buy coffee futures to reduce the risk that a rise in commodity prices will cut their profits.

Leverage gives the investor an opportunity for a large profit with a small stake. Options, futures and warrants all provide the chance of leverage because their prices vary more sharply than those of the underlying commodities to which they are linked. These concepts are more fully explained in Chapters 13 and 14.

The City's International Role

The City, of course, plays a role that far exceeds the dimensions of the national economy. It is this role that the supporters of the City invoke when they defend its actions and its privileges. And it is to preserve this role that the City is undergoing so many changes at the moment.

In the nineteenth century the City's importance in world financial markets reflected the way in which Britannia ruled the waves. Britain financed the development of Argentinian and North American railways, for example. By 1914 Britain owned an enormous range of foreign assets, which brought it a steady overseas income. Much of the world's trade was conducted in sterling because it was a respected and valued currency.

The two world wars ended Britain's financial predominance. Foreign assets were repatriated to pay for the fighting. As the Empire disintegrated, so too did the world's use of sterling as a trading instrument. Just as the USA emerged as the world's biggest economic power, so New York challenged London for the market in financial services and the dollar took over from sterling as the major trading currency. It seemed that Britain and the City would become backwaters on the edge of Europe.

One thing saved the City. The USA, which had regarded banks with suspicion since the Great Crash of 1929, did not welcome the growth of New York as a financial centre. The US authorities began to place restrictions on the activities of its banks and investors. International business began to flow back to London, where there were fewer restrictions. The Euromarket (see Chapter 11) grew into the most important capital market in the world and made London its base.

The revival of the City has brought many foreign banks to London and a steady stream of income. But other centres are hoping to increase their share of the world financial markets. New York, in particular, has abandoned some of the restrictions and is challenging London again. If London is to keep its place as the major centre of the international capital markets, it must change some of its practices to suit the new financial techniques which are sweeping the world.

It is best that we look at these changes before we examine in detail the workings of the UK financial system. Discussion of these changes requires an assumption of some knowledge on the part of the reader as to how the system works. However, this book is also designed to be read by those who know little of finance. They may well want to start at Chapter 3 and return to the first two chapters after they have read the rest.

[1] The International Financial Revolution

The world's financial markets are undergoing a revolution. Indeed, perhaps for the first time it is possible to speak of a *single* world financial market. U K investors can now put their money into Japanese shares and into bonds issued by the U S government as easily as they can invest in British companies like I C I or Cadbury Schweppes. They can pick up the telephone at night and sell those shares in Tokyo or New York, even though they may have been purchased in London or Frankfurt. In the same way U K companies looking for funds to finance their expansion can turn to investors in Switzerland or West Germany as readily as to those in Birmingham or Manchester.

A strange combination of factors – the aftermath of the 1973 debt crisis, advances in information technology and the disappearance of regulatory barriers to capital flows – has spurred these changes.

Financial markets now exist virtually independently of national boundaries and governmental regulations. As a result, funds can flow with incredible speed out of one currency or country and into another. Financial crises can spring up in minutes, and governments which fail to heed the interests of international investors can quickly find their currencies and foreign-exchange reserves suffering as a result. In today's market an independent economic policy is very difficult to follow, as President Mitterrand found in the early days of his administration in 1982–3. France attempted to expand its economy at a time when the rest of the world was restricting demand and money supply; the result was a deteriorating balance of payments and speculation against the franc in the foreign-exchange markets. It proved impossible to defend the franc, and Mitterand was forced to reverse his policies.

Countries in the Western bloc can isolate themselves from these outside influences only by installing a 'siege economy' of harsh import and capital controls. The U K has always been both a trading nation and a financial centre – it would take a radical change of policy indeed to allow it to escape the consequences of these developments. Instead it has been forced to adapt its policies and practices in an effort to maintain the City's international financial role.

The Failure of Regulation

Banking authorities around the world attempted in the late 1960s and 1970s to regulate the new international capital market, known as the Euromarket (see Chapter 11) – but they failed. There was always some offshore centre which had few regulatory scruples and therefore attracted the international financiers. Rather than continue the unequal struggle, the supervisors decided to repeal their own regulations and bring the financial markets back home. They therefore lifted restrictions on interest-rate levels, repealed taxes on foreign investments and encouraged the entry of foreign banks into their markets. This process was most noticeable in the U S A, where the Reagan administration permitted the creation of International Banking Facilities (a sort of on-shore tax haven) and repealed the withholding tax on investment in foreign bonds.

The result was that the old division between a Euromarket, centred in London, and the U S market, centred in New York, began to break down. It was now possible for borrowers to make a realistic choice between raising money in New York or in London. Even Tokyo joined in the trend as financial barriers were dismantled in response to American pressure. The Americans believed that restrictions on the international use of the yen had led to the currency being too low against the dollar, with the result that Japanese goods abroad were cheaper than their American counterparts.

The opening of the New York and Tokyo markets has created great problems for London. Both its rivals have built-in advantages as financial centres. The American economy is by far the biggest in the world and contains most of the world's largest companies. The turnover in its domestic financial markets is consequently large enough to handle the world's business. If the American economy is the biggest in the world, the Japanese economy is probably the most dynamic. Thanks to its astonishing exports record, Japan has accumulated trade surpluses which make it the world's largest net investor. Companies and governments with large borrowing needs are eager to reach Japanese investors.

By comparison, London's attractions seem flimsier. Traditionally there have been fewer regulatory restrictions on the London market, but that comparative advantage is disappearing. The UK economy is neither big nor dynamic, and its domestic financial markets (as opposed to the international market based in London) are small by the standards of New York and Tokyo. However, London can offer two distinct advantages to financial dealers: first, because of its geographical position it has a dealing day during which bankers can speak to both New York and Tokyo; secondly, it can offer the English language, the medium through which international financial deals are transacted.

If the changes in world financial markets were confined to greater freedom of capital movement, London's competitive problems would still be large enough. But financial institutions and the instruments in which they trade have also been affected. To understand the reasons for those changes we must go back to the oil crisis of 1973 and its aftermath.

The OPEC Surplus

The oil crisis of 1973 sent a tidal wave through the world economic system, and we are still experiencing the resulting choppy seas. The financial institutions rode the wave for several years, but many fear they may yet get swamped.

After the oil shock the Organization of Petroleum Exporting Countries (OPEC) nations found themselves suddenly wealthy. Thanks to the quadrupling of oil prices in less than a year, the OPEC countries' wealth far exceeded their ability to spend it. The natural place for them to deposit the surplus was with the Western banks, and particularly in the Euromarket in London.

In effect, the oil surplus was transferred to the banks. They in turn, looked for borrowers to whom to lend the money. Third World and Eastern Europe countries were desperate to expand their economies and thus eager and willing to borrow. They were also prepared to pay interest rates well above those to which the industrialized nations would agree. Some had oil of their own, which encouraged their hopes of expansion. The Arab countries had vast revenues but small populations: other oil-producing countries (like Mexico and Nigeria) had large populations keen to take advantage of the oil boom. Worst placed of all were those countries which had no oil of their own but needed to borrow to pay for their oil imports.

The banks were prepared to lend money to the governments of the developing countries because they reasoned that sovereign states were unlikely to default on their loans. In any case, the banks argued, the rates of growth of most of these economies would easily enable them to pay back the money.

The result was an explosion in the syndicated loan market, where banks clubbed together to lend large amounts to a single borrower. Loans were the chosen instrument because the developing nations were unable to raise money by issuing bonds as many had defaulted on the issues they made during the 1930s. As a result, investors were unwilling to buy their bonds.

It did seem that banks were performing an extremely useful function in the world economy – smoothing out the effects of the oil crisis in transferring the oil surplus to those nations hit hardest by the oil shock. Governments encouraged the banks in this 'recycling' role. And in the late 1970s all seemed to be going well. The world economies, and in particular those of the debtor nations, were growing fast. Yet more money was lent on the strength of the faster growth. Between 1973 and 1982 Third World debt rose from $130 billion to $612 billion.

Banks competed very hard for the new loan business. Finance is a field much subject to fashion, and in the 1970s the fashion was for asset growth. Banks' assets are not, as one might think, the deposits they obtain from customers: those are *liabilities*, since they must be repaid. Assets are the *loans* that banks make. So the banks were as eager to lend (and to expand their assets) as the Third World nations were to borrow. It was a profitable relationship for both sides – for a time.

The Debt Crisis

The second oil shock of 1979 ruined the debtor nations' hopes of growth. Rather than expand their economies to counteract the effect of the oil-price rise, the industrialized economies contracted to try to limit its inflationary effects. The world went into recession. With their export markets stagnating, the debtor nations failed to maintain the growth records that they needed to repay their borrowings.

At the same time the Western nations increased interest rates in an attempt to prevent a rise in borrowing (which they believed would cause inflation) in their economies. Much of the Third World debt was in the form of loans on which the interest payments were linked to market rates. The result was an increase in the costs of repayment at the very time when the debtor nations were becoming less able to pay. It soon became apparent that some debtor nations would be unable to repay the capital, and possibly even the interest, of their loans.

As Lever and Huhne point out, the growth in Third World borrowing was possibly only because it took place on the explicit assumption that old loans would be repaid with new borrowings.* But by the early 1980s, the banks had become uneasy about their exposure to Third World borrowers and had started to shorten the maturity of their loans. The effect was that the date of repayment grew ever closer. Something had to give, and the day of reckoning came when in 1982 Mexico announced the suspension of its debt repayments.

At this point an ancient law came into play. If you owe someone £5, you are in his power. If you owe him £1 million, he is in your power. The prospect of a major debtor defaulting on its loans was a nightmare for the banks. It was very difficult to imagine how a bank could force a country to repay its borrowings, and the negotiators of the debtor governments showed themselves very aware of that fact. The banks had collectively committed so much money in the form of loans to the developing nations that the collapse of those nations would have caused chaos in the financial system. However, it is impossible to trade without credit, and if a country does default, it finds itself ostracized from world trade and facing financial ruin. So the negotiations between the representatives of the Western banks and those of the debtor countries proved to be tough games of financial poker as each side tried to outface the other.

Peering nervously over the shoulders of the banks were the Western nations. The collapse of their banks could have ushered in a depression on the scale of the 1930s. The governments were thus committed to supporting the banks, but it was not easy to see how the problem could be solved. In some countries repayment of just the interest on their debts required the equivalent of an entire year's export earnings.

* Harold Lever and Christopher Huhne, *Debt and Danger* (Penguin, 1985).

The Role of the IMF

At this point a supranational champion of the banks came on to the scene – the International Monetary Fund (IMF). Banks did agree to a certain amount of *rescheduling* of debts – repayment over a slightly longer period or the postponement of interest payments. But they proved unable or unwilling to lend the debtor countries all the money they needed to repay their loans. Net lending to the developing countries halved every year between 1979 and 1983. The IMF seemed to be the only possible source of new loans for the debtor countries.

The Fund was set up at the end of the Second World War with funds from the member countries, with the aim of being lender of last resort to countries with balance-of-payments problems. Under the rules of the IMF countries can borrow up to a certain quota, depending on the amount of funds they contribute.

However, should countries wish to borrow funds beyond their quotas, the terms of the IMF are harsh. It usually insists on changes in economic policy to create the conditions for loan repayment. Those changes almost always involve deflationary policies – cuts in public spending, imports, devaluation of the currency and reduced wages. Such policies are unpopular with the electorates of the countries concerned, and oppositions are quick to stir up resentment of the IMF. Indeed, the IMF has imposed the same conditions on so many countries that it has become possible to argue that its recommendations are self-defeating. It is not possible for *all* countries to cut back on their imports and increase their exports at the same time.

The problem of Third World debt seemed most acute in 1982. After that year the US economy moved into top gear and started to pull the rest of the world out of recession. Economic growth helped the developing countries to increase their exports, thus giving them funds to pay off their debts. At the same time US interest rates fell, reducing the costs of debt services.

However, the debt crisis has not gone away. If the world economy were to slow down, the problem would again become acute. The US monetary authority, the Federal Reserve, has shown itself very conscious of the effects that high interest rates might have on the debtor countries and, through them, on the banks. It has striven to perform the difficult balancing act of keeping interest rates down while avoiding the risk of inflation.

Lever and Huhne argue that the current situation is perverse.* Banks no longer lend to the debtor nations. The debtors must further reduce the incomes of their already poor populations in order to repay the old loans. The effect is that the wealth of poor nations is being transferred to the rich nations. Such a process can only harm the world economy. The crisis can be solved, according to this analysis, only if the banks resume their lending to the debtors and if the regulators agree to underwrite those new loans.

In 1985, at an IMF meeting in South Korea, US Treasury Secretary James Baker came up with a new plan for solving the debt crisis. He called for commercial banks to lend a further $20 billion to the debtor nations and also called on the World Bank to assume part of the IMF's role as crisis lender. The World Bank had previously acted as lender mainly to specific Third World development projects, such as dam construction and land reclamation. One of the problems with the Baker plan was that it seemed to conflict with the aims of the banking supervisory authorities. They were arguing that the banks should reduce the amount of Third World loans on their books, since they were already over-committed in that area.

The debt crisis has brought to the surface an issue which has never been entirely submerged: to whom are the banks responsible? The banks claim that their remit is to make a profit for their shareholders. But what about their responsibility to their depositors, who may not want to see their money lent to Brazil, Mexico or South Africa? And what about their responsibility to the general public, whose economic well-being depends on a healthy financial system and who may be required to save the banks with their taxes if the banks get into trouble?

Thanks to the crisis, the status of financial institutions and their methods of operation have changed dramatically. The next two sections of this chapter describe two main themes of these changes.

Securitization

The Americans control the language of finance and thus the coining of new financial jargon. The rather daunting word *securitization* is one such piece of jargon. It refers to the process whereby untradeable assets become tradeable. Borrowers, instead of raising money through direct

* Lever and Huhne, *Debt and Danger*.

loans from banks, sell pieces of paper (securities) that grant the buyers both the right to receive interest and full repayment. They can then sell those pieces of paper to other investors if they wish.

The process of securitization began as banks withdrew from the troublesome loan commitments that they had made in the run-up to the debt crisis. Regulatory authorities added their own contribution. They were concerned that banks' assets (the loans they had made) had expanded far more quickly than their capital. The regulators asked banks to increase their capital base. The two most obvious ways of doing so were to issue shares (equity) and perpetual bonds (near-equity). The problem with the former was that the price of bank shares was very low because of the banks' credit problems. That made issuing shares an expensive means of finance. The same applied to bond issues – investors would demand high returns to accept the amount of debt that the banks were required to issue.

So the banks followed a different route to increasing their capital – improving profits. They did so by turning to fee-income products, like the arrangement of bond and share issues, rather than pursuing their loan business. Fee-income products have traditionally been the province of merchant (investment) banks. There was therefore a scramble among the commercial banks to develop their investment-banking subsidiaries. Competition to arrange issues became fierce and drove down the fees paid by borrowers.

To sustain their fee income banks needed to increase their range of products and the frequency with which they were traded. If the banks could take a cut every time a financial instrument was traded through them, they could earn the same amount of income from a larger number of transactions.

Among the new techniques that banks developed were the arrangement of swaps and the underwriting of Euronotes. Both are explained in detail later in the book (see pp. 167 and 149). Their distinguishing characteristics are that they are off-balance-sheet activities which increase profits without affecting the size of banks' assets. Regulatory authorities have become concerned about the growth in their use because they make it hard to assess banks' potential liabilities in times of financial crisis.

In addition to new debt instruments like Euronotes, banks developed a host of products to deal with interest and foreign-exchange risk. Both risks have increased in the 1980s as interest and exchange rates have moved more sharply and more often. Banks have constructed products which offer to lock in an exchange or interest rate in return for a fee (see Chapters 13 and 14).

Another aspect of securitization has been the bundling together of assets, like mortgages or hire-purchase agreements, into tradeable forms. Bonds can now be issued with home mortgages or car-hire agreements as their security. If the issuer fails to repay the loan or the interest, the bond buyer can take over as the recipient of the funds from the home or car buyers whose payments backed the issue. This is of particular help to financial institutions like the U S savings and loan associations (the U S equivalent of British building societies). Again the idea is to increase the liquidity of financial assets and thereby to strengthen the financial institutions which hold them.

Is Securitization a Solution?

Securitization has the ultimate aim of increasing the liquidity of banks' portfolios and thereby decreasing the risk of a chain reaction of default. However, Sir Christopher McMahon, former Deputy Governor of the Bank of England, argued in a speech in 1985 that in times of financial crisis the marketability of securities could be an illusion. Why should another investor buy the bond of a company in trouble? McMahon also argued that borrowers who depended heavily on securities-based finance might find it hard to restructure their borrowings in times of crisis. Unlike ordinary lending, securities finance is not based on a trusting relationship between borrower and lender, and lenders may therefore be less willing to stand behind borrowers when things go wrong.

It seems clear that securitization will not solve the problem of the fragility of the banking system. Only when banks ensure that they are not over-exposed to the default of a single borrower will the system be strengthened. Even then banks will be safeguarded only against minor rather than major shocks. If a major borrower like Brazil decides not to repay its debts – which amounted in 1985 to over $100 billion – the effects on the financial system would be catastrophic, whether those debts are in the form of loans or of bonds.

Disintermediation

Whatever the benefits which securitization may bring, many banks are still saddled, thanks to the debt crisis, with loans that may never be repaid. That fact alone has prompted talk of another development in the financial markets – *disintermediation*. What this means is that corporations have begun to realize that they do not need the banks to act as intermediaries. They can borrow direct from other companies or institutional investors, and the adverse effect of the debt crisis on the image of the banks in the eyes of investors means that many corporations can borrow at lower rates than can the banks.

Banks must charge a rate which covers at least the amount they pay for receiving their funds, otherwise they will make a loss. Thus they must charge the corporations a higher rate than their superior credit rating would warrant. When the corporations go elsewhere for funds, the banks are left with those with poorer credit ratings as potential clients. In the context of the debt crisis this is not an attractive proposition for the banks.

To sum up, long-term borrowing is now concentrated more on securities than on loans. Banks have turned to earning fees by offering securities to investors on the companies' behalf rather than channelling the funds through their own books. This activity belonged traditionally to the realm of broking (linking buyers and sellers) rather than banking.

Challenges to the Banks

Banks deal exclusively in financial products. However, some multinational companies are so large and have such frequent involvement with the financial markets that they have been able to develop in-house banks (for example, Volvo and Fiat). They lend money to their subsidiaries, use their own specialists to advise them on corporate acquisitions and deal on equal terms with the major banks. There is nothing new in the idea – after all, that is how the merchant banks developed in the UK.

The banks are threatened by more than the multinational corporations. They are also worried by competition from other financial institutions and from department stores. In the UK the biggest threat to the banks has come from building societies (see Chapter 7). With branches in the high streets of most towns, and with a tradition of attracting a significant proportion of the savings of small investors, the building societies have been seeking to extend and develop their role. Some now offer cheque facilities and cashpoint services: one society, the Nottingham, has taken an imaginative leap forward by linking up with a computer firm to offer a home-banking service for customers with personal computers. Banks have responded by attacking the societies on their home territory, the mortgage market. As the two groups grow closer and closer in activity, many now believe that they should have equivalent regulatory and taxation positions.

The challenge of the department stores is rather different. They have large numbers of customers who deal with them on a regular basis. Often customers will buy goods on credit. It has occurred to some stores that their contacts and their knowledge of the creditworthiness of their customers give them scope to offer some financial services.

In the USA Sears Roebuck has led the charge, thanks to the success of its own credit card, which is used by a formidable number of customers. The card gives it the chance to persuade customers to use other financial services and also allows it to make substantial profits from the interest charged on the balances outstanding. Sears has emphasized its commitment to the financial services market by buying a US investment bank, Dean Witter. In the UK the leading store in the field is Marks and Spencer, which has developed its own credit card, followed recently by Debenhams, with its Welbeck Finance subsidiary.

It should not be difficult for the stores to expand their financial range by offering customers life assurance schemes and perhaps consumer loans. Another potential development is the brokerage shop, in which stores would link up with banks to provide financial advice and share-dealing facilities. Whether the British public will warm to the chance of buying ICI shares with their cornflakes is open to question. Similar schemes have had success in the USA, but that country has a much wider spread of share ownership.

The Effect of New Technology

There is another (unconnected) way in which the fortunes of banks and retailers are tied together – EFTPOS, which stands for Electronic Funds Transfer at Point of Sale. The idea is simple. When you check out at Sainsbury, Tesco or even Harrods, instead of paying with cash or a cheque you hand the cashier a card with a special electronic code. When the right numbers are keyed into the machine it automatically debits your account and credits the store with the amount of the bill.

The banks will benefit from EFTPOS because they will no longer have to process through their books thousands of cheques for relatively small amounts – an extremely costly exercise. Retailers will gain because the system will allow them to deal with a greater volume of customers as the queues at check-outs shorten. Shops will also be paid immediately through the EFTPOS system rather than being forced to wait three days for cheques to clear. In addition, they will need to keep less cash on their premises, reducing the risks of robbery. However, the costs of EFTPOS will be high. Terminals must be installed in every shop and computer software devised to prevent fraud.

Who will pay for EFTPOS? Banks and retailers are arguing about the costs, but both will pass on any cost to the consumer. Most consumers are likely to perceive little benefit from EFTPOS. They can use automated teller machines to make cash withdrawals and payments at no cost. Payment by cheque gives them three days' credit; payment by credit card gives them even longer. Why pay electronically?

Ultimately, perhaps, EFTPOS will be installed everywhere, and we will experience the cashless society. Money will become merely a row of digits on a computer. Consumers will sit at home and order up goods through their terminals. It does seem a rather soulless vision of the future – where is the place for traditional street markets in such a system? It seems more likely that EFTPOS will spread gradually and will exist side by side with existing methods of payment.

EFTPOS is only one illustration of the way in which technology has affected the world of finance. Technology allows companies to be aware of their financial position in an instant. It enables investors to be aware of news across the globe moments after events occur.

Speed, and once more speed. No industry has advanced so far so fast, it seems, as the ability to transmit information, and the financial markets have been in the forefront in adapting this development. On screen a banker can now see the prices of financial products all over the world. A computer program can help to ascertain if there are any price irregularities to be exploited. A touch of the screen with an electronic pen can put the dealer through to the telephone call that clinches the transaction. A further touch enters the details of the deal into the bank's computer, so that both banker and dealer can monitor his position. If a bank is over-committed to a particular currency or client, that risk can be identified straightaway.

The result is that the majority of financial deals can now be conducted over the telephone rather than through the elaborate rituals of an investment exchange. That is already the case in the foreign exchange markets. The key question is whether the exchanges that still exist to sell shares and bonds will survive.

The Challenge for the City

The concentration on securities trading, the disappearance of regulatory controls and the advances faciliated by new technology add up to a significant challenge to the City. London must adapt to this new environment if it is to retain its role in the world financial system. The next chapter deals with its effort to do so – the 'Big Bang'.

[2] The 'Big Bang'

The City of London is attempting to carry through one of the biggest changes in its history, a change that has become known as the 'Big Bang'. At first the term 'Big Bang' referred merely to the day when minimum commissions on the London Stock Exchange (the market where shares and government bonds are traded) would be abolished. As the pace of change accelerated, however, the term began to encompass a whole range of developments. The results of the 'Big Bang' will dictate the future of the City as a world financial centre and will strongly influence the prospects of a host of banks, broking firms and their staff.

The 'Big Bang' has many root causes, but its main catalyst was a long-running case against The Stock Exchange which was pursued by the Office of Fair Trading (OFT) in the Restrictive Practices Court. The OFT was particularly concerned about the maintenance of fixed-minimum commissions, which were seen as preventing competition and thus as pushing up the costs of share-buying for investors. Fixed commissions perpetuated the division between broker and jobber – the so-called *single-capacity* system. No other major exchange had the same split between one category of dealer who bought and sold shares (the *jobber*) and one who acted as a middleman for outside investors, earning commission in the process (the *broker*). In other systems securities firms acted as both market-makers and jobbers. If a customer in the USA approaches Merrill Lynch to buy IBM shares, it will normally sell the customer shares from its own holdings. However, if Merrill wants to hang on to its existing IBM holdings, it will act as a broker and find the client shares from another dealer.

The OFT case was settled by one of the very few decisions of Cecil Parkinson in his short-lived stay as Secretary of State for Trade and Industry. He offered to bring in legislation to halt the case in return for the abolition of minimum commissions by the Exchange.

Despite the abolition of fixed-minimum commissions, The Stock Exchange hoped to maintain the separate roles of brokers and jobbers. On consulting its members, however, the Exchange found that jobbers did not believe that separate roles could persist after minimum commissions were abolished. The system relied on brokers to bring *all* their business to the jobbers. Its abolition would encourage brokers to deal off their own books and thus bypass the jobbers. They would then save the customer costs by eliminating the jobber's turn (the spread between buy and sell price charged under the old system). Minimum commissions had pre-empted that temptation, since brokers were unable to compete on price. Without fixed commissions, price would become a major factor, and the jobbing firms would never be certain that they were seeing all of a broker's business. The jobbers, accordingly, decided that they too would prefer to deal with customers direct, a privilege that they were denied under the old system.

The Evolution of the Market

The evolution of the share market was already putting pressure on the single-capacity system. The abolition of UK exchange controls in 1979 had made it possible for investors to deal in foreign shares without paying the expensive dollar premium. However, few Stock Exchange firms were able to offer a service in foreign shares, and they began to lose their business to the big overseas firms. Some people estimate that as much as 95 per cent of the overseas investments made by UK pension funds after 1979 were handled by foreign firms. City commentators began to fear that London would lose its position in the world financial hierarchy.

Shares were beginning to be traded worldwide – creating the so-called international equities market. Its equivalent for the raising of debt capital, an international bond market, already existed. Many foreign companies were already listed on the London Stock Exchange, and many UK companies were listed on exchanges elsewhere in the world. The banking magazine *Euromoney* estimated that the number of companies whose shares were traded internationally increased from 236 in 1984 to 350 in 1985.*

* *Euromoney*, May 1985.

The growth reflected the fact that the major world capital markets were concentrated more heavily than are the multinational corporations. They still are. Companies like Volvo or Fiat find that their domestic capital markets are not big enough to support their shares. There are not enough Swedish or Italian investors with the necessary investment funds.

An international equity offering broadens a company's investor base, with the theoretical result that its share price becomes less volatile. At the same time, because of the abolition of capital controls in many of the major Western economies (see Chapter 1), investors have been willing to increase their holdings of foreign equities. If one country's share market is falling, another's may be rising. Investing across several markets reduces risk.

As the international equity market grew, it became apparent that London was losing out to New York as the centre of the business. This was partly because of the restrictions imposed by the old system of single capacity and minimum commissions; it was also due partly to stamp duty, a tax payable on every share transaction in London, which does not apply in New York. Stamp duty was halved in March 1984 from 2 to 1 per cent, but that extra margin still allowed US brokers to undercut their London rivals. The size of the US market also helped – over five times as many shares were traded there in 1985 as were traded in the UK. That meant there were many more potential investors in New York than in London. By 1985 shares in ICI (one of Britain's biggest companies) were traded in greater volume in New York than in London.

The challenge to London did not come just from other exchanges. Two markets for equities were developing in parallel: a telephone (or over-the-counter) market and an exchange traded market. The speed of modern communications means that many traders now see little reason to be linked with a conventional exchange. Nor do they have to be based in London in order to trade UK shares. This can be done as easily in New York. The large American firms can bypass the London Stock Exchange and set up their own market.

The Rise of the Institutional Investor

Even before the development of the international equity market changes in the domestic share market were prompting some to question the broker/jobber division. Before World War II the majority of shares were in the hands of private individuals. Taxes on the rich and the rise of company pension schemes led to the replacement of private investors by institutional holdings (see Chapters 9 and 10). That pushed up the size of the average share deal, with the result that the costs to jobbers of carrying a large number of shares on their book increased.

As recently as 1920 there were 411 jobbing firms: by 1985 there were seventeen, of which only five were of significant size. Small firms had been forced to merge to survive in the new markets, which made it much more difficult to justify the old broker/jobber split. The theory had been that jobbers created an approximation of what economists call a 'perfect' market – lots of traders situated close together, each with the same information, trading undifferentiated products and competing on price alone. However, even after all the mergers jobbing firms were still too small to carry all the Exchange's shares on their books, and most specialized in a limited range of shares. For some shares only two jobbers made a market, which meant that there was little price competition between them. Such a market was hardly 'perfect'.

It became clear that securities firms would in future need capital backing to be able to act as market-makers. In recognition of the fact that such capital might be impossible to raise internally, The Stock Exchange accepted the need to bring in outside money. The maximum holding that any outside organization was allowed to have in a member firm was accordingly increased from 10 to 29.9 per cent in 1982. All restrictions disappeared in March 1986.

On the same date The Stock Exchange also relaxed the rules and regulations that had applied to membership. In the past, membership of The Stock Exchange had been on an individual as well as on a corporate basis. This was clearly inappropriate for a major bank. In future companies becoming corporate members of the Exchange would not need to have an individual member of the Exchange on their board or staff. Nor would firms that became members have to pay excessive entry fees.

Shopping Spree

The 1982 relaxation on outside stakes was followed by wholesale purchases of broking and jobbing firms by major banks. Barclays bought both a jobber (Wedd Durlacher Mordaunt) and a broker (de Zoete and Bevan). Midland's merchant banking associate Samuel Montagu bought brokers W. Greenwell, while National Westminster purchased jobbers Bisgood Bishop and brokers Fielding Newson Smith. It was not only the commercial banks who dusted off their chequebooks. S. G. Warburg led the race of the merchant banks, buying into two broking firms (Rowe and Pitman, and Mullens) and jobbers Akroyd and Smithers. Jobber/broker purchases were also made by Kleinwort Benson, Morgan Grenfell and N. M. Rothschild, while Baring Brothers and Guinness Mahon bought one jobbing firm each, and Hambros and Hill Samuel a broker each.

Foreign banks also joined in the rush – although only one, Security Pacific, bought a jobber. The others concentrated on brokers. Two of the biggest banks in the world, Citicorp and Chase Manhattan (never likely to do things by halves), bought a pair of broker firms apiece.

The purchases were nearly all expensive: Barclays paid around £200 million to form its conglomerate. It has little to show for its purchase in terms of physical assets – a few buildings and some office equipment. What it really bought was something that accountants call 'goodwill', the good name of the firm and the expertise of its staff. The same goes for the purchases made by the other banks. The conventional ways of valuing companies seemed to go by the board.

The Stock Exchange had helped to look after its members. In 1982 commissions on equity transactions were increased. The result was bigger profits for Stock Exchange firms and higher prices when they were sold. There was a further way to exploit the situation. Each Stock Exchange member had a share in the Exchange, and the shares could be sold to the new members. It was proposed that a ceiling of £2,000 per share should be imposed to avoid discouraging new entrants. In the end that proposal was dropped, and a motion to alter the ownership structure of the Exchange narrowly failed to get the 75 per cent membership support needed to implement it.

The Banks' Reasons

Why were banks so eager and willing to spend so much money, thus making a few stockbrokers very rich in the process? The main reason lies in the two international phenomena discussed in the previous chapter – securitization and disintermediation. No longer could the banks rely on making money merely by lending at a higher rate of interest than they paid for funds. Future profits had to come from the broking and trading of securities.

At the same time banks began to realize that all the different types of security – bonds, shares, bills – were to some extent interchangeable. Institutional investors, who were the end-buyers of so many of the securities, had worldwide portfolios, which they shifted not only between countries but also between types of security, depending on their views on the prospects for that market. In the UK banks could sell the institutions bonds and money-market deposits; the two areas of the securities market in which banks lacked a presence were equities and government securities.

The banks reasoned that those firms which would survive in the new financial markets would be those which would trade the complete range of securities, so that they could offer the institutions 'one-stop financial shopping'. If an investor wished to shift his portfolio from, say, bonds to equities, a bank could offer to arrange the sale of his bonds and the purchase of shares. At the same time The Stock Exchange and the Bank of England allowed these moves because they recognized that London's competitiveness as a financial centre depended on the success of the 'Big Bang'.

If the future is on the side of the big battalions, what will happen to those small firms which remain independent? The only London-based Stock Exchange firm which has remained independent is Casenove's, rumoured to be the Queen's broker. It believes that some investors will appreciate a firm which is purely a broker and not a market-maker. Outside London it is possible that the smaller provincial brokers will be able to survive by specializing in local stocks which have too small a market to attract their bigger rivals.

Following in New York's Footsteps

What will happen after the 'Big Bang' occurs on 27 October 1986? One guide to the likely changes is the example of New York. There minimum commissions were abolished in 1975. Commission rates immediately fell by 25 per cent and were 40 per cent down by 1977. Since the amount of work necessary to process a 20,000-share order is little more than is needed to process a ten-share order, a shift in commissions would fairly reflect the costs involved. This will be of most benefit to the big British institutions that have the power to demand lower commissions. It is possible that discount brokers will emerge who will charge for a dealing-only service without research or advice. In the USA such brokers now account for 20 per cent of the retail market. However, until the discount brokers establish themselves it seems likely that the charges paid by the small investor will increase.

Another market which has been forced to change because of the 'Big Bang' is the gilts market. Gilts are UK government bonds, and they have traditionally formed the major part of the volume of The Stock Exchange. In the past all stock was sold through the government broker, always the senior partner of the stockbroking firm Mullens and Co. The government broker would sell the stock to jobbing firms on The Stock Exchange. The two jobbing firms, Akroyd and Smithers and Wedd Durlacher Mordaunt, which controlled 85 per cent of the market, would then sell the gilts on to one of the specialist gilts brokers – e.g. W. Greenwell, Grieveson Grant, Hoare Govett and Phillips and Drew.

The disappearance of the distinction between brokers and jobbers has meant that the old system can no longer be used. The Bank of England has therefore been forced to change its procedures, although it was quite happy with the way things used to work. Under the new system the government broker has left Mullens and joined the staff of the Bank. The duopoly of jobbing firms has been replaced by a system of primary gilts dealers. After the Bank had asked for applications twenty-nine firms were appointed as the new dealers; two later dropped out. As from October 1986 the Bank offered new issues to those dealers alone: in return the dealers must always be prepared to make a market (indicate a price at which they will buy or sell) in all gilt stock. This may well result in better prices for the government, since it will have many more bids to choose from than two or three under the old system.

How will twenty-nine dealers make a market when only two did before? It seems clear that they will depend on an increase in turnover to make money. The government's abolition of capital gains tax on gilts will help, but the widening of the circle of investors is vital.

Overseas investors own only about 10 per cent of the total of gilts outstanding, perhaps because they are discouraged by sterling's volatility. (A 10 per cent drop in sterling could wipe out all the interest on most gilts for an overseas investor.) But the new market players hope that international investors will take advantage of the possibilities for exploiting price differentials between gilts and the US Treasury bond market.

Each market player must commit a certain amount of 'dedicated' capital, which must be kept in the market at all times. The firms will not be able to transfer their resources to another area of their operations. That will mean that capital will be tied up unprofitably at times when the market is quiet, making it even more difficult for the twenty-nine dealers to make a profit.

The consensus seems to be that only one-third – about ten or twelve – of the original market-makers will survive. Whether they will be the specialist brokers, the US giants or the UK clearers will be the subject of intense speculation from the moment the market opens.

Inter-dealer brokers (IDBs) will match willing parties over the telephone and will display the prices of the main firms on electronic screens on every trader's desk. If they are owned by an established securities firm, they will have to keep their broking business quite separate from their trading arm. Stock Exchange money brokers will also be established. They will give liquidity to the market by lending money to market-makers and accepting gilts as security.

Not only will the style of trading alter after the 'Big Bang' but its surroundings will alter also. In the new market the old Stock Exchange floor, with hexagonal pitches where jobbers plied their wares, is likely to disappear. In its place there will be a row of dealing desks and screens. There is really no need for a physical floor to exist at all. Traders could just as easily contact each other on the phone from different offices. Tradition, however, indicates that the floor will survive for a few more years.

The Stock Exchange has been forced into the era of high technology. Its electronic system, Stock Exchange Automated Quotation System

(SEAQ), will cover 3,500 securities and will be able to handle 70,000 deals an hour. On screen brokers will be able to see the up-to-the-minute quotes of market-makers. However, even here The Stock Exchange will face a challenge. The information company Reuters is the biggest electronic information provider in the financial markets and will put the prices of shares on screen.

Regulation

The bringing together of brokers, jobbers and bankers within the same groups presents a problem of regulation. A company which is attempting a takeover may be cautious about taking advice from a bank which is also advising investors which shares to buy and is actively buying and selling shares itself. Similarly, groups with the financial muscle of a commercial bank to support them can manipulate share prices in their own interest if they have inside knowledge of a company's financial position.

The private investor could also be cheated by a new conglomerate. If the jobbing part of a securities conglomerate has invested unwisely in depreciating shares, it can feed those shares to the public through its broking arm. The broker would have every incentive to be less than truthful about the prospects of the shares when talking to clients.

Such potential conflicts of interest did not exist with the old broker/jobber system. The broker had no reason not to get the best price for his client – his commission would remain roughly the same whatever the price. Similarly, the jobber had an interest in keeping his prices competitive in order to attract business.

The new financial groups have argued that by setting up within their companies a series of 'Chinese walls' – theoretical barriers which will prevent members of one department from giving vital information to members of another – they can prevent abuses. The cynical counter-argument is that if 'Chinese walls' were really effective, there would be no point in bringing together banks, brokers and jobbers in one group.

The Gower Report and the SIB

The department of Trade and Industry asked Professor Gower to examine the whole question of City regulation. It produced its first discussion document in 1982 and a full report in January 1984. Professor Gower proposed a new Investor Protection Act, which would be administered by a Quango under the Department of Trade. Each body of dealers would set up a self-regulatory organization whose rules and regulations would have to be answerable to the Quango.

The government took some notice of the Gower Report but decided against a Quango and in favour of a *private* regulatory authority, the Securities and Investments Board (SIB), to which the Department of Trade and Industry (DTI) will delegate its powers. For some time the government considered establishing two organizations. The second existed for some time as as the Marketing of Investments Board and would have overseen the life assurance and unit trust business. In the end all involved seemed to feel that one body would make the system simpler. The final recommendations were produced in December 1985.

All investment business will have to be authorized. They can be recognized either directly by the SIB or by one of the self-regulatory organizations (SROs). In turn no SRO will be recognized unless its rules are at least as strict as those of the SIB and are designed to ensure that private investors get a fair deal and to allow for problems of conflicts of interest. If an SRO fails to meet the criteria, SIB can force it to amend its rules.

The SROs so far established are The Stock Exchange, the Financial Intermediaries, Managers and Brokers Association (FIMBRA), the Association of Futures Brokers and Dealers (AFBD), the Investment Management Regulatory Organization (IMRO), the International Securities Regulatory Organization (ISRO) and the Life Assurance and Unit Trust Regulatory Organization (LAUTRO). This confusing crop of initials has already changed once and may yet do so again as the City sorts itself out.

The Stock Exchange will regulate firms dealing and broking in securities and some related options (instruments which give the right to buy or sell another instrument at a future date – these are described in detail in Chapters 13 and 14). The AFBD, as its name implies, will watch over firms dealing and broking in futures. FIMBRA is a merger of two earlier groups, NASDIM and LAUTRO, and will cover a wide range of securities firms and brokers in the fields of life assurance and unit trusts. IMRO will also regulate investment managers and advisers, trustees of investment schemes and in-house pension-fund managers.

If the above divisions are confusing to the amateur, they are also perplexing for many professionals in the market. Many of the SROs appear to have overlapping functions. It seems that it will be up to City firms to choose which SRO to join, and this has led some commentators to fear that firms will join the SRO whose rules are least onerous. The SIB will, in consequence, be encouraging SRO mergers. A different problem is that some organizations which offer a full range of financial services will have to join several SROs and thus report to several different authorities. Banks will also have to be authorized by, and must report to, the Bank of England.

Investment exchanges – like The Stock Exchange and the London International Financial Futures Exchange (LIFFE) may also be recognized under the new regime. This will be an option rather than a requirement for exchanges.

The Stock Exchange will thus become both an SRO and an investment exchange. It may hope to set up a joint investment exchange with the ISRO to head off the challenge of the big overseas firm.

The SIB's Critics

The creation of the SIB was a step that was much criticized by those in the City who had long argued that self-regulation is the best form of investor protection and have feared the introduction of a body with the sort of teeth possessed by the USA Securities Exchange Commission (SEC). Nevertheless, after the Johnson Matthey case, a series of scandals at Lloyd's and a rash of share-price gains immediately prior to takeover bids there has been much press criticism of City morals.

Will the Bill protect the small investor? It has impressive-looking authority. Soon it will be possible to bring criminal charges against any firm found guilty of making reckless or false statements about investments. Inspectors will be appointed and given powers to question on oath and to confiscate documents. A complaints system, under an Ombudsman, will be established and a compensation fund set up with a £30,000 limit on individual claims.

Before it disappeared the Marketing of Investments Board's Organizing Committee set out proposals for controls on the marketing of life assurance and unit trusts. It recommended that all salesmen should be licensed; that there should be two categories of intermediary – the independent and the company employees; that an independent should be just that and should not tie himself to any one particular company – he should recommend the best possible product to the client and should tell the client if he earns a higher commission from any one product or company; that company employees should market the wares of a particular firm and that firm only, unless the company does not have a full range of products; that no agent could tie himself to more than one company.

The recommendations (particularly those concerning the disclosure of commissions) aroused controversy in the life assurance business. Those most distressed seem to be independent salesmen who market the wares of several companies. However, City critics argued that the Bill protected salesmen because they were not required to reveal the total level of commissions. The main criticism of the Bill's provision from those outside the City are that the new bodies would lack the authority to enforce their codes. Regulation would be in the hands of old City employees – 'poachers turned gamekeepers'. In the eyes of those outside the City, the regulators would be disinclined to discipline their old pals. They point to the fact that the Lloyd's scandals took place in a self-regulated market.* In the eyes of the government, however, the new regulators would be the best people to watch over the market because they know the tricks of the trade.

Banking Supervision

At the same time as regulatory authorities had to be devised to cope with the 'Big Bang', the government was forced to deal with the aftermath of the Johnson Matthey affair, which necessitated a review of the whole apparatus of bank supervision. That issue is considered in Chapter 5, on the Bank of England, while the recent changes in the powers of building societies are considered in Chapter 7.

The Salaries Explosion

One effect of the 'Big Bang' has been to exaggerate the dichotomy between the City and the rest of the economy. As the major banks have

* Lloyd's was not included in the scope of the Bill. It had its own Act in 1982 (see Chapter 12).

fought to capture a niche in the equity and gilts markets, they have tried to buy expertise: sometimes that has meant firms and sometimes people.

A partner in a jobbing firm was reputed to have said that he would not move firms for less than £1 million. Such payments, which are separate from salaries, are known as 'golden hellos'. On top of the transfer payment, the salary would have been in six figures. Even at the lower end of the scale a 21-year-old bond dealer can earn over £50,000 a year. Bonuses can be as much as annual salaries and can be in the form of 'golden handcuffs', paid only on a deferred basis in order to give employees an incentive to stay with the firm. One senior banker told me, 'I feel rather ashamed when I go and visit a Midlands industrial firm and see a finance executive there who works all hours of the day and night and earns about as much as my firm would pay a young graduate.'

Whether or not firms will find themselves able to support such salaries is one question; whether they will continue to seem reasonable in the light of the City's contribution to the economy is another. However, the same argument can apply to footballers and pop groups. There is little doubt that the life of a bond trader is extremely pressured and that the rewards to a company of a successful trader can be substantial.

[3] Money and Interest Rates

Money

Primitive societies did not have money, since they did not trade. When trade began it was under a barter system. Goats might be exchanged for corn, or sheep for axes. As society became more complex, barter grew inadequate as a trading system. Goats might be acceptable as payment to one man but not to another, who might prefer sheep or cattle. Even then it was easy to dispute the question of how many sheep were worth a sack of corn.

Gradually precious metals and, most notably, gold and silver were used as payment and became the first money. Precious metals had several advantages. Money had to be scarce. It was no good basing a monetary system on the leaf. Everyone would soon grab all the leaves around and the smallest payment would require a wheelbarrowful. Money had also to be easy to carry and in divisible units – making the goat a poor monetary unit. Gold and silver were sufficiently scarce and sufficiently portable to meet society's requirements.

Of course, it soon become inconvenient to carry gold and silver ingots. Coins were created by the kings of Lydia in the eighth century BC.* From the days of Alexander the Great the custom began of depicting the head of the sovereign on coins.

There are a variety of functions which money serves. It is a *measure of value*. Sheep can be compared with goats and chalk with cheese by referring to the amount of money one would pay for each product. Money is also a *store of value*. It can be saved until it is needed, unlike the goods it buys, which are often perishable. Creditors will accept money as a future payment, confident that its value will remain stable in the meantime.

Of course, today's money is made from neither gold nor silver. Coins

* J. K. Galbraith, *Money: Whence it Came, Where it Went* (Penguin, 1976).

are made from copper or nickel, and the most valuable monetary units are made of paper. There are two main reasons for this. The first is that supplies of gold and silver were outstripped by the demands of society. If money is scarce, it is difficult for the economy to expand and for us to get richer. The second reason is the so-called Gresham's Law that 'bad money drives out good'. When money was in the form of gold coins, it was tempting for those with a large number of coins to shave off a tiny fraction of each coin. The resulting shavings could be melted down to make new coins. Gradually some coins contained less gold than others. Anyone who had a coin with the maximum amount of gold would have been foolish to spend it lest he received a coin with less gold in return. So the best coins were hoarded and the worst coins circulated. Bad money drove out good.

The earliest issues of money that was not backed by gold were known as *fiduciary* issues. Money is now totally divorced from its precious-metal origins. It will never regress. Imagine the political problems involved in basing a monetary system on a commodity whose biggest producers were South Africa and the Soviet Union.

Banknotes and Cheques

The next stages of the development of money – banknotes and cheques – are dealt with in Chapter 4, on the banks. It is sufficient to point out here that banknotes were, in origin, claims on gold and silver. Now money depends on the confidence of its users in the strength of the economy. When economies break down (as they occasionally do in wartime) money disappears and is replaced by some other commodity such as cigarettes.

As money has grown more sophisticated, so it has grown farther away from its origins. For large sums, payment by cheque is far easier and safer than payment by notes and coins. The money is debited from the payer's bank account and credited to the payee's. Even if someone presents a cheque for cash at a bank, he or she will be paid in banknotes, which are, in origin, only a claim on the real assets, gold and silver. The system depends on the confidence of all those concerned. Shopkeepers accept cheques because banks will honour them. Bank accounts are therefore money in the same sense as notes and coins are, since they can be used instantly to purchase goods.*

* Credit cards are a further stage in the development of money.

Banks can thus create money. This is because only a small proportion of the deposits they hold is needed to meet the claims of those who want to withdraw cash. Much of the need is met by those who deposit cash. The rest of the money can be lent out by the banks to earn interest. A simple way for a bank to lend money is to create a deposit (or account) in someone's favour.

Suppose that a country has only one bank, which finds that it needs to keep 20 per cent of its deposits in the form of cash. It receives an extra £200 worth of cash deposits. The bank then buys £160 of British Telecom shares, leaving £40 cash free to meet any claims from depositors. The person from whom it bought the shares now has £160 in cash, which is deposited with the bank. So the bank has £360 in deposits (the original £200 plus the new deposit of £160), of which it needs to keep only £72 (20 per cent) in the form of cash. The bank is therefore able to increase its total investments to £288 (£360 − £72) and can buy a further £128 of BT shares. Once again the person from whom it buys the shares will receive cash, depositing this with the bank. This process will continue until the bank has deposits of £1,000, of which £200 is held in the form of cash. The bank's balance sheet will then look like this:

Assets		*Liabilities*	
Cash	£200	Customer deposits	£1,000
BT shares	£800		
TOTAL	£1,000		£1,000

(Note that customer deposits are a liability, since they might at any time have to be repaid.)

To find out the total amounts of deposits that can be created from the original cash base, divide 100 by the percentage which the bank needs to hold as cash (known as the *cash ratio*). Then multiply the result by the amount of the original deposit. Thus, in this example, dividing 100 by the cash ratio of 20 per cent gives 5, and multiplying that by the original deposit equals £1,000.

The cash ratio is therefore very important. If, in the example, the ratio had been only 10 per cent, the amount of deposits created from the original deposit would have been £2,000 and not £1,000. In practice, banks find that they need to keep around 8 per cent of their deposits in the form of cash.

This relation between the money which banks need to hold in liquid form and the amount which they can lend has been used by the Bank of England to control the level of credit in the economy (see Chapter 5).

Defining the Money Supply

As money has become increasingly sophisticated, so it has become more and more difficult to define exactly what it is. This issue has assumed particular importance with the prominence of the monetarist school of economics, which believes that the level of inflation is closely related to the rate of increase of the money supply. In the late 1970s and early 1980s many Western governments, including the UK's, were strong adherents of the monetarist school and attempted to base economic policies on its theories. Accordingly, they needed to define the money supply before they could control it.

The Bank of England publishes several definitions of money. M1 is defined as notes and coins in circulation with the public, plus sterling current accounts held by the private sector. M2 is M1 plus private-sector sterling deposit accounts held with the deposit (commercial) banks and the discount houses (see Chapters 4 and 6). The broadest definition, M3, includes virtually all the deposits held by the private and public sectors in both sterling and foreign currencies. Sterling M3, which was for many years the government's principal monetary target, is M3 minus the foreign currency element. As something of an afterthought, the Bank has recently devised a very narrow definition of money, M0, which consists purely of notes and coins.

By defining money solely by reference to deposits held in banks, the Bank of England realized that it was failing to take into account other deposits which might be substitutes for those in banks. For example, building society deposits are not strictly compatible with bank deposits. Traditionally it has not been possible to write a cheque on a building society account, although this too is changing. However, if building society rates are more attractive than those offered by the banks, depositors will switch their money from their bank accounts to a building society. Most society accounts will let their depositors withdraw cash instantly, and many creditors will accept a building society cheque as payment. To call bank deposits money and building society accounts non-money would be to paint an inaccurate picture of credit levels in the economy.

The Bank of England accordingly established a new set of definitions of money, the Private Sector Liquidity (PSL series). PSL1 includes notes and coins, sterling bank deposits, certificates of deposits (defined in Chapter 6), Treasury and bank bills and similar instruments. PSL2 adds in building society deposits and shares and deposits with similar institutions like the Trustee Savings Bank (TSB). However, the PSL definitions have attracted little attention from economic analysts.

In the middle of 1985 the Chancellor of the Exchequer effectively abandoned sterling M3 as a target figure for his monetary policy. It had been growing at 20 per cent a year at a time when inflation was falling. It was announced that M0 would continue to be watched (along with short-term interest rates and the exchange rate), but it seemed that the difficulty of defining money had defeated the best efforts of the monetarists.

Interest Rates

Money on its own is a very useful but, in the long run, unprofitable possession. That £200 stashed under the mattress will in five years' time still be only £200. In the meantime inflation will have eroded its purchasing power, so that it may be able to purchase only half as many goods as it could five years before. Had the money been deposited with a building society, however, interest would have been added every six months. At 10 per cent a year the original cash deposit would have increased to £322.10 at the end of the five-year period. This interest rate is essentially the *price* of money. The price is paid by the borrower in return for the use of the lender's money. The lender is compensated for *not* having the use of his money.

There are two alternative methods of calculating interest: *simple* and *compound*.

Simple interest can be easily explained. If a deposit of £100 is placed in a building society and simple interest of 10 per cent per annum is paid, then after one year the deposit will be £110, after two years £120 and so on. Nearly all interest is paid, however, on a compound basis.

Compound interest involves the payment of interest on previous interest. In the above example the depositor would still receive £10 interest in the first year. In the second year, however, interest would be calculated on £110, rather than on £100. The depositor would thus earn £11 interest in the second year, bringing his deposit to £121. In the third year he would earn £12.10 interest and so on. The cumulative effect is impressive. The same £100 deposit would become £350 after twenty-five years of simple interest but £1,083.50 with compound interest. Most savings accounts operate on the principle of compound interest, but most securities pay only simple interest. A bond may pay 5 per cent a year but only on the principal amount borrowed. That amount does not increase over the bond's lifetime.

When dealing with a bond or with a share, it is more important to talk of the *yield* than merely of the interest rate or dividend.

Yield

A deposit account in a building society carries an annual interest rate. The money deposited will always be returned in full with the accumulated interest, but the lump sum (capital) will not grow. Other investments, like shares, bonds and houses, are not as safe as a building society account but offer the potential for capital growth. Shares, bonds and property can all increase in price as well as provide income in the form of dividends, interest or rent. Since the price of these securities can alter, the interest rate or dividend will be more or less significant as the price falls or rises. The interest rate or dividend, expressed as a percentage of the price of the asset, is the *yield.* A security with a price of £80 that pays interest of £8 a year has a yield of 10 per cent. If the value of the security rises to £100, the yield will fall to 8 per cent. In assessing the profitability of various assets, calculating their yield is very important; articles in the financial press will talk about equity yields and bond yields as much as about dividends and interest rates.

In theory, the yield on shares should be higher than that on most bonds, since shares are a riskier form of investment. However, in recent years equities and property have offered lower yields than bonds or savings accounts because the prospects of capital growth are much greater with the former investments.

Probably the best way of showing the importance of yields is to cite the bond market. Suppose that in a year of low interest rates the Jupiter Corporation issues a bond with a face value of £100 and an interest rate (normally called the coupon) of 5 per cent. In the following year interest rates rise and bond investors demand a return of 10 per cent from newly issued bonds. Those investors who bought Jupiter bonds are now stuck with bonds which give them only half the market rate. Many of them will therefore sell their Jupiter bonds and buy newly issued bonds.

Who will they sell the bonds to? Potential buyers of Jupiter bonds will be no more willing to accept a yield of only 5 per cent than the sellers. Bond sellers will therefore have to accept a reduced price for the Jupiter bonds. The price will have to fall until the returns from Jupiter and other bonds are roughly equal. If the bond price fell from £100 to £50, then each year bondholders would still receive £5 on a bond which cost them £50 – a return, or yield, of 10 per cent. The Jupiter bond would be as attractive as a bond priced at £100 with a 10 per cent coupon, which would also yield 10 per cent.

Calculating the yield on a bond is not quite that easy, however. The bond will be repaid at some future point. Say, for example, it has a nominal value of £100, sells for £96, pays £5 interest a year and has one year to go before it is repaid. Over the next year the bondholder will receive £5 interest and £4 capital – the difference between the £96 it sells for and the £100 which will be repaid. So the bond yields £9 on a price of £96, just under 10 per cent. A yield which is calculated to allow for capital repayment is called the *gross yield to redemption*. Going back to the Jupiter issue, the bonds would not have to fall in price as low as £50 to keep their yields in line. If they had a five-year maturity, they would have to fall only to around £83 to have a gross yield to redemption of about 10 per cent. Most bond traders use a pocket calculator to work out the gross yield to redemption because of the complexity of the calculation.

This process of adjusting prices to bring yields in line gives bond investors the prospect of capital gain (or loss) on their holdings. An investor who buys Jupiter bonds at £100 would lose £25 if the price fell to £75 because of the yield adjustment. That would more than wipe out any interest earned on the bond. However, if the interest rate offered on other bonds fell back to 5 per cent again, then Jupiter's bonds would climb back to their face value of £100. An investor who bought at the low of £75 would have made a capital gain of 33 per cent and still earned interest in the process.

Because of the yield factor, bond prices have an inverse relationship with interest rates: bond markets are euphoric when interest rates are falling, depressed when they are rising.

Interest-rate Determinants

Having understood the difference between simple and compound interest and the importance of yields, we can now look at the factors that determine an interest rate. In fact, it is more correct to talk of interest *rates*. At any one time a host of different rates are charged throughout the economy. So it is important to distinguish the determinants of specific interest rates as well as those which affect the general level of rates in the economy.

First, let us look at the determinants of specific rates. One of the principal elements is risk. There is always the chance, whomever money is lent to, that it will not be repaid. That risk will be reflected in a higher interest rate. This is one of the general principles of finance. The riskier the investment, the higher the return demanded by the investor. It is a principle which can be challenged, mainly because investors do not always assess risk adequately. Nevertheless, it is a useful principle to bear in mind, especially when it is stood on its head. Those investors who seek extremely high returns would be wise to remember that such investments normally involve extremely high risk.

Governments are usually presumed to be the least risky debtors of all, at least by lenders in their own country. (Other countries' governments are a different matter, as many banks who lent to Brazil and Argentina have discovered.) But the government of a lender's country can always print more money to repay the debt if necessary. In any case, if the government does not repay debt, it is reasonable for investors to presume that no one else in the country will.

Banks and building societies have traditionally been rated next on the credit ladder. Nowadays, however, as we noted in Chapter 2, because of banks' exposure to the international debt crisis, many large corporations are considered better credit risks than even the biggest banks. For the benefit of potential investors, some agencies have devised elaborate rating systems to assess the creditworthiness of banks and corporations (see Chapter 11).

At the bottom of the ratings come individuals like you and me. Individuals have a sad tendency to lose jobs, get sick, over-commit themselves and default on their loans. Unless they are exceptionally wealthy, individuals thus pay the highest interest rates of all.

One of the other main elements involved is liquidity. The housebuyer with a mortgage has to pay a higher rate than is received by the building society depositor because the society needs to be compensated for the loss of liquidity involved in tying up its money for twenty-five years. The society faces the risk that it will at some point need the funds that it has lent to the house buyer but will be unable to gain access to them. As I mentioned in the introduction, this is another of the basic principles of finance. The more liquid the asset, the lower the return. The most liquid asset of all, cash, bears no interest at all.

Logical though the above arguments are, it often happens that long-term interest rates are below short-term rates. To understand why, we must look at the yield curve.

The Yield Curve

We have already proposed a general principle of finance – that lesser liquidity demands greater reward. That being the case, longer-term instruments should always bear a higher interest rate than short-term ones. This is not always true. Long-term rates can be the same as, or lower than, those of short-term instruments.

A curve can be drawn which links the different levels of rates with the different maturities of debt. If long-term rates are above short-term ones, this is described as a *positive* or upward-sloping yield curve. If short-term rates are higher, the curve is described as *negative* or *inverted.*

What determines the shape of the yield curve? The three main theories used to explain its structure are the liquidity theory, the expectations theory and the market-segmentation theory.

The *liquidity theory*, which has already been outlined, states simply that investors will demand an extra reward (in the form of a higher interest rate) for investing their money for a long period. They may do so because they fear that they will need the funds suddenly but will be unable to obtain them, or they may be worried about the possibility of default. Borrowers (in particular, businesses) will be prepared to pay higher interest rates in order to secure long-term funds for investment. Thus, other things being equal, the yield curve will be upward-sloping.

The *expectations theory* holds that the yield curve represents investors' views on the likely future movement of short-term interest rates. If one-year interest rates are 10 per cent and an investor expects them to rise to 12 per cent in a year's time, he will be unwilling to accept 10 per cent on a two-year loan. It would be more profitable for him to lend for one year and then re-lend his money at the higher rate. A two-year loan will therefore have to offer at least 11 per cent a year before the investor will be attracted. Thus if interest rates are expected to *rise*, the yield curve will be *upward-sloping*. If investors expect short-term interest rates to *fall*, however, they will seek to lend long-term. That will increase the supply of long-term funds and bring down their price (i.e. long-term interest rates). Thus the yield curve will be *downward-sloping*.

What determines investors' expectations of future interest-rate movements? Over the past few years the monetarist bent of most Western governments has meant that the outlook for interest rates has been tied to the growth in the money supply. If monetary figures have indicated a faster than expected expansion in the money supply, then investors have expected governments to increase interest rates. On the other hand, if the money supply appears to be under control, investors have expected interest rates to fall.

Keynes constructed a more elaborate theory which depended on the yield of securities. If people expect interest rates to rise, Keynes argued, they will hold on to their money in the form of cash, in order to avoid capital loss. But if they expect rates to fall, they will invest their money to profit from capital gains. Of course, this principle applies to bonds rather than to interest-bearing accounts. As we have seen, if interest rates rise, the price of previously issued bonds falls until investors earn a similar yield from equivalent bonds. Thus a bond investor who expected rates to rise will sell his bonds before the rise in rates and the resultant fall in the bond price occurs. The investor will hold the funds in the most liquid form available so that he can reinvest them as soon as rates rise. If the same investor expects interest rates to fall, he will hold on to the bonds because their price will rise as rates fall.

The third theory of the yield curve is the *market-segmentation* theory. This assumes that the markets for the different maturities of debt instruments are entirely separate. Within each segment interest rates are set by supply and demand. The shape of the yield curve will be determined by the different results of supply/demand trade-offs. If a lot of borrowers have long-term financing needs and few investors want to lend for such periods, the curve will be upward-sloping. If borrowers demand short-term funds and investors prefer to lend for longer periods, the curve will be downward-sloping.

Economic Theories on the General Level of Interest Rates

We have already looked at the factors which affect the level of interest rates for different maturities, instruments and borrowers. It is also worth considering theories which concern the general level of rates in the economy.

The rate of inflation is generally accepted to be a substantial ingredient of interest rates. Lenders normally expect interest rates at least to compensate them for the effect of rising prices. They therefore watch closely the *real* interest rate – that is, the interest received after inflation has been taken into account. Historically, real interest rates have averaged around 2 per cent; that is, if inflation were 7 per cent, interest rates would be 9 per cent. However, this relationship is far from permanent: real interest rates have been, at times, negative (below the rate of inflation), and in the middle of 1985 they were as high as 8 per cent, making that a very good time to lend.

The most important inflation rate is the rate which a lender *expects* to occur during the lifetime of his or her investment. The inflation rate which is published by the government, the consumer price index, gives only the *previous year*'s price rises, but it is *next year*'s price rises which will affect the value of the lender's investment. So lenders must undertake a difficult piece of economic forecasting.

It is very important to remember that financial markets are now international. Rates in Britain cannot be separated from those in other countries. UK investors can invest abroad if there is the chance for higher rates overseas, and foreign investors can invest here if UK rates are above their own. Both decisions are linked with the level of exchange rates. An investment in the USA might yield a high dollar rate of return, but if the dollar fell against sterling, investors would find themselves worse off.

Governments concerned about the level of interest rates will often intervene to try to influence their movement. They may be concerned about the exchange rate and may push interest rates up to defend the pound. Alternatively, they may be concerned about the amount of credit in the economy. People may be borrowing because interest rates are low, with the result that excessive demand is leading to inflationary pressures.

The classical explanation of the level of interest rates is associated with the theory of supply and demand. Thus the interest rate is the balancing point between the flow of funds from savers and the need for investment funds from business. If more funds become available from savers, or if industry has less need to borrow, interest rates will fall. If the funds available from savers are reduced, or if industry has a greater need to borrow, interest rates will rise. The demand for funds is likely to be affected by businessmen's expectations of future profits. If they believe that they will achieve a high rate of return on investment, they will be willing to borrow.

The supply of funds for borrowers depends largely on the willingness of the personal sector to save. Why do people save? One of the main reasons is to provide for old age or for children and spouses in the event of early death. This form of saving normally takes the form of investment in pension funds and life assurance and is helped by tax advantages. There has been a substantial growth in this form of saving since the 1960s. Another reason is to guard against rainy days caused by illness or unemployment: by its nature, such saving needs to be very liquid and is normally placed in building societies or interest-bearing bank accounts. A third reason for saving is to allow for major purchases or for holidays: again, such savings need a liquid home like a building society account.

Just as important as the reasons why people save are the reasons why the proportion of their income that they save changes over time. A certain amount of wealth is necessary before people can save – if all someone's income is needed just to pay for food and rent, there will be no money left to save. However, it is not correct to assume the reverse: that the larger a person's income, the more he or she saves. The highest income-earners are often among the biggest *borrowers*, since banks will extend credit only to those who they think will be able to repay. The greater a person's income, therefore, the greater the possibility for incurring debt. Debt is negative saving. In fact, the cautious middle classes have traditionally been the biggest savers.

However, academic explanations of movements in the savings ratio (the proportion of income which is saved) have focused on income levels. If income rises, according to theory, there will be a larger increase in the level of savings; if income fails, savings will drop disproportionately as people run down their incomes to pay for their expenditure.

During the inflationary 1970s the savings ratio increased sharply, much to most economists' surprise. Since inflation erodes the purchasing power of savings, it was assumed that consumers would run down their cash balances and deposits, which bear a negative real interest rate, and would prefer to hold physical assets such as property, the value of which tends to increase in line with inflation.

What seems to have happened instead is that savers, perhaps for the rainy-day reasons outlined above, were concerned to maintain the purchasing power of their savings. Because of the rate of inflation, they needed to save a greater proportion of their income merely to keep the value of their savings constant. The rise in the savings ratio in the 1970s was followed by an equally sharp decline in the 1980s as inflation fell and it became easier to maintain the value of savings.

In analysing savings patterns an important distinction to recognize is that between committed and discretionary savings. Committed savings are made up of contributions to life assurance and pension schemes and, as such, are relatively inflexible to changes in income. Discretionary savings represent payments into building society accounts or perhaps small shareholdings. Such savings adjust much more quickly to income movements. Repayment of a mortgage represents committed savings in that it is an investment in the value of a real asset (i.e. a house).

The puzzle over changes in the savings ratio has led some economists to abandon it as a serious tool for analysing economic change. Instead they now attempt to quantify the personal sector's holdings of liquid assets (cash, bank and building society deposits). Such a technique shows that in 1979, for example, when inflation was 17 per cent despite a nominal savings ratio of 2 per cent, the personal sector's holdings of liquid assets actually fell by 2.6 per cent in real terms as the value of savings was eroded by inflation.*

* J. Maratko and D. Stratford, *Key Developments in Personal Finance* (Basil Blackwell, 1985).

[4] The Banks

Banks are at the heart of the financial system. They are the one type of financial institution with which all of us are bound to come into contact at some point in our lives. To appreciate their importance, we must look first at their origins.

The First Bankers

Gold and silver have traditionally been the two predominant monetary metals, for the reasons outlined in Chapter 3. As a result, goldsmiths and silversmiths became the earliest bankers. Nervous citizens, who were well aware of the dangers of keeping their gold under the mattress, began to use the premises of the smiths, who had safes in which to store their wares, as places to keep their wealth. In return the smiths would give depositors handwritten receipts. It soon became easier for the depositors to pay their creditors with the smiths' receipts rather than go through the time-consuming process of recovering the gold or silver and giving it to the creditor, who might only re-deposit it with the smith. Creditors were willing to accept the receipts as payment provided that they were sure that they could always redeem the receipts for gold or silver when necessary.

These receipts were the first banknotes. Their legacy is visible today in the form of the confident statement on banknotes: 'I promise to pay the bearer on demand the sum of . . .' Despite having the image of the Queen to back it up, that statement is of no value today, and anyone attempting to redeem a £5 note for gold at his local bank will be disappointed.

Smart goldsmiths were able to take the development of banking one stage further. They noticed that only a small quantity of the gold stored in their safes was ever required for withdrawal, and that amount was roughly matched by fresh deposits. A substantial quantity of money was therefore sitting idle. That money could be lent (and interest earned) in the knowledge that the day-to-day requirements of depositors could still easily be covered (see Chapter 3).

The Italian Influence

Among the earliest bankers were goldsmiths and silversmiths from the Lombardy region of Italy who were granted land in London by King Edward I. One of the sites they received, Lombard Street, is at the heart of the modern City of London. Back in Italy the moneylenders had conducted their business from wooden benches in market places. The Italian word for bench, *banco*, was corrupted by the English into bank. The Italians were also responsible for introducing the symbols that were synonymous with British money until 1971 – £, s. and d, or *lire*, *soldi* and *denarii*.

Many of the early bankers misjudged their ability to absorb 'runs' – times of financial panic when investors rushed to claim back their gold. In such cases bankers had insufficient funds to meet the claims of depositors upon them and thus become 'bankrupt' (literally 'broken bench'). Such runs could easily become self-fulfilling. As soon as depositors feared that a bank might become bankrupt, they would flock to the bank in order to demand their money back, thus accelerating the bank's deterioration into ruin. Because of the nature of banking, no bank could stand a lengthy run. Some tried ingenious methods of doing so. One bank arranged for a few wealthy depositors to arrive by carriage at the front of the bank and withdraw their gold ostentatiously. The queueing small depositors were impressed. Meanwhile, the wealthy depositors sent their footmen round to the back to re-deposit the gold, so that it could be used to meet the claims of the other depositors.

Bankruptcies did not reduce the total number of banks. The seeming ease with which it was possible to make money from banking soon attracted others to take the places of the institutions that had failed. Gradually depositors regained confidence in the trustworthiness of the banks. Thus began a regular banking cycle of boom and bust. Professor Galbraith explains that the length of these cycles 'came to accord roughly with the time it took people to forget the last disaster – for the financial geniuses of one generation to die in disrepute and be replaced by new craftsmen who the gullible and the gulled could believe had, this time but truly, the Midas touch'.*

In the UK Charles I, that unlikely saint, gave banking an unwitting boost in 1640 by seizing £130,000 which merchants had unwisely committed to his safekeeping by placing it in the Royal Mint. Merchants decided that in future it would be rather safer to deposit their funds with the bankers in the City. It was not until 1694 that the government's financial reputation could be restored and the Bank of England established: by that time the crown was on the head of that sober and respectable Dutchman, William of Orange.

Modern Banking

The history of the Bank of England is considered in Chapter 5. This section considers the modern banks which have grown out of the early activities of the gold- and silversmiths.

There are many varieties of bank, but the two types that are most generally encountered in Britain are the retail and the merchant banks. Merchant banks are discussed later in this chapter and are best known for arranging complex financial deals and for financing trade. Retail banks take deposits from customers and lend them out, via overdrafts, to companies and insolvent individuals.

The banks which most people know, and are indeed at the heart of the UK financial system, are the clearing banks, so called because individual transactions between them are cleared through the London Clearing House. This saves the banks (and therefore the customers) a lot of time. Rather than have Lloyds pay over £20 to Barclays for Mr Brown's gas bill and Barclays pay £15 to Midland for Mrs Smith's shopping, the clearing house tots up all the individual transactions and arrives at a net position for each bank at the end of the day. Lloyds might owe Nat West £20,000 and Midland owe Barclays £15,000 – the important fact is that on a daily basis each bank is involved in only one clearing-house transaction with any other.

* J. K. Galbraith, *Money: Whence it Came, Where it Went* (Penguin, 1976).

CHAPS

The clearing process has been speeded by the introduction, in February 1984, of the Clearing Houses Automated Payment System (CHAPS). Its aim is to replace the old manual system of clearing cheques and bankers' payments. Rather than laboriously adding up the total of each bank's payments and receipts by hand, a CHAPS payment results in an adjustment to a running total held on the system. At the end of the day each bank has logged up a deficit or surplus *vis-à-vis* the other banks in the system. Payments are cleared in a few minutes rather than the hour and a half of the old system.

The workload of the clearing banks is huge. On an average day the clearing system handles a staggering 6 million transactions. In addition, nearly all the cash we use for payments is distributed through the banks.

The number of clearing banks has recently been increased to include the Royal Bank of Scotland,* Standard Chartered and Citibank, although the last named is not allowed on to the Committee of London and Scottish Clearing Banks. This has eliminated the convenient use of the shorthand term 'clearing banks' for the big four banks, Lloyds, National Westminster, Midland and Barclays. The three new clearing banks and the Trustee Savings Bank are also beginning to challenge the big four's dominance of the retail banking market.

The big four banks are still easily the best-known banks in England, with over 10,000 branches between them. They handle around four-fifths of all bank accounts in Britain. Although the services they provide are virtually identical, each has its own personality and problems.

Barclays Bank was originally an amalgamation of Quaker family banks. It is the biggest of all the British banks and can claim credit for being the first to introduce such ideas as the credit card and the automated teller machine. However, it has also acquired a reputation for being heavily involved in South African investment, which has brought the bank into the forefront of the political battle over apartheid. Periodically Barclays' annual meetings have been disrupted by dissident shareholders and its branches picketed by protesters. During the South African riots in 1985 Barclays took the opportunity to reduce its presence

* This chapter deals with the English banking system. The principles involved apply to both England and Scotland. In Scotland the big banks are the Royal Bank of Scotland, Clydesdale Bank and the Bank of Scotland.

in the country, and it adopted a tough line on the repayment of South African loans. Barclays has made perhaps the biggest investment of all the big four in the new securities revolution, joining a firm of stockbrokers and jobbers to its investment banking arm in a new group, Barclays de Zoete Wedd.

Lloyds has had its problems overseas, with its subsidiary, Lloyds Bank International, disappearing amid rumours of fraud and of dissension between executives. In 1985 it set up its own merchant bank and has refrained from making any expensive purchases of stockbroking firms, preferring to concentrate on developing in-house expertise. Lloyds has a large portfolio of loans to Argentina, which gave it many problems during the Falklands War. However, it has had better luck since its move into the property field, when it set up the successful Black Horse estate agency.

Midland Bank committed perhaps the biggest folly of all the UK banks in recent years by taking a share in the California-based Crocker Bank. Crocker soon resembled a bottomless pit down which the Midland was forced to pour more and more money, and it was eventually sold in early 1986. Midland's star has waned somewhat since the days before 1947, when it was the world's largest bank. It bought a substantial stake in a merchant bank, Samuel Montagu, but in 1984 Montagu's go-ahead chief executive, Steffan Gadd, left over policy disagreements. A sign of a possible change in Midland's luck occurred in 1985, when it introduced free banking to those customers who stayed in credit. To the surprise of its rivals, it attracted an extra 450,000 depositors that year, with the result that its competitors were forced to follow suit.

National Westminster Bank, the second biggest UK bank, was formed when the National Provincial and Westminster Banks merged in 1968. It survived a crisis of confidence in 1974, when it made the unwise step of issuing a statement assuring investors that it was not in trouble (a sure way of making people believe the opposite). It is now most famous for the 600-foot-high tower which dominates the City skyline and from the air resembles the Nat West symbol of three irregular hexagons. Nat West also has a separate and quite successful merchant banking arm, County Ltd.

The Importance of Retail Deposits

The big four banks are retail banks with a built-in advantage over their rivals – the current accounts of ordinary depositors like you and me. Such accounts pay no interest, whereas the banks can charge as much as 20 per cent on overdrafts – a fairly hefty profit margin. Banks without retail deposits have to borrow in the money market at market rates in order to obtain funds. In justification of the retail banks it can be said that the costs of such a large network of branches, in terms of buildings, staff and paperwork, take a substantial slice of that margin. Nevertheless in inflationary years, when overdraft rates rose well above 20 per cent, the major retail banks were able to announce record annual profits of £500 million or more.

The reliance on ordinary depositors to provide funds makes the banks well aware of the threat from the building societies, which have taken a larger and larger slice of personal savings during the past twenty years. Since all building society accounts earn interest, a lot of private customers have been careful to ensure that the minimum necessary balance is kept in their current accounts, while the rest is invested in a building society. That tendency has been encouraged, thanks to the introduction by some societies of chequing accounts and automated teller machines: one of the first to do so was the Abbey National. As a result, the banks tend to be left with accounts which are expensive to run but have very small balances.

Retail banks have counter-attacked the building societies with high-interest cheque accounts, Saturday opening and deposit accounts with no withdrawal penalty. They were helped by tax changes in the 1984 Budget (see Chapter 7). However, such changes reduce banks' profit margins by increasing the cost of their funds, so they have attempted to cut costs by trimming back their branch networks and increasing automation.

The Credit Card

Retail banks were also at the forefront of one of the most striking developments in personal finance over the last twenty years – the credit card. Barclays was the first with the Barclaycard (Visa); the other three big banks have responded with Access (Mastercharge). However, the most famous credit card of all, American Express, comes from the United States.

Using a credit card is an extremely expensive form of borrowing, with an interest rate of around 25 per cent per annum. But a card is very easy to obtain. There are very few forms to fill in. It is also convenient for the shopper. As a result, there are now over 20 million credit cards in the UK.

Credit card companies rely for profit on the fact that consumers do not pay off their balances at the end of the month. The sum outstanding may be very small, but the interest rate is high. There are surprisingly few bad debts among credit-card holders – fraud is much more of a problem. The fact that large items can be bought with a card (a cheque can normally be used only to cover items of up to £50) makes credit cards very attractive to the sneak thief, who can run up a bill of several thousands of pounds in the course of a few hours. However, the problem of the forgery of the cards themselves seems to have been solved by the incorporation in the design of holograms and computer codes.

Assets and Liabilities

Banks' assets are the loans and investments that they make with the deposits provided, which earn them interest. Those assets are held in a variety of forms. A substantial proportion must be lent out short-term – either at call (effectively overnight) with a special set of institutions called the discount houses or in the form of short-term deposits in the money markets (see Chapter 6). The rest is in the form of loans – to individuals and to businesses. Individuals and companies both borrow mainly in the form of overdrafts (see Chapter 8). Banks like overdrafts because they can, in theory, recall them overnight. That gives them further flexibility to deal with runs. The banks also lend longer-term, both domestically and internationally. In the UK loans are vital to the development of industry. Most companies start with the help of a bank loan, usually secured on the assets of a company. That means that if the firm folds, the bank has a claim on the firm's fixed capital, such as machinery or buildings. Internationally the banks' lending activities exploded in the 1970s, and, as we saw in Chapter 1, many of them now regret it.

The proportion of the banks' assets which they need to hold in the form of cash is known as the *cash ratio*. The ratio has from time to time been set by the Bank of England to ensure that banks remain sound. It determines to some extent the total amount that banks can lend. Other factors are involved, however.

One of the most important is the supply of creditworthy customers. Banks are normally cautious about the people to whom they grant overdrafts. If we assume that the number of people who are good credit risks (i.e. those who have a steady job, good references and a good financial record) remains fairly constant, that puts a limit on banks' expansion.

The general state of the economy will also affect the growth of bank lending. If the economy is healthy, more businesses will seek to borrow funds to finance their investment plans. If the economy is in recession few industries will be prepared to invest and, therefore, to borrow. Banks may seek to attract more borrowers by lowering their interest rates, but there is an obvious limit to such a process. The banks cannot afford to allow the return from their lending to fall below the cost of their borrowing. The return from lending must always be significantly higher because of the substantial costs involved in running a branch network.

Other Deposit-taking Institutions

The TSB

The big retail banks have faced increasing competition for the deposits of individuals. The challenge of the building societies has already been mentioned. The banks have other long-standing competitors, of which perhaps the most important are the Trustee Savings Banks (TSB), which were set up in the nineteenth century to collect the savings of small depositors who did not have enough money to be attractive to the larger banks. The banks were run by 'honorary trustees' who invested depositors' funds in gilt-edged securities and paid to the depositors the interest thus earned. In the 1860s there were over 600 banks, but this number fell to twenty by the mid-1970s as the banks merged.

In 1982 their organization was changed from a federal structure into that of a holding company (TSB Group plc) with subsidiaries. Thanks to the Trustee Savings Bank Act of 1976, they no longer have to invest all their money in government securities and can now lend to private customers. The new TSB is pushing hard to rival the traditional banks, helped by its long-standing hold on the savings of the working classes.

The TSB was due to go public in 1986. In the latest of a series of privatization measures it was to be floated, and the £1 billion of likely proceeds were to be swallowed by the bank. The process was brought to an abrupt halt in November 1985, when a depositor with the TSB Scotland successfully brought an action in the courts which claimed that the TSBs were owned by their depositors and that any profits from flotation should therefore accrue to them. However, the TSB successfully appealed and floated in the autumn of 1986. Now it has gone public, its shares and services will be very similar to those of the high-street banks.

The Post Office

It occurred to nineteenth-century governments that small savers (some of whom were depositors at the TSBs) were a very useful source of funds for the National Debt (the gap between the government's revenue and expenditure). At the time the nation's private banks served only a very select band of customers. The government accordingly opened up the Post Office Savings Bank to tap these funds. It soon became the nation's largest repository for savings, thanks to the advantage of a large number of branches. Not always the most competitive of banks, it paid a standard interest rate of 2.5 per cent from about 1900 until 1970. In recent years, however, the government has offered a wide variety of savings schemes through the Post Office, from index-linked Save As You Earn (SAYE) to 'granny bonds'. (A fuller discussion of the types of account on offer can be found in Chapter 15.)

The National Girobank

The National Girobank is really more a wire payment system than a bank. It is designed to appeal to the unbanked section of the community (estimated to be 40 per cent of the UK adult population) by allowing people to pay bills and to receive non-cash payments without the need for a bank account.

Such credit-transfer or giro systems are widespread in some Continental countries. In the UK the system has been able to develop because, like the National Savings Bank, it is based on post offices. Those without bank accounts have been able to pay their rent, gas, water and electricity bills over the counter at Post Office branches six days a week.

In the interests of a more efficient economy, possibly the most useful function that the Girobank could perform is to encourage the payment of wages by cheque rather than by cash. Cash payment of wages involves an enormous waste of time and money and is extremely prone to robbery and fraud. However, the growth of the National Girobank has not been as fast as its early enthusiasts hoped, perhaps because the clearing banks, building societies and Trustee Savings Banks have been competing for the same customers.

Finance Houses

The finance houses have traditionally been involved in the financing of hire-purchase agreements between customers and retailers. The interest on such agreements is quite high and the business potentially profitable. However, over the years successive governments have placed increasing restrictions on consumer credit as an anti-inflationary measure. Many consumers have switched to credit cards as a means of financing large purchases. As a result, finance houses have become less significant in the consumer market and have concentrated on lending to companies through techniques like leasing and factoring (see Chapter 8).

Merchant Banks

The high-street banks are household names. Although most people have heard of the term 'merchant bank', few can name specific institutions, such as Morgan Grenfell or S. G. Warburg. In general the merchant banks have a bad image and are associated with asset stripping and hard-hearted capitalism in many minds; yet for some they also offer the suggestion of adventure and romance in the financial system.

It is very difficult to define exactly what a merchant bank is: one of the main guides to the business says that merchant bankers are now 'seldom merchants and by no means always bankers'.* The other name by which merchant banks have been known is that of *accepting houses*, referring to their habit of accepting bills of exchange as a means of financing

* C. J. J. Clay and B. S. Wheble, *Modern Merchant Banking*, 2nd edn., rev. L. H. L. Cohen (Woodhead-Faulkner, 1983).

companies' trading activities, but that term is far too narrow as a definition of their activities.

The main difference between the clearing banks, like Lloyds and Barclays, and merchant banks is that the former have access to a vast pool of customer deposits. Although merchant banks do accept deposits from individual customers, these are not their major source of funds. Their profits depend on financial expertise – earning fees is as important to them as the traditional banking process of earning more from investment than is paid for deposits. This means that they are considerably smaller than their retail cousins. Merchant banks claim that they alone have the skills to pilot complicated financial deals, so they are frequently involved in share listings, bond issues and company takeovers.

In the early 1970s some merchant banks began to grow extremely fast. However, those which grew the most quickly proved to be the so-called 'fringe' banks – those which had invested in the property boom. The subsequent collapse of the property market in 1973–4 led to the secondary-market banking crisis and the downfall of such gurus as Jim Slater. The weakness of the fringe banks was that they depended for funds on the money markets, which meant that their liabilities were short-term. Property is a long-term investment. When the value of their property holdings fell, other banks in the money markets refused to lend to them. The Bank of England was forced to arrange a 'lifeboat' scheme to rescue the affected banks.

In the aftermath the longer-established merchant banks recognized that it was more prudent to concentrate on their advisory skills than to commit their own money in an attempt to grow too big too fast. In the event the competition came from the other direction as the clearing banks set up merchant-banking subsidiaries (e.g. Barclays Merchant Bank and County Ltd, the merchant-banking arm of the National Westminster Bank).

The Growth of Merchant Banking

Before the development of a worldwide banking system much international trade depended on trust – trust that goods would be delivered and that they would be paid for. It was much easier for overseas clients to trust merchants with whom they had traded before or those with whom their friends had traded. Thus the larger, well-established merchants found it easier to trade than did their smaller and less experienced competitors.

The smaller firms needed some way of assuring their clients that they were trustworthy and of raising money to cover the interval between the time at which goods were delivered and the time when they were paid for. The normal method of raising finance in this period was for the exporter to draw up a bill of exchange, whose value was a large proportion of the value of the goods being sold. The exporter could then sell the bill to a local banker at a discount and receive a substantial proportion of the money in advance. The extent of the bank's discount would represent two elements, a charge equivalent to interest on what was effectively a loan and a charge reflecting the risk of non-payment.

Small exporters found that banks would often charge a very large discount to advance money on their bills, if they agreed to do so at all. So the smaller merchants began to ask their larger brethren to guarantee (or accept) their bills. In the event that the small merchant failed to pay up, the large merchant would be liable. In return for the service the large merchants charged an acceptance commission, based on a percentage of the bill.

Eventually some of these large merchants found that they could earn more money from their finance activities than from their trading and became full-time merchant banks, or accepting houses. For a long time their business centred on the financing of trade, but gradually, as they developed a reputation for financial acumen, they extended the corporate finance side of their activities.

Many merchant banks were begun by immigrants, refugees or Jews, shut out of the rather stuffy world of the clearing banks. The wheeling and dealing appealed to more adventurous spirits. However, after the early inspiration of maverick leaders the merchant banks quickly became absorbed into the mainstream establishment. Nowadays the merchant banker who was not educated at Oxford or Cambridge is a rarity.

The Activities of Merchant Banks

Acceptance business is a way of lending a bank's name rather than its money – the bank is liable only if the client fails to pay up. Although they rarely grant overdrafts, the accepting houses do make loans to businesses, usually for fixed terms. It has been estimated that more than half the commercial advances made by merchant banks are made to overseas companies.*

The merchant banks are tied up particularly with the financing of trade, and apart from acceptance credits they are active in areas like cross-border leasing (a form of international hire purchase), project finance (when a loan is tied to a particular scheme, and the profits from the scheme are used to repay the loan) and factoring (when a company borrows money on the strength of its customer invoices – see Chapter 8).

Merchant banks do not normally seek to attract business or deposits from the general public: you would need to be pretty rich before a merchant bank would think it worth while to accept your custom. The most important clients of merchant banks are large companies, government institutions and other banks. The merchant banks obtain their funds either from these clients' deposits or by borrowing from other banks in the money markets (see Chapter 6). Most of their deposits have fairly short maturities (i.e. less than a year), and as a result merchant banks prefer to lend money only for short periods.

If a client wishes to borrow funds for more than a year, a merchant bank will normally set up a credit facility. Under such a facility the maximum amount that can be borrowed will be carefully controlled, and the interest rate will vary throughout the lifetime of the loan, according to some agreed formula. Should a borrower wish to borrow more than any one bank wants to lend, a merchant bank will arrange for others to join the facility.

Although these lending activities bring in the bulk of the profits for the merchant banks, the business which gives the banks the most publicity is their corporate finance work. Probably the most important part of this business is the handling of new issues of company shares on The Stock Exchange. There are fifty-five members of the Issuing Houses Committee (the club for merchant banks which are involved in new issue activity) but only fifteen accepting houses. The mechanics of a new issue are described in Chapter 10. The fees involved in arranging a new issue can be substantial. (Kleinwort Benson was rumoured to have been paid over £1 million for its part in the British Telecom issue.)

This traditional activity of merchant banks may well be challenged by the 'Big Bang'. The retail banks have bought up the stockbroking and jobbing firms and are developing their merchant-banking subsidiaries.

* Clay and Wheble, *Modern Merchant Banking*.

They will be competing hard for new issues business. The merchant banks certainly did not have it all their own way before the 'Big Bang'. The stockbrokers had a significant presence in the market, particularly with those small firms joining the Unlisted Securities Market. Some merchant banks have responded by attempting to copy the example of the American investment banks and becoming securities houses, offering a wide range of financial services. The most notable example is S. G. Warburg, now part of the Mercury Securities Group, which also includes Akroyd and Smithers and Rowe and Pitman. Warburgs has long been regarded as one of the most innovative merchant banks and was heavily involved in the beginnings of the Eurobond market (see Chapter 11).

Company Takeovers

Corporate mergers and acquisitions have been more important even than new issues in keeping the merchant banks' names in the public eye. Over the past few years such deals have become increasingly acrimonious, with charge and counter-charge flying back and forth in national newspapers. The growing importance of American banks in this field is extending the use of the rather less 'gentlemanly' tactics used in US takeovers.

Both the company which is attempting to make a takeover and the company defending itself against one usually employ merchant banks to advise them on tactics. The fees involved can be substantial (in some cases, over £1 million), but the stakes are also pretty high. Recent bids have offered sums approaching £2 billion.

The process of making a takeover bid is long and complex. Virtually every company will reject the first offer made for it, purely as a matter of principle. The merchant bank's first task, if acting for a predator, is to try to put a price on the company that the client is trying to acquire. Having done so, it then has to make an offer price which is sufficiently attractive for the target company to worry that some of its shareholders may be tempted to accept it. The target will then be forced to divulge extra information about its finances, which can be used as further ammunition in the predator's attacks. The acquiring company will argue that the management of the defending company is poor and that a new team would greatly increase the return to the shareholders.

The merchant bank of the defending company will be seeking to use the same figures to persuade its shareholders that it is worth considerably more than the price offered. It will announce that profits are about to improve, whereas the outlook for the predatory company is dim. It will attempt to ensure that the shareholders are given enough information to keep them loyal, while not divulging any hint of financial weakness to the predators. Not only will this information be sent via the mail to known shareholders: companies will also often advertise in the national press. (Thomas Tilling is reputed to have spent £1.5 million on advertising while attempting, unsuccessfully, to fight off a bid from British Tyre and Rubber.) In some circumstances a company may apply to the Office of Fair Trading, arguing that a merger of the two companies would create a near-monopoly, which would prejudice consumers' interests. And, if all else fails, it may encourage another company, a so-called 'white knight', to take it over to avoid the predator's clutches.

Companies are almost always bought and sold not for cash alone but for a whole range of financial assets. The merchant bank should advise its client as to which particular package of financial instruments will prove most attractive to the target shareholders. Apart from cash, the predator might offer its own shares, bonds which pay fixed or floating rates of interest, bonds which are convertible into shares or even a fixed asset such as property. If a large proportion of the price offered consists of bonds or other debt instruments, this can cause problems if the bid is successful. The new conglomerate company may find its financial position weakened because of the debt it has taken on.

Takeover Fever

In 1985 and 1986 there was a spate of takeover bids for some of Britain's largest companies, which provoked much press comment. British Tyre and Rubber took over Dunlop, the tyre company. British American Tobacco took over Hambro Life, the assurance company. Habitat and Burton joined together to buy up Debenhams, the retail group. Imperial Group attempted to merge with United Biscuits only to fall foul of an offer from takeover specialists Hanson Trust. Argyll pursued the whisky makers Distillers and then lost out to a counter-bid from Guinness. Perhaps the most significant of all the bids, however, was the offer, worth slightly over £1.9 billion, by the Australian company Elders IXL for Allied Lyons.

Elders was a company valued somewhere over £500 million. It was able to make a much bigger offer for Allied Lyons only because of backing from major banks, including Citibank. The banks lent Elders the money, expecting to be repaid with the profits from the sale of the various parts of the Allied Lyons empire. It was the first time that a consortium bid of this kind had been made in the UK. In the USA they are far more common.

It seems likely that other US takeover practices will be imported. In that country defensive tactics are extremely sophisticated, including such exotic-sounding ploys as the 'poison pill' defence and the 'shark repellent'. The UK's most experienced takeover merchants, Hanson Trust, had to battle through the US courts to overcome the resistance of target company SCM in late 1985.

Theoretically, all mergers and acquisitions are bound by the restrictions of the City Takeover Code. In addition, takeover bids can, if they are likely to lead to an industry dominated by one firm, be referred to the Monopolies and Mergers Commissions by the Office of Fair Trading subject to the approval of the Secretary of State of the DTI. However, the City takeover code is only voluntary; it has failed to restrain some less salubrious takeover activities, and the decisions of the Office of Fair Trading on referral have been, to put it mildly, erratic.

The takeover spree was typical of a bull market (one in which share prices rise continuously). Most takeovers are achieved by giving shareholders of the target company shares in the acquiring company in exchange. The acquiring company's shares are much more valuable at the top of a bull market. The early 1980s saw improving profits for companies, which gave them cash to spend on acquisitions. However, in the middle of 1986 the market began to fear that the end of the bull market was in sight, and several takeovers, most notably Dixon's bid for Woolworth, failed.

Fund Management

A third and important area of merchant banks' work is fund management. Many of the investment and unit trusts advertised in the daily papers are run by merchant bankers. Among companies with large pension funds there is also a growing trend towards spreading the management of such funds among several banks rather than managing the funds within the companies themselves. The merchant banks, with their reputation for financial expertise, have been ideally placed to take advantage of this trend (see Chapter 9). In total, Clay and Wheble estimate that merchant banks manage over £20 billion worth of funds.* However, the figure may be considerably greater: Robert Fleming, one of the largest merchant banks, estimated in 1985 that it alone manages or advises over £11 billion worth of funds.

The existence of fund-management and corporate finance departments within the same bank permits potential conflicts of interest. A merchant bank which is advising on a takeover knows that it is more than probable that the share price of the target company is certain to rise when the bid is announced. It must be tempting to inform those members of the Bank who have funds to invest in the stock market. In fact, an article in the *Economist* in 1985 revealed that there was a tendency for the share prices of target companies to increase *before* the announcement of a bid. Merchant banks are very sensitive to criticisms on this score and claim that 'Chinese walls' effectively separate their departments.

After the 'Big Bang' a few merchant banks will become part of financial conglomerates which will have substantial share portfolios that might benefit from insider knowledge. Some commentators believe that the merchant banks will lose business to independent fund managers who have no trading or corporate finance activities. However, any losses may be compensated by the growing tendency for U S pension funds to invest abroad. They may well call on U K investment management expertise to help them.

Other merchant banks (like Lazards) have decided that survival after the 'Big Bang' will lie in independence rather than in absorption into a conglomerate. They will pursue the traditional merchant-bank activitiy of living on their wits by wheeling and dealing. One of the big questions posed by the 'Big Bang' is whether the large conglomerates (like Warburg) or the small independents (like Lazards) will be the winners.

* Clay and Wheble, *Modern Merchant Banking*.

[5] The Bank of England

The Bank of England, sometimes known as the Old Lady of Threadneedle Street, was founded in 1694, when King William III needed money to fight Louis XIV of France. A Scottish merchant, William Paterson, suggested that a bank should be formed which could lend money to the government. The Bank was founded, after an Act of Parliament and a Royal Charter, with start-up capital of £1.2 million. Only fifteen years later the Bank was given the monopoly of joint-stock banking in England and Wales. This ensured that it remained the biggest bank in the country, since those banks which were *not* joint-stock could by law have no more than six partners, which severely limited their ability to expand. However, that monopoly was eroded by Acts in 1826 and 1833, and the Bank's pre-eminent position was not really cemented until the Bank Charter Act of 1844. The Act followed a succession of banking failures, which was blamed on the over-issue of banknotes. Until 1844 any bank had the right to issue its own notes, opening up the risk not only of fraud but also of inflation. The Bank Charter Act restricted the rights of banks other than the Bank of England to issue notes; this restriction became total (in England and Wales) in 1921. Scottish banks can still print notes.

By that time the Bank's position as one of the country's most prestigious institutions had been estabished, and the inter-war governor, Montagu Norman, was one of the most influential men of his age. Such was the power of the Old Lady that the Attlee government thought it right to nationalize it in 1946. It is now answerable to the Treasury, although it maintains a certain amount of independence.

The Governor of the Bank of England still holds a very influential post. The present incumbent, Robin Leigh-Pemberton, formerly Nat West's Chairman, was a controversial appointment because of his Conservative Party links. (To be fair to Mr Leigh-Pemberton, if all Tory bankers were to be excluded from consideration for the post, there would be few applicants in the running.) Mr Leigh-Pemberton runs a bank with a vast range of responsibilities. The one for which it is perhaps most famous is the printing of banknotes. Before the phasing out of £1 notes the Bank was printing 7.5 million new notes every day (and withdrawing around the same number). That was equal to almost thirty new notes each year for every person in the country. British people are notoriously unwilling to handle old banknotes; in Germany only nine new notes are printed per person per year.

The watermark and the metal strip are not the only reasons why notes are hard to forge; the hand-engraved portraits and intricate geometric patterns are also extremely difficult to reproduce. The man whose signature appears on the bottom of notes, David Somerset, is the head of the banking department at the Bank of England.

The most important of the Bank's duties, however, is its role as banker to the government. All the main banking accounts of the government are held there, and our taxes eventually end up there, in the accounts held by the Exchequer. The Bank has few branches outside London and is therefore not able to hold the accounts of all the government departments; indeed, departments are encouraged to bank where the charges are lowest.

As well as holding the government's money, the Bank is its agent in influencing the financial system. There are three broad financial indicators which the government, through the Bank, regularly attempts to influence: the level of interest rates, the amount of credit in the economy (i.e. the money supply) and the exchange rate of the pound.

For much of this century the Bank made its view of the correct level of interest rates abundantly clear through the announcement of bank rate or its successor, Minimum Lending Rate (MLR). This was the rate that the Bank set for lending to the discount houses, the institutions which (as will be explained in the next chapter) acted as a buffer between the Bank of England and the retail banks. If the discount houses were short of money, they could borrow from the Bank of England, which could increase or reduce the bank rate or MLR according to whether it wanted rates to rise or fall. Like any other financial institution, the discount houses had to charge more to lend than to borrow. So when they lent money (usually in the form of discounting bills) they increased their interest rates. In this way the rates were passed on through the rest of the economy.

Since 1981 the Bank of England has changed its method of attempting to control interest rates. It now announces daily whether it will buy or sell bills within four bands of maturity: 0–14 days, 15–33 days, 34–63 days and 64–91 days. By altering the supply and demand for these bills the Bank hopes to affect the price of borrowing (i.e. interest rates) and, in particular, the relationship between the various bands of rates. However, since the Bank officially likes to proclaim that it is the market which sets rates, it does not publish the spread of rates that it would like to see. It reserves the right, however, to re-establish MLR at any time and, indeed, briefly did so during the sterling crisis of January 1985.

The government's activities are inextricably linked with the level of credit in the economy. It is the country's largest borrower. Each year the government spends considerably more than it raises from the public in the form of taxes. Even after a prolonged regime of spending cuts by the Conservative government, the public-sector borrowing requirement (PSBR), as the government's deficit is generally known (see Chapter 8), was in 1985 still as much as £10 billion.

The Bank of England is responsible for managing the government's debts, and its task is not confined to managing the annual deficit. Over the years the number of times that the government has spent more than it has received has vastly exceeded the occasions when it has been in surplus. As a consequence, some £116 billion-plus of government debt is outstanding. When this debt matures (that is, when it needs to be repaid) it must be refinanced.

Fortunately, the government finds it quite easy to borrow money, since, as we noted in the Introduction, it is regarded as a very good credit risk indeed. When the government borrows long-term the bonds it issues are known as *gilt-edged securities*, or gilts, partly because of the certainty that they will be repaid and partly because the original certificates were literally edged in gold.

Gilts

Each year not only does the Bank of England have to issue new gilts to cover that year's budget deficit but also old gilts become due to be repaid and must therefore be refinanced. To keep gilts attractive to ordinary investors, the Bank attempts to issue them in a wide range of varieties. Some will not be repaid for as long as twenty-five years, others in less than five.* Some gilts are index-linked, which means that the interest rate they pay varies with the rate of inflation. Others are offered with only a very low interest rate but are sold at less than face value in order to give the investor the prospect of capital gain.

The Bank wants to ensure both that it can sell enough gilts to cover the government's debt and that the gilt market is 'orderly' and not subject to violent fluctuations in prices. If the market became 'disorderly', people might become reluctant to purchase gilts, making it difficult for the government to fund its debt. One way in which the Bank attempts to control the market is by holding back some of its stock and selling it whenever there seems to be excess demand for gilts. The Bank will always try and keep one such issue (known as a *tap issue*) on hand.

Not all of the government's borrowing is financed long-term in the form of gilts. It also issues short-term instruments, known as *Treasury bills*. The bills generally have a life of three months and are issued at a discount to their face value. The bill buyer receives the full face value when the bills are repaid by the Bank.

Under the Conservative government the importance of the Treasury bill market has been much reduced. Now only £100 million of bills are issued each week, compared with £500–600 million previously. The reason is that between 1981 and 1985 the Bank used a technique known as *over-funding* to help it to control the money supply.

How does over-funding work? As we noted in the Introduction, it is very difficult to define exactly what money is. However, it is clear that the more liquid an asset, the more nearly it approaches the status of money. Gilts, being very long-term and illiquid assets indeed, are included in none of the definitions of money. If the government sells gilts to the non-bank sector therefore, those that buy them will run down their bank deposits in order to pay for gilts. Since banks are careful to maintain the relationship between their loan volume and their deposit volume, they will call in their loans if their deposits fall. The result is a drop in the money supply. Conversely, if the Bank buys back gilts from the non-bank sector, then the public will have cash in the form of a bank deposit where once it had gilts. This increase in deposits will result in an increase in bank loans and will thus increase the money supply.

When the Bank wants to cut back the money supply it issues more gilts than are needed to fund the government's deficit: it *over-funds*.

* For special reasons some gilts will never be repaid at all.

However, this is a tactic that leads to problems. If the banks are short of cash because of over-funding, they recall the funds they have lent to the discount houses. The latter are entitled to borrow from the Bank of England as *lender of the last resort*; the Bank buys bills from the discount houses. Four years of doing so led the Bank of England to accumulate a bill 'mountain', which has distorted the money markets. Although the Bank could theoretically charge a high interest rate (i.e. pay a low price) on these bills, it does not, since that would push up the level of interest rates in the economy. As a result it is now normally cheaper for companies to borrow by issuing a bill than by seeking a loan from a bank.

The type of the bills that the Bank of England has accumulated has therefore been subject to change. As we have already seen, the Bank has reduced its issue of Treasury bills. Commercial bills have taken their place in the discount houses' holdings.

The commercial bills which the Bank of England is prepared to buy from the discount houses are more strictly known as *eligible bank bills*. A bank bill is a bill sent from a creditor to a debtor, which is guaranteed (accepted) by a bank.* The creditor can take the bill to another bank, which will give him money in advance of the time when the debtor is due to pay. The creditor will not, of course, receive all his money: the accepting house will charge a fee for giving its guarantee; the buying bank will buy the bill only at a discount. Often the buyer will be a discount house. Because of the problems caused by its over-funding the Bank of England in 1981 increased the number of eligible banks from a handful to over a hundred.

So the Bank issues gilts and Treasury bills to cover the government's debt and, at the same time, to influence economic trends. Treasury bill policy was traditionally used to affect the level of short-term interest rates. After 1981 the Bank of England used its vast holdings of commercial bills to influence rates. However, in late 1985 the Chancellor of the Exchequer announced that over-funding would be no longer used as a monetary policy. This may yet lead to the re-emergence of the Treasury bill as the major part of the short-term market.

The Bank of England has other policy options for controlling the money supply. Retail banks make wealth more liquid by turning long-term assets into liquid funds. This concerns the Bank of England, since bank deposits count as money, while shareholdings do not. Over the

* That is, the bank will pay the bill holder if the exporter fails to.

years, therefore, one of the Bank's most common weapons for affecting the money supply has been the control of the ratio of liquid to illiquid assets in the portfolios of commercial banks. This weapon has been particularly effective because of the multiplier effect of the ratio. If the liquid asset ratio is 10 per cent, a £1 million drop in a commercial bank's liquid assets will force it to cut its assets by £10 million.

The Bank of England's current regulations are probably more relaxed than at any time since the war. Banks need hold only 0.5 per cent of their eligible liabilities in cash. No longer is it mandatory for banks to hold a certain percentage of their funds with the discount houses. However, these regulations are in force not so much to control the amount of money in the economy as to ensure that the Bank of England has funds with which to finance its activities. In addition, banks are required to 'consult' with the Bank of England about their liquidity policies, although that is a requirement which is designed more to ensure that banks stay solvent than to affect the money supply.

The Bank also manages the Exchange Equalization Account, through which it can intervene in the foreign-exchange markets to affect the value of the pound. If the government feels that the pound is too low, the Bank will intervene by buying pounds and selling foreign currencies, hoping that the laws of supply and demand will push the pound up. However, if sentiment against the pound is strong, the Bank will merely succeed in losing money.

If the pound is felt to be too strong, the Bank will intervene by selling pounds and buying foreign currencies. The size of the flows in the foreign-exchange markets now means that the Bank will not normally intervene unless it is acting in concert with other central banks.

Before 1979 the role of the Exchange Equalization Account was much broader – the Bank was involved in every foreign-exchange transaction of any size. However, when the Conservative government came into office in that year it abolished exchange controls, and individuals and institutions can now undertake foreign-currency transactions without notifying the Bank.

Supervision

In addition to these varied duties, the Bank also has to keep a watchful eye on the economy. This supervisory role draws it into a wide variety of areas. It reported its concern about the activities of the London Metal Exchange some eighteen months before the tin market collapsed, for example, and scandals at Lloyd's forced it to intervene and to appoint an outside Chief Executive (see Chapter 12).

The Bank's most important supervisory activities, however, relate to the banking system. The 1979 Banking Act defined not only the word 'bank' but also the Bank of England's statutory powers of supervision. As we have already seen, it has often used its powers to regulate the asset portfolios of banks. It is also concerned to ensure that bank depositors are protected from collapse. This role was brought into the public eye in 1984, when the Bank was forced to step in and buy Johnson Matthey Bank, for the nominal sum of £1, to save it from insolvency.

The Johnson Matthey scandal forced the Bank to revise and strengthen its supervisory functions. George Blunden, the man who guided the banking system through the secondary banking crisis of 1974–5, came out of retirement to take on the Deputy Governor's post. He and the Bank were faced with dealing with two problems: the prevention of fraud and the protection of bank depositors.

A White Paper was produced in December 1985 with the aim of bringing in a Banking Bill to replace the 1979 Banking Act. A special board, the Board of Banking Supervision, was set up. The board will have eight members, three from inside the Bank (the Governor, the Deputy Governor and the executive director in charge of banking supervision) and five outside members, who will probably be ex-private-sector bankers and accountants. The Chancellor of the Exchequer will be involved in the selection of the Board's members, a step which has been widely seen as a diminution of the Governor's powers. (It is well known that Chancellor Lawson was less than happy with the Bank of England's handling of the Johnson Matthey affair.) The Board will be responsible for advising the Governor on a wide variety of issues, including the development and evolution of supervisory practice, the administration of banking supervisory legislation and the structure, staffing and training of the Banking Supervision Division.

The two-tier system of banks and licensed deposit takers (LDTs), established only in 1979, will be abolished. Under the old system there were 300 banks and rather more LDTs, which varied considerably in size and function. Supervising them all will greatly increase the Bank's workload and its supervision department has accordingly been extended.

Under the new system authorized institutions will need to have minimum net assets of £1 million, and issued capital of at least £5 million, to be able to call themselves a bank. They will have to report to the Bank certain information about their lending patterns. It will be a criminal offence 'knowingly or recklessly to provide information to the supervisor which is false or misleading in a material particular'.

One of the trickiest areas in banking supervision is the role of bank auditors. The Bank of England had hinted that auditors might be required to report to it directly – a breach of the time-honoured tradition of confidentiality between auditors and audited. According to the White Paper this will happen only in the most exceptional circumstances (i.e. when the auditor suspects fraud). Auditors will have no *statutory* obligation to report serious wrongdoing to the Bank. However, the Bank will have powers to appoint a second firm of accountants if it is dissatisfied with the work of the first.

The White Paper recommends that the Bank of England should be notified of any exposure to an individual customer which amounts to more than 10 per cent of a bank's capital (equity and near-equity) and that exposures of over 25 per cent require *prior* notification to the Bank. (As mentioned in the Introduction, Johnson Matthey Bank lent 115 per cent of its capital to just two borrowers.)

The whole issue poses an awkward dilemma for the Bank. To what extent will the knowledge that the Bank can act as a safety net encourage banking managers to follow the reckless policies of Johnson Matthey? However, if the Bank of England were to allow a bank to fail, would that shatter confidence in the UK banking system? And if it imposes too tight constraints on banks, will that drive the banks away to less watchful financial centres?

[6] The Discount Houses and the Money Markets

The business of most financial institutions is to borrow money from one source and lend it to another at a profit. The most obvious case is the commercial banks. They receive the bulk of their funds in the form of current accounts, which pay no interest but may be withdrawn at any moment. Although the banks make loans to companies and buy some long-term securities, they want to keep a substantial proportion of their money in liquid form. In order to earn interest on this money and thus to make a profit, they lend it out to other financial institutions in the so-called money markets.

Banks can also find themselves short of the cash needed to meet their obligations and therefore have to *borrow* in the money markets. Thus the markets are one of the main channels through which banks can iron out day-to-day fluctuations in their cash flow. The money markets are a particularly important source of funds for the dealings of the merchant banks, since these do not possess the customer deposits of the clearing banks. To distinguish them from the retail markets, the money markets are often known as the *wholesale markets*, and the deposits or bills involved are usually denominated in large amounts. A typical deal might involve a loan of, say, £5 million.

Transactions in the money markets are normally in the form of either deposits or bills. Deposits are made (with the exception of money-at-call) for set periods of time at an agreed rate of interest. Bills are pieces of paper which are issued at a discount to their face value. The bills can then be traded by their holders after issue.

The Discount Houses

The discount houses are so called because the bulk of their business is the discounting of bills. From companies or banks they buy bills at a discount to their face value only to be repaid with the full amount when the bills mature. The difference between the face value and the discounted value is the equivalent of an interest payment.

Traditionally, as we saw in Chapter 5, the discount houses have formed a buffer between the Bank of England and the commercial banks. The houses have been a vital link in the chain which converts the funds of short-term depositors into funds for long-term borrowers.

As already noted, banks have to lend a substantial proportion of their deposits for very short periods in case a 'run' occurs and a large number of depositors decide to withdraw their funds. Discount houses enable the commercial banks to do this by borrowing from them 'on call' (i.e. overnight). The houses then invest the funds they borrow from the banks in Treasury bills and in other short-term instruments which generally pay a higher rate of interest.

Virtually all of the money borrowed by the discount houses is technically at call, but in practice they will offer higher rates to those prepared to enter into a gentlemen's agreement not to withdraw their funds for a fixed term. The bulk of the money is borrowed from the banks, but nowadays 15–20 per cent of the total is borrowed from corporations. The discount houses need to pay a competitive rate to attract company funds, since, unlike the banks, companies have no legal obligation to invest with them. Banks have traditionally, though not currently, been required by the Bank of England to hold a proportion of their liabilities with the members of the London Discount Market Association (LDMA). As a consequence, discount houses have not had to be quite so competitive in offering rates to their banking customers, paying well below (typically about 1.5 per cent below) bank base rates. As the regulations on their holdings have slackened, banks have continued to lend to the houses because the funds are so liquid.

Every day those banks and companies which do deposit funds with the discount houses must decide by midday whether they will recall their funds. The representatives of the discount houses call on the major banks in the morning, dressed by tradition in top hats, to discover whether or not they will do so.

By borrowing overnight and investing in Treasury bills (which normally have a maturity of three months) the discount houses are committing the classic financial sin of borrowing short-term and lending long-term. If for some reason overnight rates rose dramatically, the price of Treasury bills would fall. (Bond and bill prices fall as interest rates rise.) That would leave the houses with dramatically increased borrowing costs *and* much less valuable investments.

Because they run this risk the houses add vital liquidity to the money markets. However, the fact that their funds can be recalled instantly means that they can never be sure how much they will have. As a consequence, the discount houses can easily find themselves short of funds when the banks call back their deposits. Because of this the Bank of England gives the discount houses a further privilege. The Bank will act as lender of last resort and will lend them funds if they need them, whether through a straight loan or through the rediscounting of commercial or Treasury bills. As we shall see, this gives the Bank considerable power to influence the level of interest rates in the market.

In return for these privileges the discount houses are required to 'make a market' in Treasury and commercial bills. (Making a market means that you are always ready to buy or sell a particular product.) Each week when the government offers its Treasury bills the discount houses are required to tender for all the bills on offer. They effectively underwrite the issue – all those bills which are not bought by outside institutions will be bought by the discount houses. This system pleases the Bank of England because it ensures that the government can always fund its debt.

As we saw in Chapter 5, the Treasury bill tender is far less important for the discount houses than it once was. In the 1970s the Treasury's weekly offer was sometimes over £500 million. In the 1980s the figure has been fairly steady at £100 million a week.

As a result, the discounting of commercial bills has become a much more important part of the discount houses' work. These are bills issued by companies to allow them to borrow short-term. If commercial bill rates fall below those in the money markets, this can lead to the process known as 'roundtripping', which occurs when companies borrow by issuing commercial bills and invest the proceeds in the money markets, making a guaranteed profit in the process. It is a practice frowned upon by the Bank of England.

In addition to Treasury and commercial bills, the discount houses also invest in certificates of deposit issued by the major banks (see below). Like commercial bills, certificates of deposit offer the houses the opportunity for both interest income and capital appreciation. The discount houses also invest in short-term gilts, particularly in the last few months before the gilts mature.

The fact that the discount houses receive the greater proportion of their funds from the banks and then invest heavily in bank paper illustrates how closely the fortunes of the two groups are tied together. Indeed, it also indicates how fine are the margins on which the discount houses work. Making a profit by borrowing from and lending to the same institutions requires agile financial management.

Discount houses tend to hope for interest rates to fall, since they then make a capital gain on their investments. If rates rise, the value of the discount houses' assets falls while the cost of their funds rises.

Repurchases

One investment technique which the discount houses use, when the Bank of England allows them to, is the repurchase agreement or *repo*. The houses sell part of their portfolio of commercial or Treasury bills to the Bank of England and agree to buy them back the following day or at some future date. The repurchase price will be higher than the selling price, to reflect the interest that the securities will earn in the meantime. The discount houses hope that the money obtained through repos will be reinvested at a rate higher than that paid to the Bank.

The Future of the Discount Houses

The long-term effects of the 'Big Bang' may hit the discount houses particularly hard. Competition in the money markets will increase, and it may be difficult for the smaller discount houses to survive. Some small houses have been bought by outside institutions to give them a foothold in the money markets.

The most notable purchase has been that of Seccombe, Marshall and Campion by Citicorp, the largest bank in the world. Seccombe, although the smallest of the houses, had immense prestige because of its role, until early 1986, as the Bank of England's special buyer. The chairman of Seccombe acted for the bank by buying back bills from the houses when they needed the money. With Seccombe's acquisition by Citicorp, its former role has been assumed by the Bank of England. In February 1984 Alexander Discount was bought by Mercantile House, and the latter added Jessel, Toynbee and Gillett to its financial services group a few months later. Another house, Gerald Quin Cape, was bought by Banque Belge. Some felt that the Bank of England had 'encouraged' the outside institutions to rescue the houses from ignominy.

The number of discount houses had been steadily diminishing, and by 1985 the two largest houses accounted for around 50 per cent of the market's capacity. For the independent houses that remain the short gilts area of their portfolios will become even more important. The two largest discount houses, Union Discount and Gerrard and National, have been appointed market dealers in the new expanded gilts market. However, they are among the smallest of the twenty-eight potential gilts players, and may yet find it a struggle to keep up with the market giants.

Discount houses are peculiar to the UK financial system, and their usefulness has often been questioned. The 'Big Bang' may prove their death knell, but their obituaries have been read before only for the houses to disappoint their undertakers.

The Money Markets

Although the discount houses have traditionally been the focus of textbook explanations of the money markets, it is important to remember that the bulk of the markets' business consists of banks lending to and borrowing from each other. In March 1984 the total of loans in the interbank sterling market amounted to around £34 billion. Most of the loans made had maturities of three months or less.

Much of this trading takes place via the telephone, with traders watching market prices move on electronic screens. Each trader will be seeking to manage a bank's money for profit. He or she will attempt to do so in one of two ways. As in the foreign-exchange markets (see Chapter 14), dealers charge a spread between rates: they lend at a slightly higher rate than the rate at which they borrow. The spread may be as small as $\frac{1}{32}$ of a percentage point. Because of the size of the deals involved, the cumulative effect of spreads can add up to a sizeable profit.

However, the dealer cannot rely on the spread alone. Interest rates are constantly fluctuating. This can wipe out the dealer's spread. For example, a dealer may agree to lend at $8\frac{1}{32}$ per cent and borrow at 8 per cent. He accordingly lends money at $8\frac{1}{32}$ per cent. While he is making the deal, the market moves to $8\frac{1}{8}$–$8\frac{3}{32}$ per cent. If the

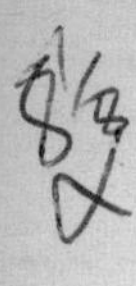

dealer now borrows the money that the bank needs to cover the loan, he or she will now have to pay $8\frac{3}{32}$ per cent, $\frac{2}{32}$ per cent more than the bank is receiving, even allowing for the spread.

The second way in which money-market dealers make money, therefore, is by trying to anticipate these moves in rates. If they expect rates to rise, they will borrow more than they lend (in market parlance, 'go short'). If they expect rates to fall, they will lend more than they borrow ('go long'). So in the above example the dealer went long at the wrong time – when markets were rising. Had he or she gone short and borrowed at 8 per cent, then when rates rose the dealer could have lent the bank's money at the new higher rate.

Money Brokers

Linking the activities of the money-market dealers are the money brokers. They wheel and deal on the telephone, linking lenders and borrowers in return for a commission. Unlike the dealers, they do not lend and borrow themselves. They depend on high turnover to make money. Fortunately for the brokers, turnover has grown considerably over the past few years as interest rates have fluctuated more violently. The commission that brokers earn is tiny (less than 0.02 per cent). However, all those small percentages add up to a lot of money when the principal sums involved are large. Even the advent of negotiated commissions at the start of 1986 did not prevent the larger brokers from maintaining their profits.

The 'Big Bang' led the largest brokers to recognize the need to diversify into the broking of securities, particularly gilts. Mercantile House, Exco, Tullett and Tokyo, Mills and Allen, and Charles Fulton, five of the six biggest broking firms, have been made interbank dealers in the new gilts market (see Chapter 2). They will be linking those who wish to buy and sell government securities.

Mercantile House is a particularly interesting broker because it is one of the new financial conglomerates. It owns two discount houses, Alexanders and Jessel, Toynbee and Gillett, and the stockbroking firm Laing and Cruickshank. These it can add to interests in US brokers Oppenheimer and smaller stakes in Japanese money brokers. It will be a primary dealer in the new gilts markets and may yet prove to be one of the most successful conglomerates.

Certificates of Deposit

The money markets have four further components: certificates of deposit (CDs), local authority loans, commercial paper and the Euromarket. The latter, because of its size and international scope, is considered in Chapter 11. The simplest definition of a CD is that it is a tradeable document attesting that the holder has lent money to a bank or building society. In March 1984 the size of the CD market was around £11 billion.

CDs are a highly important form of investment in the money markets. If an investor puts his or her money into a term loan, it cannot be withdrawn until the loan matures. A CD, however, can be sold by an investor if the funds are needed suddenly. They are dealt with on an interest-accrued basis – that is, the money that the CD would have earned is added to the CD's face value. However, the rate which the investor will actually have earned will depend on the way that interest rates have moved since the CD was purchased.

For example, an investor buys a three-month CD for £100,000 at an interest rate of 10 per cent. If the CD is held until maturity, the bank will repay the investor £102,500.* That sum will be repaid to whomever holds the CD when it matures. After a month the investor decides to sell the CD. Its price will not necessarily be one-third of the difference between £100,000 and £102,500 (£100,833); it will be so only if interest rates have stabilized and if investors expect interest rates to stay at 10 per cent. If rates have dropped (or are expected to drop), the price will be more than £100,833 because the CD will be more attractive to other investors. If rates have risen (or are expected to rise), the price will be less than £100,833 because investors will be able to get more attractive interest rates elsewhere. In either case the price will settle at the level at which it is equivalent to other prevailing market rates.

In return for receiving the extra liquidity that the CD provides, investors are ready to accept a slightly lower interest rate than on the equivalent term deposit. Borrowers (mostly banks) get the benefit of the slightly lower interest rate and are still guaranteed that the money will not have to be repaid until the CD matures.

CDs may be issued for periods between three months and five years, normally in amounts ranging from £50,000 to £500,000. In the UK the size of an individual certificate is at least £10,000. In the USA, however,

* A year's interest would be £10,000. Divide by four to get the three-month figure of £2,500.

CDs have been issued in smaller denominations in order to attract individual investors.

Local authority loans represent one of the oldest sectors of the money markets. In March 1984 local authority loans outstanding in the money markets amounted to around £4.5 billion. It is a steady and unspectacular business, but the recent storms over ratecapping have highlighted the fact that local authorities can look to the City for funds.

So far our coverage of financial institutions has focused only on banks. In the next chapter we shall look at a rival set of institutions, the building societies.

Commercial paper is a funding mechanism which is extremely popular in the USA but became permissible only after the 1986 Budget. It is the equivalent, for companies, of the bank CD – that is, a short-term security. It has the advantage over the commercial bill that it does not have to be linked to a particular transaction.

When a company arranges a commercial-paper programme a bank will agree to sell the paper to end investors. Note that this is another step in the process of disintermediation, whereby companies borrow from investors rather than from banks. Large companies in the USA borrow via commercial paper at rates well below those charged by banks.

[7] Building Societies

Building societies are among the few financial institutions which have retained a good public image over the years. They have been the repositories of the small savings of millions of people and the providers of finance for the vast majority of home purchases. Few societies have folded because of financial mismanagement. Newspapers are unable to run adverse headlines about the societies' excessive profits because they are mutual organizations and any surplus of revenue over expenditure is added to a society's reserves rather than distributed to shareholders. Now, however, the societies are on the brink of some immense changes in their functions – changes which may lose them the friendly image of old.

Origins

The original building societies were literally that – groups of individuals who subscribed to a common fund so that they could buy or build themselves a house. Once the house or group of houses had been built the societies folded up.

After a rather shaky period in the late nineteenth century, when a spate of society collapses sapped public confidence in the movement, the building societies established an important place in the financial community. But it is in the last twenty years or so that their advance has been phenomenal. In the early 1960s the societies' share of private savings was less than half that of banks; by the early 1980s societies had replaced banks as the main repositories for personal-sector savings. At the end of 1984 50.9 per cent of all personal-sector liquid assets were held in building society accounts compared with 33.2 per cent in banks and 15.7 per cent in national savings. The number of society shareholders rose from 4 million to 39 million between 1960 and 1984, and the value of their holdings rose from £3 billion to £96 billion over the same period.

That advance was aided by a special privilege extended to the societies by the government. They were allowed to pay their depositors interest net of tax. In addition, that tax payment could be calculated by referring to the average tax status of depositors. Since some depositors paid no tax at all, the tax rate charged was less than the basic rate. But in advertisements the net rate could still be 'grossed up' at the standard rate to provide a very attractive package. The effect was that societies could offer to basic and higher-rate taxpayers higher rates of interest than could the banks. However, banks could offer higher rates to those not paying tax.

In 1984 banks were given the same privilege as the societies, with the result that competition for the personal sector's savings increased. In addition, the tax treatment of the profits or surpluses of banks and building societies is gradually being equalized – part of a process known as 'fiscal neutrality'. For example, building societies have had their favourable tax treatment on gilts investment withdrawn.

The scramble for personal savings increased as the Building Societies Association's control over the mortgage and savings rates charged by members gradually weakened. The result was that building societies began to compete more aggressively among themselves for funds, with extra interest accounts offering instant withdrawal without penalty for the saver. The proportion of building society deposits obtained from ordinary share accounts fell from 90 per cent in 1974 to just 32 per cent in 1984. Short-notice and immediate-access accounts were introduced in 1980 and made up 45 per cent of all deposits, and term accounts paying premium rates of interest for long-term deposits now make up about 20 per cent of all deposits.

The Growth of Societies

Since building societies do not make profits as such, it has been traditional to judge their success by the growth of their assets. However, although the excess of building societies' revenue over expenditure is called a 'surplus' rather than a profit, it is taxed as if it were the latter. Often those societies which have grown more slowly have been more profitable because they have been less aggressive in offering 'premium' interest rates to attract deposits. Many societies invested heavily in new branches, which increases deposits but is very costly in the short term. A survey of buiding societies* showed that the faster grower at the time, the Cheltenham and Gloucester, was ranked only 133rd in terms of profitability. Both the fastest-growing and the most profitable societies were among the smallest. However, the slowest-growing and least profitable societies were also small in size. The biggest society at that time, the Nationwide, was ranked only fortieth in terms of growth and sixty-fourth in terms of profit.

The concentration on growth has meant that many smaller societies have combined, and now a few building societies dominate the market. More than 50 per cent of societies' assets are held by the five largest societies – the Halifax, the Nationwide, the Leeds, the Alliance and Leicester (formed after a merger in 1985) and the Abbey National. The total number of societies fell from 726 in 1960 to 190 in 1984 as smaller societies were subsumed into large ones.† But over the same period the number of branches collecting deposits rose sharply from 985 to 6,815. There is scope for further reduction in numbers, since of the societies remaining thirty-six have assets of less than £2 million.‡

As a result of their privileged position in the savings market and the growth in the mortgage market, building societies doubled their assets in the 1970s. They were still very small compared with the big banks, but their success encouraged banks to enter the mortgage market. The percentage of mortgage loans made by banks rose from under 7 per cent in 1980 to 35 per cent in 1982, before dropping back to 14 per cent in 1984.§ That percentage has since increased again as foreign banks have battled for a slice of this lucrative market.

Building societies have responded to the banks' counter-attack in two ways. First, they now show a willingness to lend to home buyers whatever the level of interest rates. Previously societies responded to high interest rates by attempting to protect existing borrowers from an increase in the mortgage rate and by imposing mortgage rationing on new buyers. That option is no longer available because the banks will absorb the unsatisfied demand. The consequence of this change has been that building societies have been forced to alter mortgage rates much more often. The second

* Article by T. J. Gough in the *Banker*, March 1985.

† *Building Societies Factbook*, 1985.

‡ A merger between two of the biggest societies, the Nationwide and the Woolwich, was considered and then ruled out in 1985.

§ Article by Nikki Tait in the *Investors Chronicle*, 4 October 1985.

change is that societies have decreased the extra interest provisions placed on mortgages (e.g. for large purchases or for endowment mortgages).

As already noted, the abolition of societies' tax advantages has allowed banks to compete hard for the former's share of personal-sector deposits. That competition has forced societies to abandon some of their long-established practices. In November 1984 the Building Societies Association Council decided to stop recommending specific interest rates to its members, bringing an end to the interest-rate cartel which the societies had practised for so long. The resulting competition has led societies to increase the number of so-called 'premium' accounts which grant savers extra interest if they fulfil certain conditions. They have also attacked the banks head-on by offering withdrawals from automated teller machines, cheque facilities and home banking. The latter developments, as we have already seen, have had profound effects on UK monetary policy.

The twin phenomena of competition in raising money from depositors and competition in mortgage lending has increased societies' costs and put pressure on their revenues. The amount received from depositors each month has been subject to violent fluctuations.

Societies are now also ready to make good any shortfalls in their deposits by borrowing in the main financial markets. They have issued CDs and borrowed in the Euromarket. In September 1985 four building societies raised over £600 million between them by issuing Eurobonds. That was more than the average net monthly total of deposits attracted by *all* building societies that year. It was only legislation under the 1985 Finance Act that allowed them to do this.

The Mortgage Business

As noted in the Introduction, building societies perform a piece of financial magic by turning customers' deposits, which can be withdrawn at any time, into home loans extending up to thirty-five years. To guard against sudden shortfalls in deposits, they also have limited investments in safe short-term instruments like short-dated gilts. Societies can pull off this feat of legerdemain because of the creditworthiness of so many house buyers. Only 0.13 per cent of mortgages were over twelve months in arrears at the end of 1984.* Even if home owners do default, societies

* *Building Societies Factbook*, 1985.

have the houses themselves as security. The average life of a home loan is only six years, which means that most home buyers will have paid off no more than a fraction of the capital borrowed and will have to borrow again. Mortgage lending is a profitable business.

It has also been an expanding business, thanks to the fact that home ownership became increasingly popular in the 1960s and 1970s. Governments have been keen to encourage owner-occupation and have accordingly given tax relief on the first £30,000 of house prices, with higher rate relief allowable for higher taxpayers. Property is most Britons' major investment, and house prices have more than kept pace with inflation. As a result, home ownership rose from 44 per cent in 1965 to 61 per cent in 1984. Building societies played a major part in the increase. Their gross lending through mortgages more than doubled, from £12 billion in 1981 to around £26 billion in 1985.

There has been much debate over the question of whether tax relief on mortgages has introduced a distortion into the housing market and encouraged the subsidy of the better-off by the poor. Such points were made by both the Duke of Edinburgh's Commission (1985) and the report by the Church of England, *Faith in the City* (1985). The effects of the tax system are quite complex. If relief were withdrawn overnight, house prices would certainly fall, and there would be an increase in the number of mortgage defaults as borrowers struggled to meet the extra payments. Some argue that the relief has increased mortgage rates because people can afford to pay more interest. Certainly Marc Boleat, Secretary General of the Building Societies Association, believes that tax relief on mortgage interest payments has reduced the cost of home ownership but has increased the cost of houses and mortgage rates. In the end, the effect has been to increase the rates that housing finance institutions can pay to investors.*

The Mortgage Rate

What determines whether the mortgage rate goes up or down? More than ever before, it is the general level of rates in the economy. The building societies cannot stay separate from the other financial institutions, since they must compete with them for depositors, and they must sometimes borrow from them. As the cost of raising their funds rises and

* Article in *Building Societies Gazette*, December 1985.

falls, so must the mortgage rate. In general, however, the mortgage rate is slower both to rise and fall than bank rates.

Chapter 3 has already described some of the theories of interest-rate movements. However, it is important to remember that rates can rise for reasons external to this country – as a response to a run on sterling by overseas investors, for example.

Banks Versus Building Societies

In the early 1980s, as competition between banks and building societies for deposits and for mortgages increased, some societies complained about the restrictions placed upon them. The most onerous requirement, in their opinion, was that building society lending was restricted to the mortgage of freehold and leasehold property in the UK. Some societies wanted to widen their businesses to compete even further with banks in the way that their US equivalents, the savings and loans institutions (S&Ls), had done. The fact that many S&Ls had run into financial difficulties in the process did not deter the bolder building societies. They argued, with some justification, that the problem which hit US S&Ls was that their investments were in fixed-rate mortgages which were left behind, as interest rates rose, by the increased costs of the S&Ls' borrowings. In the UK there has been little tradition of fixed-rate mortgages – if interest rates rise, so does the return from the building societies' investments.

The Building Societies Bill

The Conservative government recognized that the societies had some cause for complaint. It had an ideological commitment to increasing competition in the financial markets. In 1985 it accordingly introduced the Building Societies Bill, which was designed to allow societies to expand the range of their activities.

Under the new legislation societies will be allowed to devote 5 per cent of their lending to so-called Class 3 assets, which cover unsecured loans and other activities such as residential property investment and investments in estate agencies, insurance brokers and other subsidiary activities. Up to 10 per cent will be permitted to be devoted to Class 2 assets, which cover second mortgages, equity mortgages and other secured lending. However, at least 90 per cent of the total portfolio must be devoted to first mortgages to owner-occupiers. A newly formed body, the Building Society Commission, will be allowed to raise the ceilings but only to 20 per cent for Class 2 and 10 per cent for Class 3. The limits will mean that only the big societies will find it worthwhile to devote funds to the new activities. Societies will also be able to raise 20 per cent of their funds from the wholesale (i.e. money) markets. Once again, the Commission will be able to raise the level from 20 to 40 per cent.

The Bill will give societies the freedom to become limited companies. However, there are various restrictions on this freedom. A society can become a company only if the move is approved by 75 per cent of voting investors, 50 per cent of voting borrowers and 20 per cent of all investors. Some societies may see advantages in becoming public companies, though legally they will cease to be building societies if they do so. As public companies, societies will become attractive takeover targets for banks. Building societies have 26 million customers and 7,000 branches. Banks like Citicorp and Standard Chartered, which are seeking to build up retail banking business in Britain and which lack a branch network, have already said that they would be interested in buying a society.

What will happen if the societies do go public and raise money through a share offering? Will it be the societies or the depositors who keep the proceeds? Will a society be owned by the depositors or by no one? As we have seen, this is a question which plagued the flotation of the Trustee Savings Bank. It may well be that a building society flotation will be challenged in the courts to determine the question of ownership.

One problem involved in giving the money to the depositors is that many people might open a small account for a few days and claim all the benefit. If more restrictive conditions were imposed – say, a large amount in an account or a minimum period of tenure – that would reduce the number of depositors who could benefit. Those left might be easily enticed by a bank which wanted to take the society over. So, although it may be disappointing to building society depositors, there is unlikely to be a bonanza. Instead it seems probable that depositors will merely receive preferential treatment when shares are allocated.

The new legislation will allow one society that wants to take over another to appeal directly to its members, over the heads of the target society's management. However, the bidder will have to wait three months before it can gain access to the list of the target society's members. In addition, a society which becomes a public company will be partially protected against predators. No one investor will be able to hold more than 15 per cent of the shares, and takeover bids will be subject to the rules of the Takeover Panel.

Building societies argue that there are great benefits in mutuality and that they have been able to grow very fast as deposit-taking institutions. However, critics argue that growth has been due to the tax-subsidized development of the mortgage market, in which building societies have had a virtual monopoly. Will building societies lose their favourable public image if they become companies rather than mutual organizations?

One-stop Shopping

Some societies have been arguing for the right to set up a comprehensive house service, in which societies could act as estate agents, conveyancing agents and lenders. The new Bill allows the Lord Chancellor to draw up rules so that the societies can conduct conveyancing. Such rules are likely to restrict the societies to conveying only those purchases which they do *not* finance.

Will houseowners benefit from an integrated service in any case? There are a number of potential conflicts of interest, as Ian Oddy, Vice President of the Royal Institution of Chartered Surveyors, has pointed out:* 'Suppose a borrower wishes to sell his or her house and approaches the building society requesting it to act as his or her estate agent; and suppose that the building society decides to accept the instruction to sell.' According to Oddy, the questions which then arise are: 'Is the building society permitted to make a loan on the house to the new purchaser of the property? How does it reconcile the valuation it gives when advising the vendor as against the value it accepts when making the advance to the new purchaser? What advice will it give to either party in the case of a defect which might affect a further resale? How will it handle the interest from a late bidder who actually proposes to introduce a mortgage from a different society?' Oddy goes on to list some further potential contradictions before stating: 'It is both a practical and a moral impossibility that there can be one-stop shopping in this field.'

* Speech to the Wales and West of England Association of Building Societies Conference, October 1985, reported in the *Building Societies Gazette*, December 1985.

Whatever the outcome of the one-stop shopping debate, it seems certain that building societies will no longer be the safe and steady members of the financial community that they have been for most of this century. The differences between building societies and banks will become less and less apparent, especially if societies become companies and get taken over by the big banks.

[8] Borrowers

The financial institutions described in the last few chapters fulfil the function in the economy of channelling funds from those who wish to lend to those who wish to borrow. In the next two chapters we will look at the lenders and the borrowers. There are three main groups of borrowers in the economy: individuals, governments and companies. The job of the financial system is to channel funds to those borrowers from investors. Of course, in playing that role banks and other financial intermediaries must both borrow and invest. However, this chapter examines those borrowers who are not financial institutions and the alternatives open to them.

Individuals

Individuals borrow for a host of different reasons. Perhaps the most common is that income and expenditure are rarely synchronized. Christmas comes but once a year but drives many people into overdraft. Few people can afford to buy large consumer durables (like washing machines) without borrowing the funds involved. Unplanned events, such as illness or redundancy, can reduce income without a corresponding effect on expenditure. Food must still be bought, and rent and mortgages must be paid.

Most people borrow by taking out an overdraft from a bank or by carrying a credit-card balance. Banks will also lend money for more specific projects, like study courses or home improvements. Finance companies and big businesses will lend money to those buying expensive goods. However, the most important debt which most people incur is the purchase of a home with a mortgage. As we saw in the last chapter, the biggest providers of mortgages are the building societies, though banks have recently begun to compete with them.

Governments

British governments have historically spent more than their incomes and, like anyone else, they have to borrow to cover the difference. They borrow, as we saw in Chapter 5, in the form of long-dated securities called gilts and short-dated securities called Treasury bills. Money is also borrowed direct from the public through the various national savings schemes on offer (see Chapter 15). The government can give itself a built-in advantage in the market for personal savings because it can allow savers to escape tax. It does so on some schemes. However, the loss of tax income increases the government's cost of borrowing. As a result, it tries to maintain a balance between the amount it borrows in various different forms.

The total amount that most governments have had to borrow has increased in post-war years because of the growth of welfare economies in the West, with the resulting in-built increases in expenditure. Few governments have been willing to take the unpopular step of raising taxes to cut the deficit. The expenditure side of the equation has accordingly suffered. The result in the UK has been continuous battles over cuts in spending between those Ministries with escalating budgets (particularly the Department of Health and Social Security, Environment and Defence) and the Treasury.

The difference between the government's total revenue and its expenditure is known as the public-sector borrowing requirement (PSBR), and it is the size of the PSBR that has been one of the central points of the Conservative government's financial strategy. (Indeed, so frequent was the mention of this acronym in the speeches of Sir Geoffrey Howe that one wag suggested that he was 'unable to tell his PSBRs from his elbow'.) The economic rationale behind the government's desire to reduce the PSBR is that a fall in government borrowing will stimulate the economy. If the PSBR is too high, they reason, the available funds for investment will flow to the government (a safe credit) rather than to industry. Companies will be able to borrow only by offering investors penally high rates of interest, discouraging them from investing in new plant and machinery. Without new investment the economy will not grow. The government will effectively have 'crowded out' private-sector borrowing. A low PSBR, the government argues, will result in low interest rates. Businesses will be encouraged to invest, and the economy will grow.

Unfortunately for this line of argument, interest rates have also been used by the government as a weapon in two other policy areas, combating monetary growth and supporting sterling. In the second Thatcher term of office both policies required the government at intervals to push up interest rates. The government's success in controlling the size of the PSBR has been accompanied by real interest rates which have reached record levels.

Nor is the US experience positive evidence for proving a relationship between the level of interest rates and the size of the government deficit. Since President Reagan took office in 1981 a combination of tax cuts, increased defence spending and Congressional reluctance to cut programmes elsewhere have brought record budget deficits of over $150 billion.

The US government has had little problem in funding its deficit. Overseas investors have been eager to own dollar-denominated assets. Although real interest rates did rise to unprecedentedly high levels in 1982–3, they then plummeted. The Federal Reserve, the US's equivalent of the Bank of England, was conscious of a need to keep rates low in order to encourage economic growth and to ease the burden on Third World debtors.

So in the country where the government has struggled to control its deficit, interest rates have risen. And in the country where the government has turned a blind eye to the deficit, interest rates have fallen. In the circumstances the relationship between the size of the PSBR and the level of interest rates appears to be very slight.

Is it not immoral that government should pile up debts which must be paid for by future generations? The image comes to mind of the philandering nineteenth-century gentlemen who drank and gambled their families into ruin. Does not the money that the government pays in interest each year constitute an unacceptable tax imposed by the irresponsibility of past politicians?

The mistake that many people make when worrying about the national debt is to draw an analogy between a nation and a family. The proper comparison is with a business. The UK is one enormous and extremely complicated business and, like other businesses, it has to borrow to expand. Borrowing to finance investment is perfectly acceptable in a business, provided that in the long term the return on the investment is greater than the cost of the borrowing. For a nation the problem is deciding how to calculate the return on the investment.

The proportion of national income which constitutes debt is considered by some economists to be the most important factor. If it is steadily increasing, that would indicate that the cost of borrowing is greater than the return on our investments and that the government has been borrowing too much (or investing in the wrong things). If the proportion is decreasing, then the government is using its borrowings wisely and increasing national wealth. Those who propound this argument argue that money spent on the so-called *infrastructure* (investment in roads, railways or airports) is wise expenditure which is increasing our wealth. Debt in such circumstances is not a burden to future generations but a contribution to their standard of living.

In opposition to this argument many economists would point out that the majority of government expenditure is used for consumption rather than for investment. The biggest element of the public expenditure bill is the salaries of its employees and the benefits paid to the sick and unemployed. The cost of paying these wages and benefits is subtracted from the incomes of the private sector of the economy. Less expenditure by government would mean more money for the private sector to invest.

Whatever the merits of the opposing arguments, the evidence seems to be that government debt, though increasing in nominal terms, has been steadily falling, *as a proportion of national income*, since World War II. (Remember, debt is not the same as public expenditure.) On that basis it could be argued that the country has been investing wisely rather than recklessly.

Companies

Why do companies borrow? Unlike individuals, for whom borrowing is often a sign of financial weakness, borrowing is a way of life for most corporations, no matter what their prospects. Firms which are very successful often have substantial amounts of debt. There obviously comes a point beyond which companies can be said to have borrowed too much, but frequently corporate borrowing merely indicates a willingness to expand.

What routes are open to a company which wishes to finance expansion? It might be imagined that the ideal method would be to generate the funds from past profits (retained earnings). In other words, the company would finance itself and thus reduce its costs by avoiding interest payments. However, self-financing is not always possible. While companies are in their early years they have little in the way of previous profits to draw on, since many of their investments will not yet have generated a return. Nevertheless, in order to establish themselves companies must continue to invest in further projects, necessitating capital outlay. If they were forced to wait until funds were available internally, they might miss profitable opportunities and spoil their long-term prospects in the process. Company results are often judged by their profitability in relation to their equity base (the value of the combined shareholdings). Debt can be used to increase the return on equity (a process known as *leverage* or *gearing*) by allowing companies to seek profitable investment opportunities when retained earnings are insufficient.

Another way in which a company may generate cash for expansion is to sell existing assets or, alternatively, not to replace old and worn-out assets. Both, however, are one-off ways of raising money and are indicative more of a company which is winding down than of one which is expanding.

A company can increase its capital base by issuing new shares or equity. However, it may not wish to do so because that would weaken the control of the existing shareholders. In companies where control is exercised by a small majority of shareholders' votes, this could be particularly important.

It is also possible for a company to have too much equity. It is in the nature of equity (see Chapter 10) that, unlike debt, it cannot be redeemed. If a company issued more equity and then failed to expand, it would be left with large cash balances. Paying those balances back to shareholders in the form of increased dividends would have severe tax disadvantages.

So companies tend to borrow. Debt, as a financing technique, has some distinct advantages. Interest is tax-deductible from company profits, so the effective cost of borrowing is reduced. In addition, debt is reversible. If a company finds itself flush with cash or lacking in investment opportunities, it can repay some of its borrowings. Most shareholders will accept the need for a company to borrow, provided that they expect that the project in which the borrowed funds will be invested will yield a higher return than the cost of borrowing the funds. As already noted, a company can be described as inefficient if it achieves a very low return on equity – borrowing can increase that return.

Company analysts tend to watch the debt–equity ratio, which is very roughly defined as the company's borrowings versus its shareholders' funds. Ideal debt–equity ratios vary from industry to industry, but most analysts would be alarmed if the size of the company's debts approached the size of its equity – in other words, if the ratio approached 1.

How Companies Obtain Extra Finance

Which are the debt instruments most used by companies? For small and medium-sized firms the overdraft is probably still the most common method of borrowing. The overdraft has built-in advantages – it is very flexible and easy to understand. An upper limit is agreed by the bank and the borrower: the borrower may borrow any amount up to that limit but will be charged interest only on the amount outstanding at any one time. The rate charged will be agreed at a set margin over the bank's base rate, and thus the cost of the overdraft will move up and down with the general level of rates in the economy.

The overdraft is a very British institution. In the USA it is virtually unknown. There companies borrow term loans, the amount and duration of which are agreed in advance, and interest is charged on the full amount for the full period of the loan.

UK companies have found that the 'hard-core' element of their overdrafts has increased over the years, suggesting that they are funding their long-term needs with short-term loans. Accordingly, many companies have begun to switch to funding with term loans from banks instead of overdrafts. Term loans are normally granted by banks for specific purposes, such as the acquisition of machinery, property or another company, rather than for the financing of working capital needs, such as the payment of wages or raw-material costs.

Overdraft financing was probably the only source of funding for the smaller companies up to fifteen years ago.* Many companies now borrow in the money markets, often using the services of a money broker to find a willing lender, which is likely to be a bank. In return, the broker (who never lends or borrows money himself) receives a commission. Money-market loans are for set amounts and periods and are therefore less flexible than overdraft facilities. However, interest rates in the money markets are generally below those for overdrafts.

* Daniel Hodson (ed.), *Corporate Finance and Treasury Management* (Gee & Co., 1984).

Longer-term finance for large firms is most frequently obtained by the issue of debentures, bonds which pay a fixed rate of interest to the investor. Debentures usually have maturities of over five years. Multinational firms which have very large financing needs may turn to the international and Eurobond markets (see Chapter 11). Those markets give firms access to a very wide investor base and allow them to raise tens of millions of pounds at a stroke.

The more sophisticated financing techniques of the Euromarket are not open to the small and medium-sized British firm. Their long-term financing needs are normally satisfied by some kind of bank loan. However, there are a variety of options open to firms seeking shorter-term finance. One in particular is the acceptance credit or banker's acceptance. A bank agrees that it will accept bills drawn on it by the company, in return for a commission. When the company needs funds, it will send the bills to the bank, which will then discount them – that is, it will pay the company less than the full amount of the bills' value. The amount of discount is equivalent to the rate of interest charged by the bank. So, if the company sends the bank a three-month bill with a face value of £100 and the interest rate on such bills is 12 per cent a year, the bank will discount the bill to £97.* As with other loans, the credit rating of the company will affect the cost of the borrowing: the poorer the credit rating, the bigger the discount.

The Financing of Trade

Many of the more specialist methods of raising finance revolve around the financing of trade. The key principles are that it is better to be paid by debtors as soon as possible and to pay creditors as late as possible. It is also important to ensure that debtors settle their debts. This is a particular problem for exporters who are dealing with customers out of reach of the UK legal system.

There are four main methods of paying for exports: (1) cash with order; (2) open-account trading; (3) bills of exchange; (4) documentary letters of credit.†

The best method for the exporters is cash with order. That way the exporting company already has the money before it sends off the goods;

* Because it is a three-month bill, the discount is a quarter of the full year's rate.

† This explanation owes a lot to articles by David Bowen and Arthur Day.

however, importers may not be keen to pay by this method, and it is rarely used.

Open-account trading is the opposite end of the scale – the exporter sends the client the goods and then waits for the cheque to arrive. It offers the least security of all the payment methods but is still the most widely used, at least in trade, between industrialized countries.

Bills of exchange offer rather more security to the exporter. The firm will send the bill ('draw' it) to its foreign customer with the invoices and the necessary official documentation (referred to as a *documentary bill*). Then the firm will inform its bank, telling it to obtain the cash from the client. The bank will send the documentary bill to a bank in the importer's country. Under some arrangements the buyer pays for the goods as soon as he receives the documents. Often, however, he is given a period of credit. He must accept the bill (otherwise he will not get the goods), and accepting a bill is proof of receipt of goods in law. When the credit period is up, the bank presents the bill to the buyer once again.

Bankers' documentary credits, normally known as letters of credit, are the most expensive of the forms of payment but offer a great measure of security. The onus is on the importer to open a credit at his bank in favour of the exporter. The importer's bank then informs the exporter's. The credit tells the exporter that if he presents certain documents showing that the goods have been shipped, he will be paid.

There are many different types of letters of credit. *Revocable* credits can be cancelled or amended by the importer without the exporter's approval. They are therefore very risky for the exporter. *Irrevocable* credits, despite their name, can be altered but only with the approval of both parties. *Confirmed irrevocable* credits are guaranteed by the exporter's bank in return for a fee. As long as the exporter has kept to his side of the bargain, the bank will ensure that he is paid. If the importer fails to pay, it is the bank's job to pursue the debt. These credits are the normal method of payment for goods shipped to risky countries. *Revolving* credits allow two parties to have a long-term relationship without constantly renewing the trade documentation. *Transferable* credits are used to allow goods to be passed through middlemen in order to give security to all three parties – exporter, middleman and importer. With all these payment instruments the finance comes from the exporter or his overdraft. If he has to wait for, say, sixty days before being paid, he is, in effect, making an interest-free loan to his customer. Only when the credit is medium-term (more than six months) will the customer normally be expected to pay interest.

There are three further methods of trade finance which involve the exporter in passing to another institution part or all of the responsibility for collecting his debts. One is to use an export credit agency in return for a premium (see Chapter 12). The other two are factoring and forfaiting.

A company which is involved with all the problems of designing, producing and selling a range of products may feel that it has enough to do without the extra burden of chasing its customers to settle their debts. Instead it can call on the services of a factor. Factors provide both a credit-collection service and a short-term loan facility. Their charges therefore have two elements, the cost of administration and the charge for the provision of finance. Most factoring covers domestic trade, but it plays a distinct role in exporting.

Companies who have called on the services of a factor invoice their clients in the normal way but give the factoring company a copy of all invoices. The factors then administer the company's sales ledger in return for a percentage of the turnover. They despatch statements and reminder letters to customers and initiate legal actions for the recovery of bad debts. In addition, some companies provide 100 per cent insurance protection against bad debts on approved sales.

Factoring is a particularly important service for expanding companies which have not yet developed their own full accounts operation. Factors also provide short-term finance for corporations short of cash. When a company makes out its invoices, it can arrange to receive the bulk of the payments in advance from the factor. Effectively, the factor is making the company a loan backed by the security of a company's invoices. In return the factor will discount the invoices, paying (say) only 90 per cent to the company. The extra 10 per cent covers both the factor's risk that the invoices will not be paid and the effective interest rate on the 'loan'.

Like factoring, forfaiting is a method of speeding up a company's cash flow by using its export receivables. Forfaiting gives exporters the ability to grant their buyers credit periods while receiving cash payments themselves. Factoring can be used for goods sold on short-term credit, such as consumer products or spare parts; forfaiting is designed to help companies selling capital equipment, such as machinery, on credit periods of between two and five years.

Suppose that a UK company has sold goods to a foreign buyer and has granted that buyer a credit period. A forfaiting company will discount the exporter's bills, the amount of discount depending on the period of credit needed and the risk involved to the forfaiting company. In order for the exporting company to make the bills more acceptable to the forfaiting company, it will ask the buyer of the goods to arrange for the bills to carry a guarantee, known as an *aval*, from a well-known bank. The more respected the bank involved – and the less risky the country in which it is based – the cheaper the cost of forfaiting. Unlike factoring companies, forfaiters often sell on these bills to other financial institutions. Their ability to do so helps reduce the cost of the service. (In general, the more liquid the asset, the lower the return.)

In the past forfaiting has been used mainly by companies seeking to finance medium-term trade commitments (three to five years). In the past few years forfaiting has been used increasingly as a means of financing short-term payments of three to six months.

This chapter has discussed the needs of the major borrowers in the UK economy. In the next chapter we will look at individuals and institutions with funds to invest.

[9] Investment Institutions

Nowadays the majority of the nation's shares are held not by wealthy individuals but by institutions – pension funds, life assurance companies, unit and investment trusts. They are also the biggest holders of gilts and wield significant power in the property market. The investment institutions are now among the barons of the land. One estimate has suggested that the institutions had £20,000 million of *new* funds to invest in a year, the equivalent of £400 for every person in the country.* Such is the influence of the institutions that one of the reasons why the City has been forced into the 'Big Bang' is in order to meet their needs. The abolition of fixed-minimum commissions seems certain to bring down the costs of share-dealing to the big investors. Previously they had shown signs of being enticed away from The Stock Exchange and into the telephone-based, over-the-counter markets made by the big securities firms.

Most fund managers do not feel very powerful. Each of the investment institutions has outside forces to which it is beholden. Pension-fund managers must look to the trustees of the companies whose funds they administer, life assurance and insurance companies to their shareholders and policyholders and unit and investment trusts to their unit- and shareholders respectively. Conspiracy theorists can follow the chain of ownership back and back without finding a sinister, top-hatted capitalist at the end of it.

In theory, investment institutions could combine and could start altering the policies of the companies in which they have substantial holdings. However, the reality is that they rarely exercise their power to intervene in the day-to-day running of firms. That does not mean that managers can ignore their wishes: if institutions dislike a company's policies, they will sell their shares, bringing down the price in the process. Too low a share price will attract predatory rivals, who will buy up the company, and the management will lose its cherished independence.

* William Clarke, *Inside the City*, rev. edn (Allen & Unwin, 1983).

The time when institutional investors are most powerful is during takeovers, when both sides bid for the institutions' favours. The sizeable holdings of the institutions means that the way they jump will decide the success or failure of the bid. In recent years the institutions have shown little tendency to be loyal to existing managements and appear to be more than willing to sell out to the highest bidder.

The Growth of the Institutions

The extraordinary growth of investment institutions is due in part to the increased wealth and longevity of the population. In the past few people survived into old age, and those that did often had independent means. As people have lived longer there has been a greater need for pensions. Few people have been satisfied with the pension provided by the state, so occupational pension schemes have evolved, with both employees and employers making tax-free contributions.

Each pension fund is run by a trust, which can either manage the funds itself or appoint outside fund managers. The outsiders can be banks, brokers or specialist fund-management companies. The pension-fund trustees generally split up the fund between several managers to ensure that a bad set of decisions by one manager does not affect the solvency of the whole fund.

The wealth of the country has also allowed savings to be more widely distributed than ever before. In late Victorian times the population was divided into a few people with a lot of savings and the mass who had no savings at all. Seventy-five years of redistribution taxation, and a growth in the nation's wealth, mean that many more are now able to save. Until 1984 life assurance was a very tax-efficient means of savings. Premiums could be offset against income tax. Despite the withdrawal of the tax privilege, it is likely that life assurance will continue to be popular.

Around 75 per cent of the households in Britain already have some form of life assurance. The common idea of all policies is that the policyholder pays regular premiums in return for a lump sum at the end of a set period. This distinguishes *assurance* from *insurance*. An assured sum *will* be paid, and an insured sum *may* be paid, in certain circumstances (e.g. death). However, there is an element of insurance in most assurance policies, since if the policyholder dies before completing the payments, the sum will be paid immediately to his or her dependants.

The most common life policy is the endowment mortgage, whereby a mortgage is linked to a life assurance policy. When the policy matures the mortgage is repaid. If the policyholder dies, the mortgage is paid off. Life companies have also introduced unit-linked policies, which offer investors the growth potential of unit trusts and a modicum of life protection.

Added to this group are the general insurance companies (see Chapter 12), which collect premiums in return for insuring property holders against risk. As the nation has grown more wealthy, people have had more property to insure. Car insurance has been a particular growth area since the war. These three sets of institutions make up a distinct branch of the institutional investment family.*

They all have essentially long-term liabilities – pensions to be paid, life assurance policies to mature. They create portfolios of assets with the contributions they receive – portfolios which are designed both to be safe against loss and to provide capital growth. If the institutions invested in one company or in one type of security, they would be exposed to the chance of loss.

Portfolio Investments

What are the ingredients of these portfolios? A significant proportion is invested in government securities. Although this figure varies from company to company and from fund to fund, it is on average between one-quarter and one-third of the total portfolio. Gilts, because of their long maturities, can be used to match long-term liabilities. However, because of the need to achieve a profitable return in the short term the funds will also purchase short-term gilts in the hope of making capital gains. The government would have enormous difficulty in funding itself without the gilt purchases of these two sets of institutions, which in March 1984 owned 62 per cent of long-dated gilts between them.

A further chunk of the funds' investments goes into property – buying land and then leasing it to industry for the building of factories, offices and shops. Property investment represents about one-quarter of the average portfolio. The boom-and-bust cycle of the early 1970s has perhaps discouraged some institutions from venturing into the property

*Often life assurance and insurance companies are one and the same thing, but there are specialized companies in each sector.

field. Nevertheless, property has a tradition of being a safe, long-term investment and of more than keeping pace with inflation. Perhaps this is because of the tax advantages given in the private housing market, which enable demand for private housing to outstrip supply. The rising prices for private and new houses, encouraged by the tax system, force prices up in the rest of the market.

The biggest proportion of institutional investment (somewhere between one-third and half) goes into equities, and in the next chapter we examine the effect of institutional investors on the share market. Equities have traditionally more than kept pace with inflation, which explains their appeal to the institutions.

The spare cash of the investment institutions goes into the money markets. Although their immediate outgoings are usually met by the premiums and contributions, the institutions still need liquid funds to meet any disparities. So they invest in bank CDs, commercial bills issued by major companies and wholesale deposits from the banks and discount houses. At certain times, when the yield curve is inverted (see Chapter 3), the proportion invested in the money markets increases.

Overseas Investment

Not all of this institutional investment takes place in the UK. In 1979, as we noted in Chapter 2, the government abolished exchange controls. This allowed the institutions to invest substantial sums abroad. The overseas portfolios of the UK non-bank private sector rose from £11 billion at the end of 1979 to an estimated £63 billion at the end of 1984. Of the £52 billion increase only £22 billion was new money. The remaining £30 billion consisted of capital gains on previous investments.* The proportion of the portfolios of pension funds and insurance companies held overseas increased from 5 to 14 per cent in the same period.

This move has aroused some political controversy (see Chapter 16). Investment abroad, it is argued by those on the left, deprives UK industry of the funds that it needs. Those on the right argue, however, that pension funds should invest abroad. Foreign investment diversifies their assets, thus reducing the risk that a slump in UK industry will cut pensions and insurance pay-outs. On economic principles they also point out that investment abroad must accompany a current account surplus

* All figures from the *Lloyds Bank Economic Bulletin*, October 1985.

(see Chapter 14). The balance of payments must balance, and if we are selling more exports than imports, we are paid in the form of foreign assets. Those assets are equivalent to a flow of investment abroad that is recorded as a capital account deficit, which matches the current-account surplus.

The Labour Party is unimpressed by these arguments and proposes that the proportion of funds invested overseas should be reduced to 5 per cent. Investors will be allowed to invest more overseas, but if they exceed the 5 per cent limit, they will lose tax privileges (like the right to deduct pension contributions for occupational pension funds).

The next main set of institutional investors are the trusts. They are divided into unit and investment trusts, but both serve roughly the same function – to channel the funds of small investors into the equity markets.

Investment Trusts

An investment trust is a public company like any other company except that its assets are not buildings and machinery but investments in other companies. Investors buy shares in the trusts and rely on the expertise of the fund managers to earn a good return on their investments.

The origins of the investment trust movement lie in Scotland. Many of the entrepreneurs who made money out of the Industrial Revolution found themselves with surplus funds which could find few profitable homes in their area. So they looked for advice to help them invest elsewhere and turned to their professional advisers – the lawyers and accountants. A few smart people from both professions realized that they could pool the funds of their clients and invest in larger sums. That early development was complemented by the growth of Scottish life assurance companies and pension-fund managers, and today Edinburgh is still a very significant force in international fund management.

Nowadays all investment trusts must be approved by the Inland Revenue. They raise money through preference shares and loan stock as well as through equity. There are around two hundred operating in the UK, managing assets which range in value from £1 million to £750 million. Investment trusts have invested around 90 per cent of their portfolios in equities. They represent about 5 per cent of the whole UK stock market, managing a total portfolio of assets worth over £16 billion. On average around half of their portfolios are based in the

UK, but there are also trusts which specialize in overseas investment.

There are a few restrictions on the way in which trusts can invest. No single holding can constitute more than 15 per cent of their investments. Capital gains must be reinvested in the business and not redistributed to shareholders.

The trusts have the advantage that they can borrow money to finance their investments, and the interest on their borrowings can be offset against tax. This is known as *gearing* and relies on the rate of return on the trusts' investments exceeding the cost of borrowing. If it does, the trusts' profitability increases substantially; if it does not, losses multiply.

Many of the trusts are at a discount to their assets. This means that the total value of their share capital is less than the value of the investments they hold. In theory, a big investor could buy up the shares and sell off the assets at a profit. If this does happen, those individual investors who hold shares in the trust can come out very well.

Investment trusts are not allowed to advertise their shares. Because of the rival attractions of unit trusts and the claims on savings of contractual schemes like life assurance and pensions schemes, their importance in the total share market has declined since the war.

Unit Trusts

Like investment trusts, unit trusts bundle together the assets of small investors in order to give them a less risky opportunity to invest in the equity markets. Rather than buy shares in a company, investors buy units whose prices rise and fall with the value of the assets held by the trust. The unit trust managers earn their money through the spread between the buy and sell prices of the units and through a management charge.

Unit trusts – which, unlike investment trusts, are allowed to advertise themselves – have been one of the investment successes since the war. At the end of November 1985 there were 796 unit trusts operating in the UK, including sixteen launched that month. The total of funds under unit trust management was almost £20 billion. They have always invested almost all their portfolios in the equity market, the only change in recent years being a greater concentration on overseas shares. Many specialize investing in, say, US equities or in small companies. By doing so some can achieve spectacular rates of growth.

All unit trusts must be authorized by the Department of Trade and Industry. There must actually be a trust, whose trustees are normally either banks or insurance companies. The trustees' job is to ensure that the fund is run properly and not to supervise its investment policy. The latter task is organized by specialist managers who often are also supervising the funds of insurance companies or merchant banks.

There are thus strong links between members of the investment institution fraternity. At a merchant bank the people who run the unit trusts might work in the same office as those who advise the pension funds and life assurance companies. In part this explains the herd mentality of institutional investors, who tend to desert unpopular sectors of the economy and pile into fashionable industries. If Johnny across the room and Bernie at the club say, 'Sell ICI', their colleagues and friends will listen. After all, Johnny and Bernie are advising clients with stakes worth millions of pounds. A good example of the herd mentality was the plunge into high-technology stocks in the early 1980s and the subsequent retreat in the middle of the decade.

Government Agencies

A large number of government agencies provide investment funds for industry. Their importance waxes and wanes with the ideology of the government in power. The National Enterprise Board (NEB), for example, one of the major creations of the 1974–6 Wilson government, is now only part of the British Technology Group (BTG). The old NEB had an economy-wide brief, but the BTG's main role is to finance high-technology projects.

Investors in Industry (3i – formerly Finance for Industry) invests in small and large companies, although its maximum stake in any one firm is £35 million. In addition to long-term finance for industry, it has a leasing division, a corporate finance department (which gives advice in the same way as merchant banks) and training and management consultancy subsidiaries.

Underwriting

The investment institutions do more than just invest in existing shares. They also play a part in the new issues and the rights issues markets by underwriting. In return for a fee, they guarantee to buy shares at a set price if no one else will. The fees can be substantial. When Abbey Life went public in June 1985 the value of the shares it issued was £243 million. Total underwriting fees were £3 million.* The underwriters had guaranteed to buy shares at the offer price of £1.80. When shares actually started trading the price jumped immediately to £2.35. The issue was a resounding success, and the underwriters pocketed their fees.

It is rather unfair to say that underwriters earn money for doing nothing. They act in the same way as insurers. Claims occur when the underwriters have to buy up shares at the offer price, and in those circumstances the loss can be considerable. Had Abbey Life's share price fallen to £1.50 immediately after the issue, the underwriters would have been faced collectively with a loss of 30 pence a share (around £40 million), several times their fee. For the underwriters the knack is to ensure that the sums earned from successful deals outweigh the costs of supporting failures. If underwriters tried to avoid the bad deals, the brokers who put the business their way would cut them out of the likely successes.

At the beginning of 1986 underwriting fees were around 1.25 per cent of the issue value of share issues. Following the 'Big Bang' underwriting fees may drop. The big new financial conglomerates will be able to buy up all of the rights issues and place them with end-investors direct. They will have the capital to carry the shares if they sell badly.

As we have seen, investment institutions tend to invest a large proportion of their funds in equities. The next chapter looks at the market for stocks and shares.

* Article in the *Investors Chronicle*, September 1985.

[10] Stocks and Shares

When most people hear the terms 'finance' or 'the City' they tend to think of those two great financial commodities, stocks and shares. Although the terms are generally used synonymously, some people use the word stocks to denote interest-paying instruments like bonds. In the UK bonds are usually known as *debentures* if they are issued by companies and as *gilts* if issued by the government. The interest that stocks pay is normally fixed. *Shares* pay dividends rather than interest and are literally shares in a company's assets. If a company folds, shareholders will be repaid only after all the other creditors have been attended to. Since the equity of a company is defined in law as that which is left over when all other claims have been met, the terms 'share' and 'equity' are usually interchangeable.

Shareholders therefore own a part of the company in which they invest. Their ownership could, theoretically, continue for ever. Bonds, however, will eventually mature and be repaid. A company's first responsibility is to its shareholders; indeed, in theory the sole rationale for the existence of companies is to provide their shareholders with profit.

Shares and shareholders are unique to the capitalist system. Under the communist system bonds are issued but never shares, since ownership of all commerce is in the hands of the state. It is not exaggerating the case, therefore, to say that shares are at the heart of capitalism. They have traditionally been the investments that are most likely to get people rich quickly and also to reduce them to poverty (remember the Great Crash of 1929). Ownership of shares is at present a live political issue: all the major parties in the UK are committed to increasing the number of individual shareholders (but by different means).

Shares also provide the means through which ownership of industry can be divorced from control. The modern industrial giants are run by boards of directors. They in turn appoint salaried managers to administer the day-to-day business of the company. Some managers sit on the board and some have shares of their own, but, except in small firms, managers rarely own a significant proportion of the company's equity. Death and taxes have gradually weakened the grip of the founders of old family-run businesses. Few individuals now have the capital to finance a firm's expansion alone.

Although managers do not own the firms they run, they are unlikely to be dismissed through shareholders' action unless they are particularly incompetent or corrupt. Nowadays, as was seen in Chapter 9, the great majority of shares are owned by investment institutions. If they dislike the policies of the firms in which they invest, they vote with their chequebooks and sell their shareholdings. Rarely do they take the positive action of trying to change the policies from the inside.

The Stock Exchange

The Stock Exchange* is the traditional arena where existing securities are traded. It has long been seen as one of the symbols of both the City and the British economy. The daily fluctuations in its index are seen as reflections of the nation's economic health. Many forget the *raison d'être* of The Stock Exchange – that it provides a marketplace in which government and industry can raise the long-term funds that they need. As we saw in Chapter 2, the Exchange is now facing strong competition from outside forces which are challenging its position as the premier European marketplace for securities.

The Exchange's origins lay in the seventeenth century, when merchants clubbed together to form joint-stock companies, like the East India Company, to conduct foreign trade. After a time some merchants sold their holdings to others, and in the process there developed a secondary market for shares in the joint-stock companies. At first the shares were traded in the coffee houses which were then fashionable, but in 1773 the different sites for trading were centralized for the first time. By 1801 The Stock Exchange was established in roughly its modern form.

Exchange members built up some of the country's most colourful traditions. Legend has it that if a member spotted an outsider on the

*The Stock Exchange is the title of the amalgamation of the old regional exchanges. Apart from London, the Exchange has subsidiaries in Birmingham, Manchester, Liverpool, Glasgow and Dublin.

Exchange floor, he would shout, 'Fourteen hundred!' (for a time, there were 1,399 members), and the offending individual would be ejected into the street, minus his trousers. Another tradition, which will vanish, is that of 'hammering', the term used to describe the financial failure of a member firm. The term arose because in the old days failure would be announced after an official had interrupted proceedings by hammering on a rostrum.

Times change, and the old gentlemanly agreements have given way to the age of the computer. Stock Exchange deals are now processed through the Talisman system. Talisman is operated through a special Stock Exchange company, SEPON Limited, which has an account in the register of every UK company whose shares are traded on the Exchange. All purchases and sales are processed through a SEPON account and recorded on a central computer. Ownership is automatically transferred from buyer to seller in the computer's records, and the computer then generates all the necessary paperwork. It also calculates the required tax payments. The system processes, on average, 14,500 deals a day.

Talisman is not the first attempt to bring computers into the world of stocks and shares. ARIEL (Automated Realtime Investments Exchange Limited) was set up in 1971 by the merchant banks in an attempt to compete on costs with The Stock Exchange by trading through computer screens. Although ARIEL had little immediate success, despite the astonishing development of its US equivalent, NASDAQ, some commentators feel that it has succeeded in keeping a check on the level of Stock Exchange commissions. However, its turnover in 1985 was still less than 1 per cent of The Stock Exchange.

In Chapter 2 we looked at the challenges which face The Stock Exchange in the light of the development of international equity markets. Despite the fact that some feel that the Exchange is a dying institution, it still has considerable influence. In the 1986 Budget, for example, the Exchange persuaded the Chancellor to cut stamp duty (the tax paid on share purchases) from 1 to 0.5 per cent. As a result, the costs of share dealing in London are now on a par with those in Tokyo, although still above the costs in New York, where no stamp duty is paid at all.

The Unlisted Securities Market

The Unlisted Securities Market (USM) was set up in 1980 to help small companies to raise capital after it had been noticed that the number of firms applying for full membership of the Exchange was declining. USM listing requires less rigorous criteria to be met than does the main Exchange (for example, only 10 per cent of the company's shares need to be sold as compared with 25 per cent on the full Exchange). In theory, the USM allows more risky ventures to raise capital and offers speculative investors the chance to have a punt on the ICIs of the future.

Ninety-seven companies were brought to the USM in 1985, raising the total of companies listed on the market to 406. By the end of 1985 forty-five companies had progressed to a full listing, and only eight had been suspended or cancelled because of company financial problems.* The brokers have been very careful about the companies they have brought to the market.

The FT Index

Every day on the television news some reference will be made to the performance of the FT index – the so-called barometer of industry's health. If the FT index goes up, that in itself is regarded as 'good' news. If it goes down and keeps falling, talk of a national crisis begins.

There are several indices in use, but the one most commonly referred to is the FT-30 Industrial. The thirty firms involved are some of the biggest in the country – the 'blue chips'. The firms currently included are ASDA–MFI, Allied Lyons, the Beecham Group, BICC, Blue Circle, BOC International, Boots, British Petroleum, British Telecom, BTR Industries, Cadbury Schweppes, Courtaulds, General Electric Company, Glaxo, Grand Metropolitan, Guest, Keen and Nettlefolds, Guinness, Hanson Trust, Hawker Siddeley, ICI, Lucas Industries, Marks and Spencer, National Westminster Bank, P & O Steam Navigation, Plessey, Royal Insurance, Tate and Lyle, Thorn EMI, Trusthouse Forte and Vickers.

The idea is to select companies of such size and range that they reflect both the industrial diversity of Britain and the shares involved in the

* Figures are taken from Peat Marwick's USM Quarterly Survey.

market. Every time a company is taken over or falls on bad times, the index must be changed, as it was in 1986 after the takeovers of Distillers and Imperial.

Because the FT-30 index is felt by some to be too narrow a base (a large move in the price of just one firm can affect the whole index), there are two further indices – the FTSE-100 and the FT All-share index. The latter, despite its name, does not include all the shares traded on The Stock Exchange, but it does include all those (around 650) in which there is a significant market. There are equivalent indices in other markets. In New York the key index is the Dow Jones Industrial, in Tokyo, the Nikkei–Dow.

Does it really matter if the FT index falls or rises? The answer is not clear-cut. Day-to-day shifts are of little importance. They may result from a chance remark of a government minister, from an opinion poll showing one or other party to be ahead, from an unexpected set of economic statistics or because investors expect any or all of these things to be good or bad. What actually happens to the economy or to the government is usually not so important as the expectations of investors about what *might* happen.

Remember that the vast majority of shares are held by investing institutions. They must judge not only the prospects of individual companies but also the prospects of the share market as a whole. If they think that, say, interest rates are about to fall, they might shift their portfolios into bond investments because the prices of bonds will rise as rates fall. However, they might feel that a drop in rates will reduce the costs of industrial companies and cause share prices to rise. Either line of reasoning would have logic behind it. The net result will be that some investors will sell shares and some will buy, moving the index up or down depending on where the balance lies. Such day-to-day shifts have little effect on the performance of business, although they may be costly for shareholders who buy or sell at the wrong time.

Long-term shifts in the index are more important. There is little doubt that the Wall Street Crash of 1929 contributed to the depths of the 1930s depression. In the UK share prices bounced back in the late 1970s from their lows of January 1975 as the economy recovered from the three-day week, the miners' strike and hyper-inflation. They have scarcely stopped rising since. A long-running reversal of that trend would make both UK and foreign investors wary of investing in British industry.

Under the auspices of the London International Financial Futures Exchange (see Chapter 13) it is possible to buy futures (see Chapter 13) based on the FTSE-100 index. If the index rises, the price of the future will also rise. Under the system through which futures are traded, a rise in the futures price benefits futures buyers, and a fall benefits the sellers. That allows institutional investors to sell futures to protect their shareholdings against a general fall in prices. However, it appears that the majority of index futures have so far been bought and sold by speculators rather than fund managers. For those who do not fancy the intricacies of the futures market, several bookmakers offer simple bets on whether the index will fall or rise.

Shares and the Rights that They Confer

Ordinary Shares

The most common form of share is the *ordinary share*: it gives the owner the right to vote (although there are non-voting ordinary shares), the right to appoint and remove directors and, most important, the right to receive dividends if and when these are declared. Remember that the dividend is to the shareholder what the coupon is to the bondholder: an opportunity to receive income rather than capital appreciation.

Most companies pay a dividend every six months. The first appears with the half-yearly results and is known as the *interim dividend.* The second accompanies the annual accounts and is called the *final dividend.* Income tax at the basic rate is deducted at source.

Because shareholders stand at the end of the creditors' queue if a company fails, shares are at the riskiest end of the risk/reward scale and can therefore attract the highest return. Like bonds, shares can increase in price, but the potential for share-price increases vastly exceeds that for bonds. Although dividends add to the attractiveness of shares, it is this chance of a sharp rise in price that makes shares such an exciting investment. A wise investor who had placed his money in Saatchi and Saatchi in 1978 would have seen the share price rise from 24 pence then to £9.36 by 1986, a thirty-nine fold increase. But – and it is a large but – success stories on such a scale are not commonplace, and a large price rise often cometh before a fall. It is necessary to go back only to 1974 to find a time when the FT-30 index was at 146, its lowest level for fifty years.

History is littered with stock-market crashes and with companies that have gone bust, from Rolls-Royce to Laker Airways. The ordinary shareholders are usually the losers from such failures.

Other Types of Share

In order to attract investors who are wary of the risks of ordinary share ownership, companies have devised other forms of share which are slightly less risky. *Preference shares* are different from ordinary shares in that they give the holder a first claim on dividends and on a company's assets if and when it is liquidated. The amount of dividend attached to a preference share is fixed. If it is not paid, this is a sign that the company is in severe financial trouble. The lesser risk attached to holding preference shares means that the return in good years is less than that of ordinary shares. In addition, the voting rights of preference shareholders are normally restricted.

Cumulative preference shares entitle the holder to be paid in arrears if the dividend is not paid one year. Since they are slightly less risky than ordinary preference shares, the yield on cumulative preference shares is marginally lower. *Redeemable preference shares* will be repaid at a future date; they closely resemble bonds and must offer a similar return to be attractive to investors. *Participating preference shares* offer a lower basic rate of return but allow for a bonus rate if the ordinary dividend is high. *Convertible preference shares* can be converted into ordinary shares at a certain price – they closely resemble convertible bonds (see Chapter 11). Again, the investor is compensated for the lower initial rate of return by the chance of future gains.

As a group, preference shares resemble fixed-rate bonds; indeed, the yield from such shares tends to be compared by investors with the yield on long-dated gilts. However, companies which issue preference shares cannot offset the dividend against tax, as they can in the case of bonds. Thus preference shares tend to be issued by companies that want to raise money but whose existing management group is concerned that a conventional rights issue will weaken its control of the company.* The managers can safeguard their position by issuing preference shares as a bonus to existing shareholders and by selling their own allotment to outside in-

* Those who are familiar with the Westland saga will know that the proposal for the minority Sikorsky–Fiat holding was to be achieved by an issue of preference shares.

vestors in return for cash. Since preference shares do not carry voting rights, the management's control over the company is not threatened.

Companies can also issue stocks called *debentures*, which are essentially long-term bonds (over fifteen years). Debentures have advantages both for the companies which issue them and for the investors who buy them. Companies can deduct the interest payments from profits before taxation and may retain the option of early repayment. Further, investors have the advantage of a high level of security, since most debentures are secured by a charge on the assets of the company; debenture holders can appoint a receiver if the firm is in financial trouble; and they rank above all other creditors and shareholders when a failed company's assets are being redistributed. Companies are obliged in law to pay interest on, and to repay the capital of, debentures regardless of whether the firm is making a profit or a loss.

Traded Options

Traded options differ from other types of equity investment because they are not issued by the companies concerned. Instead they are instruments traded on stock exchanges and are designed both to give investors greater leverage and to act as hedging vehicles for investors who are worried about future share-price movements.

Options grant the buyer the right to buy (a *call* option) or to sell (a *put* option) a set number of shares at a fixed price. The option buyer is not obliged to buy or sell at that price if it is not advantageous to do so. In return for granting the option the option seller receives a non-returnable premium.

An example will help explain the principles involved.* Suppose an investor has bought British Telecom (BT) shares at £1.50. Their price moves to £1.70 each. The investor wants to make sure that he retains some of his gain but does not want to miss out on the chance of seeing the price rise still further. So he buys a put option at £1.70, which gives him the right to sell his shares at £1.70 if he wishes. In return he pays a premium of 5 pence a share. If the share price falls to £1.50, the investor exercises the option and sells the shares at £1.70. Deducting the cost of the premium, he has retained a profit of 15 pence. If the share price rises

* Examples of two other sorts of option, based on interest rates and currencies, are given in Chapter 13 and Chapter 14 respectively.

to £2.00, the investor simply lets the option lapse. He has paid 5 pence a share but has a profit of 45 pence a share over his original purchase.

More speculative investors may try to use options for their leverage potential. Suppose an investor has no share in BT but merely believes their price will rise. In the above situation (BT shares at £1.70) he could buy a call option for 5 pence a share (on 100 shares, that would cost him £5). If the price rises to £2.00, the option will be worth at least 30 pence on the traded market because he could buy his shares at £1.70 through the option and then sell them at £2.00 on The Stock Exchange. Rather than exercise his option, the investor would sell the option and receive £30, or a 500 per cent profit on his original investment. An ordinary shareholder, buying at £1.70 and selling at £2.00, would make a profit of only 17.65 per cent. However, not all options are tradeable. The majority are part of the traditional option market and cannot be sold.

New Issues

There is an important distinction between The Stock Exchange, which is a secondary market for trading existing securities, and the new issues market, where companies (and the government) initially raise their capital. New issues must be launched according to Stock Exchange rules if they are to be traded there – buyers will be much keener to purchase an issue if they know they will be able to sell it easily. The name of the stockbroker or merchant bank which has agreed to sponsor the company may also be very important in ensuring investors' confidence in the issue.

A full listing on The Stock Exchange will not be granted unless a company has a total market value of £500,000 and unless the size of the issue is at least £200,000. The cost of raising an issue of £2 million has been estimated by The Stock Exchange at about 7.5 per cent or £150,000. That includes as much as £100,000 for a prospectus (part of the detailed documentation companies must prepare before a listing). The full list of rules and regulations is outlined in The Stock Exchange's Yellow Book.

A company wishing to make an issue must decide first, with the help of its advisers, when the issue should be made, how much should be raised and on what terms. The advisers will base their advice on their knowledge of how the issues of other companies in similar situations or industries have been received and on their assessment of the likely reaction of investors to the name and profit record of the company.

An *issue by prospectus* is the most expensive method of making a new issue, since it requires a large amount of publicity. The prospectus sets out, in very detailed form, the company's structure, trading record and prospects. It must appear in at least two daily newspapers. Despite its enormous cost (about £150,000), it is the best way of obtaining a wide market for the company's shares. The company's advising bank or broker invites investors to apply for shares by a certain day: the investors are told the price in advance.

The amount of money raised from the issue will be the number of shares times the price in the prospectus minus the fees and expenses. Any subsequent rise in price after the shares are issued will reflect well on the company and please the shareholders but will not bring the company any more cash. The bank's problems in setting the price will be exacerbated by the presence of stock market investors (called *stags*) who are eager to make a profit out of new listings.

Stags are speculators who believe that a new issue has been priced too low and who therefore attempt to purchase as many shares as possible. If they have correctly assumed that an issue is underpriced, the shares will immediately rise in value when the issue is made. The stags can then resell the shares and make a quick profit. A good example of successful stag dealing is the British Telecom issue in November 1984. The advising bank to the government, Kleinwort Benson, was particularly worried that investors might balk at such a big issue (over £4 billion). They thought it safer to err on the low side with the price. However, it quickly became obvious that the publicity surrounding the issue had been so successful that the price would rise quickly and substantially. Indeed, by May 1985 the price of BT shares had risen threefold. Despite the attempts of the government to limit the number of shares bought by any one institution, there is no doubt that some stags made a killing.

It is posssible for both the advising bank or broker and the stags to overestimate the likely demand for a company's shares. If that happens, the price of the company's shares will drop below the issue price. If that happens, a stag will have to sell the shares and take the loss or hang on to them in the hope that the price will rise. As some stags will have borrowed money to purchase the shares (planning to repay the loan with the help of the profits), a failed issue can hit them particularly hard.

The other animal members of the investor family are *bulls* and *bears*.

Bulls are optimists. They buy shares in the expectation that their prices will rise. Bears are pessimists who sell shares in the hope of buying them back at a lower price. Some bears are so aggressive that they sell shares which they haven't yet bought, hoping that the price of the shares will fall quickly enough for them to buy the shares needed. Such a process is known as *going short*.

To avoid some of the problems of setting the price and of marketing shares to a wide investing public, some issuing houses launch a company's shares through a *private placement*. For a commission the adviser will find institutional investors willing to buy a company's shares. A placing is cheaper than other methods of new issues but normally results in the firm's shares being owned by a small number of investors. If one investor then sells his shares, the effect on the share price can be considerable.

The most popular method of making a new issue is the *offer for sale*. A bank or securities house purchases all the shares from a company and then attempts to sell them to investors at a higher price. Under an offer for sale a company can get its cash immediately but may not receive as large a total return as with an issue by prospectus. The bank will offer to buy the shares at a price slightly below that which it would have recommended for a prospectus issue – the difference will be the bank's profit if the sale goes well. The bank, however, takes the risk that the investing public will fail to buy the shares at the higher price. It will usually arrange for the shares to be underwritten to cover that risk.

If it seems particularly difficult to set the right price for a company's shares, the advisers may recommend offering the shares for *sale by tender*. Applicants will be asked to state how many shares they would like to purchase and at what price. The bank will then allot the shares at a price which ensures that all the shares are sold. Tenders have not been a popular way of selling shares. One reason is that companies fear that a large investor might bid high and buy up all the shares on offer and thus become, overnight, a contender for control of the firm. Another potential problem is that the share price is as likely to fall as to rise after a tender bid, reflecting badly both on the company and on its advisers.

Whatever the chosen method of sale, the adviser will probably act as salesman for a large proportion of the shares and will perhaps underwrite some of the issue. Advisers are accordingly very careful about the calibre of the firms that they bring to the market in this way.

Raising Further Equity Capital

Rights Issues

A new issue normally takes place in the early years of a company's existence. As companies attempt to expand, however, they need more funds than were provided by the original sources. There are many avenues to raising funds in the form of debt. However, as we noted in Chapter 8, too much debt makes a company unbalanced. At some point the company will need further equity capital.

Further equity will normally be raised through a *rights issue*. Shares are offered to existing shareholders in proportion to their holdings – a typical offer might be one share for every four owned. The shareholder may then take up his or her rights and pay for the new shares or sell the rights to do so to another investor.

A major factor in favour of the rights issue as a financing technique is that UK companies legislation demands that existing shareholders should have a pre-emptive right to subscribe to any new shares on offer. If they had no such right, companies might prefer to raise money from outsiders, and the shareholders' stake in the company would be eroded. At the moment UK companies can place shares with new investors only if the existing shareholders agree.

When considering a rights issue the main questions facing a company, and the bank or broker advising it, are when to make the issue and at what price. The shares will normally have to be offered at a discount to the market price for the company's existing shares, otherwise those shareholders who want more shares will simply buy existing ones on the market. The bigger the proportion of new shares on offer (say, one to four or less), the heavier the discount will have to be in order to attract the amount of funds needed.

The company will also have to extend a grace period, usually three weeks, to allow shareholders time to decide whether or not to take up their rights. If the price of the existing shares falls too far during that period, it can ruin the prospects of the issue; the discount offered may have to be substantial in order to avoid that risk.

Timing the issue is very important. If the stock market is strong, a company can raise a lot of money by issuing fewer new shares. However, shareholders may be unwilling to take up new shares which are highly priced. If the share market is weak and a company's share price is low, then a rights issue to raise a large amount will involve issuing a large number of shares. This can dilute the control of its shareholders.

The Bought Deal

The techniques involved in making a rights issue may change after the 'Big Bang'. The so-called *bought deal* may become prevalent. A bought deal is similar to an offer for sale for new issues. A securities firm buys all the new shares and then sells them to other investors at a slightly higher price.

Two factors have militated against the bought deal in the past: first, Stock Exchange regulations protected the rights of existing shareholders; second, most UK stockbrokers lacked the resources to undertake a bought deal. The Stock Exchange has been forced to concede the former point, while the latter has been countered by the creation of the new giant financial conglomerates. The new conglomerates will have the capital needed to carry the shares while they wait to find buyers. It will be a very risky business for the conglomerates, but competition in the new market may well push them into it. Companies may benefit through a reduction in the costs of rights issues. These who will suffer most will be the small shareholders, who will miss out on the most profitable deals.

The proportion of a company's total profits, dividends and assets held by existing shareholders is unaffected by the *price* at which new shares are issued under a rights issue or the *number* of shares issued – it is the *amount raised* which is important. If the market capitalization of a company is £10 million and it issues £2.5 million of new shares (a *one-for-four issue*), existing shareholders will now hold four-fifths of the company if none of them takes up his or her rights. They will still hold four-fifths of the company regardless of whether it has issued 5 million shares at 50 pence each or 1.25 million shares at £2.00 each. The important question for existing shareholders to decide is whether to exercise their rights to the issue or whether to sell them to a more willing buyer. That decision may depend on whether they have the cash available to pay for the new shares, whether they have an interest in controlling the company and what they see as its future prospects.

How much would their rights be worth? Assume, in the above example, that the company had offered 1.25 million shares at £2.00 each and that its 4 million existing shares were trading at £2.50. The theoretical value of the rights can be calculated as follows:

4 million existing shares at 250 pence	£10 million
1.25 million new shares at 200 pence	£2.5 million
5.25 million shares in total	£12.5 million

Dividing the total value of the company by the number of shares (£12.5 million ÷ 5.25 million) gives a share price of £2.43p. Subtracting the rights issue price of £2.00 gives a theoretical price for the rights of 43 pence.

Bonus Issues

Capitalization issues, sometimes known as *scrip* or *bonus issues*, create more shares but without a resulting cash flow to the company. Each shareholder is given extra shares in proportion to his or her current holdings. These issues are essentially accounting operations, transforming retained earnings into shareholders' capital. Sometimes they are undertaken to reduce the price of shares since it is usually believed that high-priced shares are unpopular with individual investors.

Although the price of a company's shares should theoretically fall in proportion to the size of the capitalization issue (since the number of shares has increased while the nominal value of the company has remained constant), this does not always happen. Capitalization issues normally take place during periods of high company profits, and shareholders may be encouraged by news of such issues to improve their view of a company's prospects and thus bid up its share price.

How Investors Value Companies

One of the most obvious measures of a company's performance is its pre-tax profits. Calculating these profits is not quite so simple as deducting the company's costs from its revenues. A charge must also be made for the gradual fall in value of a company's fixed assets. This charge is known as *depreciation*. It is a useful concept, since it circumvents incidental accounting peaks and troughs (such as a sudden drop in profits because a firm needs a new boiler). Allowances for depreciation make it easier to judge a trend in a company's performance.

Having deducted tax, preference dividends and minority interests from profits* and divided the result by the number of shares, an analyst can arrive at a figure for earnings per share. If the share price is divided by the earnings per share, the result is the price/earnings (P/E) ratio. The P/E ratio is one of the best-known ways of valuing shares. It gives a rough guide to the time needed for the investor's initial stake to be paid back in full. If the P/E ratio is 15, then it will take fifteen years (on current earnings) to pay back the shareholder's investment. If the P/E ratio is 2, then it should take only two years. Of course, for the P/E ratio to be a perfect guide to the pay-back period, a firm would have to keep its profits constant and to distribute all of them in the form of dividends. Both events are extremely unlikely, but the P/E ratio retains its hold on investor interest all the same.

One might assume that the lower the P/E ratio (and therefore the shorter the pay-back period), the better the shares as an investment. This is far from being the case. Since all investors would prefer to have their stake repaid in two years rather than in fifteen, they would flock to buy the shares of a company with a P/E ratio of 2 if they thought that the prospects were good. As a result, the price of that company's shares would rise, and so, consequently, would its P/E ratio. Other investors would sell the shares of companies with high P/E ratios, and those companies would see their share price (and therefore their P/E ratio) fall.

The P/E ratio thus seems to reflect investors' *expectations* of a company's earnings power. If the ratio is *low*, this indicates that investors expect the company's earnings to *fall*. If the ratio is *high*, it normally means that investors expect the company's earnings to *rise*.

Another frequently consulted index of a company's performance is the *yield*, calculated by dividing the dividend by the prevailing share price. The result is a percentage figure which can be compared with the return on bonds. Some companies, when forseeing difficult times, will keep their yields high to retain investor support.

A sometimes neglected but very important statistic is the net asset value of a company. This represents the value of its fixed assets (land, machinery, etc.) and thus the sum which shareholders could expect to receive if the company were wound up. Companies whose market capitalization (that is, the number of shares multiplied by the price) is higher than their net asset value are said to be at a premium. Those which have

* It is usual to deduct an average of 35 per cent rather than the actual tax bill.

a net asset value higher than their market capitalization could be vulnerable to a takeover bid from a company that would sell all the assets.

The Decline of the Individual Investor

It is the riskiness of share ownership, combined with the distortions caused by the tax system, which has precipitated the decline in the proportion of shareholdings of private individuals. The careful saver with only £1,000 to invest has no desire to see his savings decline into nothing overnight. It is better to accept a slower rate of growth in return for safety. Over the last thirty years the share market has had the added disadvantage of being the least favoured, in tax terms, of the traditional outlets for personal investment. Tax relief has been available on mortgage interest payments, pension contributions and (until 1984) life assurance premiums.

All experts agree that the most sensible way of investing in shares is to spread risk by creating a portfolio of investments in different companies. For the small investor the transaction costs of investing in shares are high, thanks to stamp tax and commissions. It is therefore open only to those with substantial savings (£25,000 or so) to create their own portfolio. Those without such sums should spread their investments by the indirect route of investing in unit trusts and investment trusts (see Chapter 9). The trusts pool together the savings of small investors, thus enabling them to have a stake in a wide range of companies.

The British Telecom issue and the rest of the Conservative government's privatization programme have reversed the decline in individual shareholdings – but the 'Big Bang' is likely to discourage the establishment of a 'shareholding economy'. As noted in Chapter 2, the abolition of minimum commissions will result in lower commissions for institutional shareholders but will in all probability increase the commissions paid by the small investor. The government's attempts to boost individual shareownership (personal equity plans, for example) may not be enough to offset the effect of increased commissions.

[11] The Euromarket

The growth of the Eurocurrency market is probably the single most important development in the international financial markets since the Second World War, because it has created a market in which borrowers and lenders can borrow and invest funds, virtually untouched by the wishes of nation states.

What is a Eurocurrency? The first Eurocurrency was the Eurodollar – the simplest definition of which is a dollar held outside the United States. A Eurocurrency, by extension, is a currency held outside its country of origin. Eurocurrencies are normally held as bank deposits. So dollars deposited in Barclays Bank in London are Eurodollars; French francs held in the same bank are Euro-French francs; a sterling deposit in Paris is a Eurosterling deposit; and so on.

How did the Eurocurrency market begin? Some people believe that the market had its origin in the unwillingness of the Soviet Union to hold dollars in New York for fear that the US government might freeze its deposits at times of political tension. However, the Russians still needed dollars to be able to conduct international trade, and they began to borrow in Europe through a Russian-owned bank, Banque Commerciale pour l'Europe du Nord, whose telex code was Eurobank.

Where did the dollars that the Russians borrowed come from? From the late 1950s onwards there were plenty of dollars around outside the United States because of the current-account deficits run up by the Americans. If a country has a current-account deficit, it pays out more of its own currency than it receives in foreign currency. Dollars were therefore flowing out of the country into the hands of foreign exporters. At the same time the US Treasury imposed Regulation Q, which set upper limits on the level of interest rates that US banks could offer to domestic and foreign investors. Those people who held dollars outside the United States and wanted to invest them found that non-US banks were able to offer more attractive rates than their US counterparts. Thus the Eurodollar market was born.

As more currencies became convertible (readily exchangeable) following the dismantling of post-war controls, the market grew. There was a range of major convertible currencies by the late 1950s. Investors were able to put their money into Eurodollar deposits in the knowledge that they would be able to convert their holdings into their domestic currencies if they wished.

A liquid market for these deposits quickly developed, and banks began to quote interest rates for dollar loans up to a year. After a short while London became the centre of the market, restoring to the City a position which it had begun to lose to New York. This was an immensely important development: the City's financial pre-eminence, formerly a concomitant of sterling's role in world trade, had been eroded by the UK's economic problems. By comparison with its rivals, London had a distinct advantage – its position in the middle of the time zones between Tokyo and New York, which allowed London-based dealers to talk to those in other centres in the course of the working day.

Those American banks which had been precluded by Regulation Q from attracting foreign investors' deposits began to set up branches in London, enabling them to compete with the European banks in the Eurodollar market. In addition to its time-zone position, London had the extra advantage of speaking the same language as the Americans, thus making it easier for bankers to live and work in Britain. The number of foreign banks in London grew from eighty in the late 1950s to 430 in 1984.

The main participants in the Eurodollar market are banks, multinational companies and institutional investors such as pension funds and insurance companies. The Bank of International Settlements estimated that in 1984 the gross size of the Eurocurrency market was $1,753 billion. Excluding interbank deposits to avoid the risk of double-counting, the figure was 'only' $1,085 billion – more than twice the size of the UK's annual gross national product.

The growth of the Eurocurrency market was undoubtedly given a boost by the end of the system of fixed exchange rates in 1971.* The sudden changes in exchange rates which subsequently occurred could wipe out the profit margins of exporters, importers and institutional investors. One way in which these groups could try to protect themselves against such

* See Chapter 14.

exchange-rate changes was to use the Eurocurrency deposit market.

Suppose a UK car exporter has received an order from a German importer. The UK company will be paid in three months' time. If the Deutschmark falls against the pound during those three months, the UK exporter will receive less money in sterling terms. It might avoid that risk by borrowing Deutschmarks for three months in the Eurocurrency deposit market and exchanging them for sterling at the prevailing exchange rate. It now has to pay interest on the Deutschmark loan, but it can invest the money in a sterling account. There will therefore be a cost depending on whether UK interest rates are below or above German rates.

In three months' time the German importer pays over the Deutschmarks, and the UK company uses them to repay the loan. If, in the meantime, the Deutschmark has fallen against the pound, that will be reflected in the lower cost of repaying the loan (in sterling terms) as well as in the lower receipts of the car sales. The two effects cancel each other out whether the Deutschmark falls or rises. An importer due to pay out Deutschmarks could protect himself against a rise in the German unit by lending Deutschmarks in the Eurocurrency deposit market.

In each case there is a risk. If the Deutschmark rises, the exporter will reap the benefit if he has not used the Eurocurrency deposit market. By using the market and by effectively 'locking in' an exchange rate, the exporter foregoes the chance of a windfall currency profit.*

When Eurocurrencies are lent or borrowed in the interbank market, interest rates are quoted on a spread between the bid and offer rates. The bid rate is the rate which a bank is prepared to pay to borrow funds; the offer rate is the rate at which it is prepared to lend. The average of the offer rates, the London Interbank Offered Rate (LIBOR), is an important benchmark for other loans. By referring to LIBOR it is possible for banks to lend money for long periods by agreeing with borrowers to reset interest rates, every six months, at a rate above (or sometimes below) LIBOR. They thus ensure that the returns from long-term lending stay close to the cost of short-term borrowing.

It is now possible to borrow Eurocurrencies for a wide range of maturities. The most commonly quoted are overnight, one week, one month, two months, three months, six months, nine months and one year, but it is possible to borrow for other periods. Eurorates for the major currencies are quoted every day on the money markets page of the

*The same effect can be achieved by using the forward marker, as Chapter 14 indicates.

Financial Times. With the growth in the size and depth of the market, many millions of dollars can be moved between banks in anticipation of tiny changes in rates (the minimum movement is normally one-sixteenth of a percentage point).

In addition to the term deposits there is a short-term tradeable instrument, the Euro certificate of deposit (Euro CD). Since Euro CDs can be sold, they give the investor extra liquidity and thus carry a slightly lower interest rate than other comparable deposits. They also fluctuate in price like longer-term tradeable instruments, so they allow investors to take a gamble on short-term interest-rate movements.

There has been great debate over the question of whether the Eurocurrency markets cause inflation. They *could* do so if the funds invested in Eurocurrencies were then re-invested in the same market – thus making possible a spiral of credit creation. A recent major work on the subject concluded that most Eurocurrency deposits leak back to their countries of origin, and thus the market's inflationary impact is probably small.*

Whatever its effect on inflation, the market has a great importance in the world economy, since it provides a mechanism by which funds can flow quickly between one currency and another. As the market is largely outside governmental control, it can prove a potent weapon for destabilizing a currency. It is a brave government that follows an economic policy which might alarm the Euromarkets.

Syndicated Loans

The Eurocurrency deposit market described above is a short-term market. However, borrowers who need long-term finance have also been eager to tap the market. In the earliest stages the most popular means of raising long-term finance was a syndicated loan.

A syndicated loan is merely a large, long-term bank loan which a syndicate of banks club together to provide because no one bank wants to commit that much capital to any one borrower. In the Euromarket syndicated loans carry interest rates at a margin relating to LIBOR. Companies, countries or institutions with a good credit rating can sometimes borrow below LIBOR or even the London Interbank Bid Rate (LIBID), but borrowers whose financial position is not so healthy can expect to pay a considerable margin over LIBOR.

* R. B. Johnston, *The Economics of the Euromarket* (London, Macmillan, 1983).

The syndicated loan market gives borrowers access to large sources of long-term funds (often the size of loans is several hundreds of millions of dollars) in a short space of time. Another advantage for borrowers is that they can borrow as much as they want up to a certain limit. The overall limit on the loan may be $100 million, but borrowers pay interest only on the amount outstanding at any time. (This compares favourably with a bond issue, interest on the full amount of which must be paid until the bond is repaid.) Syndicated loans have been particularly attractive to nation states which wish to raise large amounts of money in a single borrowing. The advantage to banks of such loans is that they can lend long-term at rates above their normal costs of funds without committing too much capital to any one borrower.

In the early 1980s the syndicated loan market suffered a decline. The main reason seems to have been the number of loans which had to be rescheduled, or deferred, because of the international debt crisis. The banks were faced with bad debts which cut their profits and reduced their credit ratings. Banks became unwilling to tie up their money in syndicated loans and started to lend money in more liquid forms or even to act as arrangers rather than providers of borrowings (the two processes mentioned in Chapter 1 as *securitization* and *disintermediation*).

A further liquid instrument which was developed in response to the banks' worries was the transferable loan facility (TLF), which can be traded in the same way as bonds. Another development was the growth in the floating-rate note market (described below), which guaranteed a return linked to the cost of banks' funds and offered the liquidity they needed. A third development was the growth of the Euronote market, involving the issuance and trading of short-term non-bank paper.

The Eurobond Market

In parallel with the growth of the syndicated loan market in the 1960s and 1970s, borrowers issued long-term tradeable instruments – Eurobonds. A bond, as seen in the Introduction, is merely a piece of paper which promises, in return for an immediate loan, to pay the holder interest until the loan is repaid. Since the original purchaser can (and usually does) sell the bond, repayment will be made to whomever ends up holding the bond (the bearer) on maturity. Attached to each Eurobond are coupons which the bearer can tear off in order to claim the interest payment. Normally the maturity of the bond will be at least two years; the maximum maturity is around thirty years, although some bonds have been issued on the express condition that they will never be repaid.

The borrower can arrange to pay back the debt by setting aside a certain amount each year during the life of the bond through a sinking fund or by waiting until the end (a so-called 'bullet maturity'). Bonds can be repaid early if a borrower buys back the debt in the traded market or if it incorporates a call option at the time of the issue, allowing it to repay a certain amount of bonds each year. The effect of all these strategies is to minimize the impact of repayment on the borrower's cash flow.

There are bond markets in most parts of the world. Traditionally borrowers raised money only in their domestic bond markets. Formerly issues in foreign markets were the exception rather than the rule. As a consequence a bond issued by a foreign institution is known as a *bulldog* in the UK, a *Yankee bond* in the USA, a *samurai bond* in Japan and so on. As we saw in Chapter 5, in the sterling market the main issuer of bonds (in the form of gilts) is the government. In the Eurobond market a whole range of borrowers issue bonds; corporations and banks are the most frequent issuers, followed by governments and supranational institutions like the European Community.

Some companies, governments and banks have borrowing requirements which are so large that their domestic market cannot accommodate them. It is possible for them to borrow at a much better rate abroad. Domestic investors may have already bought large numbers of their bonds and no longer wish to buy the bonds of that institution unless they are guaranteed a high rate of interest. Foreign bond issues give borrowers access to other countries' investors: Eurobond issues grant access to international investors.

How did the Eurobond market develop? In 1963 the USA imposed an Interest Equalization Tax (IET) to discourage foreign borrowers from raising capital in the US market. President Kennedy was worried about continuing US current-account deficits; he considered that these were encouraged by US investment overseas. The IET was imposed, at a rate ranging from 2.75 per cent to 15 per cent, on the purchase value of foreign bonds bought by US citizens, thus making it considerably more expensive for foreign institutions to borrow money in the USA (since they had to offer higher yields to compensate investors for the tax disadvantages). Non-US borrowers were still keen to borrow dollars, however, and therefore began to look for investors outside the USA who had dollars to lend.

Although this is the subject of debate, some people regard the first Eurobond as a $15 million issue of Autostrade, the Italian motorway company. As we have seen, a Eurodollar is merely a dollar held outside the USA: a Eurobond is a bond sold outside the country of the denominating currency. The vast majority of the early Eurobond issues were denominated in dollars – a reflection of the dominant role played by the dollar in international trade.

European bankers, especially those based in London, realized that the IET had created an opportunity which they could exploit. Traditionally dollar-denominated bonds were managed by US banks, which pocketed the substantial fees involved (0.5 per cent was then standard, and on a $50 million issue that would mean $250,000). The US banks also acted as underwriters for the issues – that is, they agreed to buy any bonds which failed to be sold to outside investors. The fee for underwriting was often as much as 1 per cent. European bankers seized a portion of this lucrative business and created a London-based market to bring together international borrowers and investors.

To whom do the banks sell Eurobonds? In the markets the legend is that the typical Eurobond buyer is the Belgian dentist, the middle-class professional attempting to avoid the stringent tax laws of the Benelux countries. Indeed, an important reason for the success of the Eurobond market is the fact that bonds are denominated in bearer form, allowing the investor almost complete anonymity. Whoever presents the coupon to the bank for interest, or the bond itself for repayment, will receive payment. There is no register of owners; accordingly, they cannot be traced by regulatory authorities. As a result investors who hold bonds outside their own countries are normally able to escape tax. In fact, Eurobond investors include banks, investment management firms, pension funds and insurance companies all over the world as well as wealthy individuals like the Belgian dentists.

The main currency in which Eurobonds are issued is dollars, but they have also been issued in a wide range of units, including Deutschmarks, sterling, Canadian dollars, Japanese yen and even the Kuwaiti dinar. Borrowers are not limited to issues denominated in their domestic currency. With the help of swaps (see Chapter 13), they can issue in one currency and end up with cheap funding in another, and this explains the popularity of some currencies, such as the Australian and the New Zealand dollar.

The arranging bank has a difficult task in issuing a Eurobond. It must set a yield which will be attractive to investors but will be the lowest rate possible for the borrower. It will normally be paid its fees in the form of a discount to the price of the bond (perhaps around 1.5 per cent). In today's highly competitive market most new issues are so priced that they can be sold only at a discount. The arranging bank rarely makes a profit on a new issue and quite often makes a loss. In the *Financial Times* Eurobond column bonds will often be described as 'falling outside their issuing margin' – a sign that the arranging bank has misjudged the yield and lost money in the process. However, so much prestige is attached to the arrangement of Eurobond issues that the banks keep trying.

Growth in the Market

The advantages of the Eurobond market – the degree to which it is unfettered by regulation and the size of the investor base – have resulted in its truly phenomenal growth since that first issue in 1963. In that year the volume of Eurobond issues was just over $100 million. By 1985 it was over $100 billion. The UK government was able to raise $2.5 billion with a single issue in October 1985.

It is much easier now to raise such large amounts because there is a highly developed secondary market in Eurobonds. A primary market is one in which bonds are sold for the first time; a secondary market is one in which existing bonds are traded. Traders sit in vast dealing rooms, surrounded by electronic screens displaying the current prices of bond issues, the latest moves in interest rates and the trends in the economy. They look for bond yields which have moved out of line with the rest of the market and can therefore be bought or sold for profit. They also try to anticipate whether interest rates will fall (and bond prices will rise) or rise (and bond prices will fall). If they make the right decision, they can earn their companies a lot of money; in consequence, they are some of the most highly paid men and women in the country.

London is the centre of the Eurobond markets. The Americans have tried, without much success, to switch the market to New York by setting up international banking facilities, which allow banks to treat some of their New York offices as being off the US mainland. And in 1984 it was feared that the abolition of the US withholding tax (a tax on the investment by US citizens in bonds issued abroad) would lead to the Eurobond market drifting across the Atlantic. However, London retains the advantage of sitting between the time zones of New York and Tokyo, and it seems likely that the Eurobond market will remain focused on the City.

The location of the Eurobond market may still be London, but it is the American rather than the British banks who now have the lion's share of the business of Eurobond arranging. The early lead of the European bankers evaporated when US banks set up London-based subsidiaries to recapture their hold over the dollar bond market. According to a table compiled by *Euromoney*, the banking magazine, the top five international bond managers in 1985 were Crédit Suisse–First Boston, Salomon Brothers, Merrill Lynch, Goldman Sachs and Morgan Stanley. The last four are American; the first is a US/Swiss combination.

Although we have referred to the Eurobond market in the analysis above, it is a term which is becoming less and less appropriate. The capital controls and banking restrictions which spurred the start of the market have largely disappeared, and it is now more correct to refer to an *international* bond market in which international borrowers issue bonds and notes to international investors via international securities houses. Borrowers can now issue bonds in very sophisticated forms, some of which are described in the rest of this chapter.

Floating-rate Notes

Most people are aware of the concept of floating-rate debt. After all, nearly all mortgages are a form of floating-rate debt: a building society can (and does) frequently change the interest rate to be paid on the amount borrowed. The same is true for most people's savings. The interest paid to a lender is subject to change, largely at the whim of the deposit-taking institution.

Floating-rate bonds (more often called floating-rate notes or FRNs) have been a major part of the Euromarket only since 1970. One reason was that traditionally many UK borrowers, particularly companies, preferred the idea of fixed-rate debt because they could calculate their costs in advance. (Floating-rate debt was more common in the USA.) Another snag to the development of the FRN market was agreement on a benchmark around which FRNs could 'float'. Double-digit interest rates conquered the first problem; the development of the Eurocurrency deposit market provided an answer to the second.

When interest rates are high, borrowers become reluctant to borrow long-term at fixed rates because they would then find themselves saddled with a very expensive debt obligation should interest rates subsequently fall. The interest payments on an FRN, however, rise and fall with the level of rates in the market. This is particularly attractive to banks. Most of the money they invest (lend) is lent at floating rates, so borrowing through FRNs allows them to be sure of a constant relationship between the return on their investments and the cost of their funds.

Investors tend to be especially interested in buying FRNs at times when the yield curve is inverted – that is, when short-term interest rates are above long-term rates. Since the return on FRNs is linked to a short-term rate, they provide a higher income than equivalent fixed-rate bonds at such times. Booms in FRN issues have therefore taken place when high interest rates (which make borrowers want to issue FRNs) have occurred simultaneously with an inverted yield curve (which makes investors want to buy FRNs). Two such booms occurred in 1970 and 1974. The greatest FRN boom of all, however, occurred in late 1984 and 1985. In the latter year nearly $45 billion of FRNs were issued.

The Eurocurrency deposit market established the mechanism through which interest rates on long-term securities could be linked to short-term rates (LIBOR). It had already been used as a benchmark for long-term loans, and it was easy to use it as the base rate for FRNs. Typically, FRNs are linked to six-month LIBOR (the rate which banks charge other major banks for six-month loans) and are reset every six months. Most borrowers pay a margin over LIBOR that is related to their creditworthiness. The first issue was made by the Italian public utility Enel, which paid a margin of 0.75 per cent over the mean between LIBOR and LIBID, the rate which banks are prepared to pay in order to borrow.

Over the years nearly three-quarters of the borrowers who have issued FRNs have been banks. Recently, however, more and more types of institutions have issued FRNs, particularly governments and supranational bodies. As the credit ratings of banks have declined, borrowers have been able to borrow at lower and lower spreads over LIBOR, some at rates below it.

What about the secondary market in FRNs? As we saw in Chapter 3, the level of interest rates has a major effect on the market price of fixed-rate bonds. Because they are closely linked to the prevailing level of interest rates, one might expect FRNs to stick fairly close to their issuing price. However, this does not always happen. Although the interest rate on FRNs changes, it does so only once every six months. In the intervening period the general level of interest rates can rise and fall, affecting the price of FRNs.

If interest rates rise, investors will receive a return on the FRNs which, because it is set by an out-of-date benchmark rate, is unattractive. They will sell their FRNs, causing their prices to fall, until the yields come back into line. If rates fall, FRNs will be offering a higher return than the market rate and their prices will rise. However, because the FRN rate is changed every six months, these fluctuations are nowhere near as substantial as those on fixed-rate bonds: most FRNs trade in a range of 96–104 per cent of their issuing price.

'Bells and Whistles'

Banks have developed other variations on the Eurobond, so-called 'bells and whistles', which are designed to attract investors and thereby help the issuer to achieve a lower interest rate than would be possible with a conventional issue.

One of the most prominent 'variations' is the zero-coupon bond, which, as its name suggests, pays no interest at all. Instead it is issued at a discount to its face value. Say it is issued with a face value of £100; its selling price may then be £50. When the bond matures in five years' time, the borrower will repay the full £100. The investor has effectively received all the interest in a lump, rather than spread out over the years. This can be particularly attractive to investors in countries which have tax regimes that differentiate between income and capital gains. The difference between the prices at which the bond is bought and sold is treated by some tax systems as a capital gain; capital gains taxes are normally below the highest rates of income tax. If the investor is going to pay less tax on a zero-coupon bond, he will be willing to accept an interest rate effectively rather lower than that on a straight bond. Both investor and borrower thus benefit.

It is possible to calculate the 'interest' on a zero-coupon bond, though this sounds an odd concept. Assume that the bond has a one-year maturity and a face value of £100, and that it is sold for £80. An investor who buys the bond on issue will make a £20 gain if he holds it until maturity. A profit of £20 on an investment of £80 is a return of 25 per cent per annum. If the bond had a two-year maturity, an issue price of £64 would achieve the same return (25 per cent of £64 is £16, which, added on to £64, makes £80).

Another variation is the partly paid bond. This allows investors to pay only a proportion of the bond's face value when the bond is issued and to pay the rest later on. This gives them an opportunity for 'leverage'.* Suppose a bond is issued at a yield of 10 per cent and the investor is asked to pay only £50 on a bond with a face value of £100. If, because of a change in the market level of interest rates, the price of 10 per cent bonds rises from £100 to £110, then the price of the partly paid bond will rise to £60. The partly paid investor will make a gain of 20 per cent on his initial stake, whereas a conventional bond in the same conditions would have earned him only 10 per cent. Of course, had conventional bonds fallen from £100 to £90, partly paid bonds would have fallen from £50 to £40, a drop of 25 per cent as against 10 per cent (the risk/reward trade-off again).

A further potential advantage to buyers of partly paid bonds is the scope for currency speculation. Investors can buy a partly paid bond in another currency, believing that the foreign currency will fall against their own. If it does, they will have to pay less for the second part of the bond.

The problem of currency risk affects all investors who buy bonds denominated in foreign currencies. A US investor who buys an issue denominated in sterling will want sterling to appreciate against the dollar during the lifetime of the bond. Suppose the bond is worth £1 million when it is bought and the exchange rate is $1 = £1. If, when the investor redeems the bond, the sterling exchange rate has risen to $2 = £1, then the investor will receive $2 million (double the original investment). However, if the pound has fallen against the dollar, the investor will receive less than his original investment.

Dual-currency bonds fix the exchange rate at which the investor is paid. The investor pays for the bond in one currency but will be repaid

* As defined in the Introduction, leverage is the process of attempting to make a considerable profit from an initially small stake.

in another at a pre-arranged exchange rate. The borrower will protect this rate through the forward foreign-exchange markets (see Chapter 14).

Just as exchange-rate movements can adversely affect the investor, so can changes in the level of interest rates. Bonds have been devised to combat this risk with fixed and floating characteristics. There have been five basic types: the debt convertible, the warrant, the droplock bond, the capped FRN and the minimax.

The *debt convertible*. This is an FRN which is convertible into a fixed-rate bond at the option of the investor. The investor will exercise the option only if interest rates fall below the level offered as a fixed rate. With such a bond the borrower faces the risk that the investor will exercise the option, and hence the cost of borrowing will be fixed at an above-market rate. However, because the bond gives the investor some flexibility, the issuer can price the original FRN at a lower interest rate to reflect its extra attractiveness.

The warrant. This is similar in principle to an option. Warrants are normally sold separately from the original issue and give the investor the right to purchase a new bond, bearing a fixed rate of interest. The borrower gets additional and immediate cash from the sale of the warrants but incurs the risk of being forced to issue extra debt at above-market rates. The investor enjoys the prospect of profiting if interest rates fall but faces the risk that the warrants will be worthless when they expire because interest rates have stayed above the level available for the warrants.

The *droplock bond*. This is similar in principle to the debt convertible except that the option of conversion is taken away from the investor. If rates fall to the set conversion price, the investor is locked on at that rate for the remaining life of the bond.

The *capped FRN* and the *minimax*. These are two variants of the same principle. On the first the interest rate floats but will not go above a certain level. On the second upper *and* lower rates are set on the coupon. The bond's interest rate can fluctuate only in a narrow band (say, 9–11 per cent).

Although all the bonds described above have been fashionable for brief periods, none has been an overwhelming success. However, one type of bond which has been a constant feature of the markets has been the equity convertible.

The Equity Convertible

Equity convertibles, as their name suggests, are bond issues which can be converted into shares of the issuing company. The company issues a (normally fixed-rate) bond. The investor may exchange each bond into a given number of shares, which becomes advantageous when the shares reach a price on the stock market which is usually 20–25 per cent above their current value. The investor has two ways of profiting from a convertible issue: through the interest rate and possible capital appreciation of the bond, and through conversion into shares, which permits him or her to earn dividends and a possible further increase in the share price. The borrower will be able to offer a reduced coupon on the original bond issue because of the potential benefits to the investor of conversion. If the investor converts, the company will increase its equity base but will dilute the value of its shares.

Another means of achieving a similar effect is to issue a bond with equity warrants attached which grant the investor the right to buy the company's shares at a set price. The difference between the two methods is that with a straight convertible the borrower gets the benefit of a reduced cost of borrowing because of the lower coupon and with a warrant the borrower receives the benefit in the form of additional cash from the sale of the warrant.

Tombstones

Every day in the *Financial Times* and other papers there are several advertisements called *tombstones*, not just because of their sepulchral appearance but also because they originally appeared next to the obituary column in newspapers. They are designed to advertise, as a matter of record, bond or loan deals, and they usually show the name of the borrower, the size of the deal and the banks which have managed the deal. At the bottom are the names of the banks which participated in the loan (in the case of a syndicated loan) or the banks which sold the bonds (in the case of a Eurobond). It is a matter of great prestige whose name appears at the top of the tombstone, and once the lead managers have been listed, all other banks are listed in alphabetical order to save disputes.

Getting a Eurobond Rating

It is almost impossible for investors around the world to be aware of the strengths and weaknesses of the multitude of borrowers who issue bonds. Largely for this reason, rating agencies have assumed an important and unusual place in the financial hierarchy. The two most famous agencies – Standard and Poor's, and Moody's – are both American. Before any bond issue, and before almost every Eurobond issue, the borrowing institution will pay one of the rating agencies to rate the issue. Standard and Poor's ratings range from AAA (the ability to repay principal is very strong indeed) to D (the bond is in default and payment of interest or repayment of principal is in arrears). Only bonds rated BBB or above are regarded as being of investment grade and eligible for bank investment.

The criteria which Standard and Poor's use for rating issue made by governments are quite interesting and give an insight into the minds of international investors. The first is political risk. The agency makes an assessment of the country's underlying political and social stability: it sees the most important factors as 'the degree of political participation, the orderliness of successions in government, the extent of governmental control and the general flexibility and responsiveness of the system'.* Standard and Poor's add: 'Signals of high political risk include such events as periodic social disorder and rioting, military coups or radical ideological shifts within the government.'

Among the social factors that the agency examines are the rate of population growth, its location and its ethnic mix. The more fast-growing, concentrated and racially diverse the population, the greater the social risk. Further factors are the degree of the country's integration into the Western political system and the extent of its participation in international organizations. The more the country is enmeshed in the Western system, so the reasoning runs, the less likely it is to repudiate its debt and therefore the better its credit rating.

An economic analysis of a country's prospects is undertaken by comparing the total of the country's debt with its foreign-exchange reserves and its balance-of-payments position. This last factor is seen by the agency as one of the most important of the economic criteria, since most debt defaults have occurred when countries have incurred persistent

* Standard and Poor's *Credit Week*.

trade deficits. However, the standard of living of the inhabitants is also considered – the higher it is, the more able a government will be to cut down demand if it is faced with a trade deficit. A good economic growth rate also helps: the agency feels that 'A high rate of growth in total output and especially exports suggests a better ability to meet future debt obligations.'

The safest countries, and therefore those with the best credit ratings, are the Western democracies – Third World countries and particularly those with left-wing governments are regarded as much more risky.

Euronotes

A Euronote is a short-term (under twelve months) tradeable note sold to international investors. It resembles a CD or the commercial paper which is traded in the USA. It has become important in the Euromarket because banks have structured Euronote *facilities*, which allow borrowers to issue the notes over a period of several years. Their effect is to permit borrowers medium-term finance at short-term rates. Because the notes are tradeable, they offer advantages to both banks and borrowers.

Syndicated loans involve the banks in the actual lending of funds which will not be reclaimed until the end of the loan. If a borrower gets into financial trouble, the banks are effectively stuck with the loan. Under a Euronote facility the banks normally act as arrangers. Their profits come from arrangement fees rather than from the use of their capital. They will have to provide capital only if they are acting as underwriters. Even then the notes are tradeable and can be resold.

Borrowers can benefit from using Euronotes because they can choose how many notes they want to issue, and therefore how much they want to borrow, at any time. The notes can also offer cheaper financing. At times when the yield curve is steeply positive (that is, when short-term rates are significantly below long-term rates) Euronotes offer a cheap source of borrowing. If the yield curve shifts to negative and long-term rates fall below short-term, borrowers need not issue more notes.

There are several types of Euronote facility; the terminology is rather confusing. A revolving underwriting facility (RUF) was the most common type of Euronote in the early stages of the market. Under an RUF one bank, or a number of banks, agrees to underwrite short-term paper issued by the borrower for a period of several years. Every three or six months the borrower can decide whether to draw on its facility. If it does not need to do so, it has no need to borrow. However, if it does want to issue paper, the underwriters must attempt to sell this and buy it themselves if they fail.

Under a different sort of facility, generally known as a note-issuance facility (NIF), a panel of banks bids at a rate at which they feel they can sell the notes. Aggressive banks may well bid at a rate well below their normal costs of funds. Nevertheless, they believe they can make a profit by selling the notes at a higher rate to investors.

A third type, which is rapidly growing in importance, is Euro-commercial paper, where borrowers issue paper whenever they wish with a small group of dealers who sell the paper to investors in return for a small placement fee.

The importance of the Euronote market is that it offers borrowers a chance to bypass the banks and tap the funds of institutional investors like pension funds and insurance companies. If borrowers borrow only from banks, they must, of course, pay an interest rate at least as high as the rate at which banks themselves borrow. However, if the borrower is a multinational corporation, it may have a much better credit rating than any bank. By issuing a Euronote it can exploit that better credit rating and borrow from institutions at a rate below that which the banks pay.

Eurobonds, FRNs, syndicated loans, Euronotes and their assorted variations have flourished as borrowers have become more sophisticated about their financing programmes. Investors have had to stay alert in order to understand the range of instruments on offer. With hundreds of highly paid investment bankers in the market, it seems certain that the range of borrowing techniques will increase.

[12] Insurance

Almost everyone in the country has insurance of one form or another – whether it is for house, car or life. Most have insured all three and more besides. Companies need insurance as much as individuals – to cover themselves against damage to factory buildings or equipment or even claims for damages from aggrieved customers. The result is a multi-million dollar industry represented by insurance institutions which, as we saw in Chapter 9, play a vital part in the financial system, and in the economy, because of their role as investors in industry.

The insurance sector has, since the Second World War, been one of the country's biggest foreign-exchange earners. It plays a vital role in assuming part of the risk involved in industry. Without insurance a severe fire, for example, might render a department store bankrupt. With insurance a company can concentrate on the *commercial* risks it faces (that is, whether it can attract enough customers). In return for assuming an insurance risk, insurers charge a premium. They hope that their premium income will exceed the money that they have to pay to those with legitimate insurance claims. If an insurance company feels that the risks it runs are too great, it can pass some of them on to a second company, a process known as *reinsurance*.

Lloyd's

Perhaps the most famous (and, as a result of the recent scandals, infamous) insurance institution is Lloyd's. Lloyd's of London developed from a coffee house opened by one Edward Lloyd just before 1687. Gentlemen from the City used to meet there to discuss insurance over their beverages. By the middle of the eighteenth century they decided that they might as well make it their main place of business.

From the beginning the speciality of Lloyd's was marine insurance, helped by the fact that England has traditionally been a great naval power. Like underwriters in the other financial fields we have looked at (bonds, Euronotes and shares), Lloyd's underwriters accept a commission in return for providing against an unfortunate eventuality. In the case of underwriters of financial instruments they guarantee to buy the bond, if no one else will, in return for a premium. Early Lloyd's underwriters agreed to pay shipowners for the damage to, or loss of, their ships and cargo. For a long time Lloyd's had the best intelligence on the movements of foreign shipping. Perhaps the most famous feature of Lloyd's is the Lutine Bell, which is rung when important news is about to be announced (one ring for bad news, two rings for good).

The Lloyd's Structure

An elaborate structure has been built on the filmsy edifice of a coffee house. There are now five classes of individual involved in Lloyd's.

First and foremost there are the *clients*. Merchant shipping has long since passed its peak, and Lloyd's now provides insurance for a wide variety of customers and products, including Betty Grable's legs, potential kidnap victims and space satellites. Sometimes the clients may be other insurance companies and markets for whom Lloyd's provide reinsurance.

The second tier in the structure is the *brokers*. They link client with underwriter in return for a commission. Their business is rather less risky than the underwriters', since they are not liable to pay out for any claims. But as Lloyd's has been challenged by other insurance markets around the world, Lloyd's brokers have been forced to travel far and wide to drum up business. Not all of it goes to Lloyd's; indeed, the bulk goes to outside insurance companies. However, Lloyd's still retains the flexibility that encourages brokers to place with it substantial or unusual risks. Brokers provide a service which goes beyond merely broking: they advise clients on the best kind of insurance protection for their needs, and they act for clients by administering their insurance business and by collecting any legitimate claims they may have. The big broking firms have gradually come to dominate the market, in the process buying many underwriting agencies. As we shall see, this has led to many problems.

The next tier is the *underwriters*, who actually take on the insurance risk in return for premiums. Many underwriters put up their own capital, but it is a business only for those with strong nerves and large wallets. So great are the risks that underwriters club together in syndicates to spread the costs. There are over four hundred underwriting syndicates, divided into four main sections: marine, non-marine, UK motor and aviation. Even so, the combination of high taxes and safer alternatives has meant that there is a limit to the number of people who can become active underwriters.

To bring in the capital to allow the market to work efficiently, Lloyd's has been forced to attract outsiders. It is that development which has created the other two tiers of the Lloyd's structure: the *names* and the *agents*.

The *names* are wealthy individuals who club together in a syndicate to bear the risk of underwriting but allow the underwriting decisions to be made by a specialist (a working name) on the floor of Lloyd's. In a good year being a Lloyd's name can bring in a substantial income: in a bad year it can destroy a fortune. Only those who can prove capital of £100,000 are allowed to be Lloyd's names (although some mini-names are allowed in for a mere £50,000). There are various elaborate tests to determine which forms of wealth will count towards the total. Among those who have passed the tests and become names are Henry Cooper, Edward Heath, Tony Jacklin, Robert Maxwell and Susan Hampshire. As well as the show-business stars, there are wealthy people from more traditional backgrounds, like the Duchess of Kent and the Duke of Marlborough. Since all these worthy people have other things to do than assess insurance risk, their syndicates are managed by agents. Most names will spread their risk around by becoming members of several syndicates.

Underwriting agents decide whether to accept business on behalf of their syndicates. If they are working names themselves, the agents can underwrite business on their own behalf and earn fees from using their syndicates' money to insure a proportion of the same risk.

There are also *members' agents* who act as a sort of dating agency for names: they earn a fee in return for introducing names to Lloyd's and for placing them on profitable syndicates.

In theory underwriting can be immensely profitable. The capital employed by the underwriter can be invested so that it earns interest. Premium income results from assuming risk which can also be invested to earn interest. If premiums exceed claims, there is also a profit. An underwriter's money is thus working several times over. In addition, Lloyd's has certain tax privileges. Underwriters can carry forward losses in order to offset them against underwriting profits for tax purposes in future years.

The effect of investment earnings means that underwriters can afford to pay out slightly more in claims than they receive in premiums and still make a profit. However, if the deficit between claims and premiums becomes large, the arithmetic begins to look less healthy. That was the case in the late 1970s and early 1980s as Lloyd's returned several consecutive years of losses.

To clarify the system, let us examine a typical Lloyd's deal.* A client with an insurance risk to cover, such as a ship's cargo, will place his business with a broker. It is the broker's business to find underwriters who will cover the risk. To do so, he will go into the underwriting room.

The underwriters sit in long rows of what are called 'boxes' (these actually consist of two benches and a desk). The broker sits down next to an underwriter and hands him a slip detailing the client's insurance need, uttering by time-honoured custom the words, 'Let me broke you this,' as he does so.

The underwriter, if he accepts the risk, will set the premium and the broker's commission and then stamp the name and number of a syndicate on the slip. His names are then committed to the deal. However, the underwriter will accept only a very small percentage of the risk, and it will then be up to the broker to find other underwriters to accept the rest. If the underwriter asks questions about the nature of the risk and the client, it is up to the broker to answer as honestly as he can to ensure that the deal is made in 'utmost good faith', as the Lloyd's motto goes.

Scandals

In the late 1970s and early 1980s Lloyd's was hit by a series of scandals which caused much adverse press and parliamentary comment. The first headline case was the Savonita dispute, which concerned the loss through fire of a number of cars aboard ship. The Lloyd's underwriters sensed that the circumstances were suspicious and refused payment. That was

* This explanation owes much to Geoffrey Hodgson, *Lloyd's of London: A Reputation at Risk* (Allen Lane, 1984).

followed by news of heavy losses on computer leasing insurance and a loss to the Sasse syndicate of £21.5 million, which seemed to have been caused by the insurance of some dubious properties in the USA. The names involved protested strongly, and the Lloyd's committee eventually agreed to cover part of the losses, although the names were still expected to find the balance of £6.25 million.

The most serious scandal concerned allegations of impropriety at one of Lloyd's biggest broking firms, Alexander Howden, involving one of Lloyd's most successful underwriters, Ian Posgate, known as Goldfinger because of his Midas touch. The details, which involved the placing of reinsurance business, were complicated and need not concern us. What was of importance was the doubts that developed over the capacity of Lloyd's to regulate itself. Much of Lloyd's business came from overseas, particularly in the USA. Doubts about the market could lead to US customers withdrawing their business and turning to US-based insurers.

In response to the scandals in 1982 Parliament passed the Lloyd's Act, which reorganized the workings of the market. A new committee was appointed to which representatives from outside the market were introduced. Brokers were told to divest themselves of their underwriting interests.* At the same time, all members were asked to declare their outside interests. Special attention would be paid to the reinsurance interests of underwriting syndicates. To strengthen the market's self-regulation Ian Hay Davison, formerly with accountants Arthur Andersen, was brought in by the Bank of England in 1982 as Chief Executive of Lloyd's. He had a mandate to reorganize and reform.

Davison resigned at the end of 1985 after rumours of internal conflicts over policy. He had carried through a series of reforms but had failed to satisfy Lloyd's critics. Few people seemed to have been disciplined or prosecuted over the scandals, and many called for Lloyd's to be included in the scope of the 1986 Financial Services Bill. The government resisted those cries, arguing that the Lloyd's Act of 1982 had not had time to be judged but might yet be forced to tighten up the regulations further. It accordingly announced an inquiry into the success of self-regulation at Lloyd's.

* It is interesting that this reform runs entirely counter to the 'Big Bang'. In the capital markets financial conglomerates are being created to offer a whole range of financial services. Lloyd's is returning to the single-capacity system under which each institution offers only one type of service.

Other Insurance Markets

Lloyd's brings in only about one-tenth of the business earned by UK insurance companies, of which there are over six hundred. Some specialize in life assurance, and some cover the whole range of policies from life to vehicle insurance. Splitting them into two groups, the biggest life insurance companies include the Prudential, Legal and General, Commercial Union, Standard Life and Norwich Union. The biggest general insurers include Royal Insurance, Commercial Union, General Accident, Guardian Royal Exchange and Sun Alliance. Between them these companies represent a substantial category of the institutional investor sector, whose characteristics we examined in Chapter 9.

Most of the big companies are *proprietary* companies – that is, they are owned by shareholders in the same way as a normal business. A few, however, are mutual companies, which are owned by the policyholders just as building societies are owned by their depositors. By their nature, the mutual societies are slow to expand. There are also some *mutual indemnity associations* which sell policies to professional bodies.

The big firms are mainly insurance underwriters, but there are also some 4,000 broking firms which put clients in touch with underwriters, ranging in size from one-man high-street businesses to the giants such as the Sedgwick Group and Willis Faber, which are also involved in the Lloyd's market. The insurance companies sell directly to clients as well as through broking firms. They also use part-time agents, particularly in the fields of life and household insurance. In Chapter 2 we saw how the activity of the agents is proposed to be regulated.

Strictly speaking, life insurance is not the same as the other forms of insurance dealt with in this chapter. Death is certain, but the policies against fire and theft, etc., are covering uncertain outcomes. Life assurance is discussed elsewhere in this book (see Chapter 9 and Chapter 15). It is essentially a form of investment which must compete against other investment. General insurance is a sector on its own.

The Problem of Insurers

Since the Second World War insurers have been faced with the continuing expansion of the scale of risk. The risks of new developments like computers and space travel are very difficult to assess, since there are no track records to follow. The decline in the old heavy industries and their replacement with high technology seems, in fact, to have greatly increased insurers' risks. As one writer put it, 'Large-volume, low-unit-value, low-hazard risks have been replaced by small-volume, high-unit-value, high-hazard propositions.'* In addition to the development of these risks, there has been a growing tendency on the part of judges the world over to increase the size of industrial compensation awards. The result has been a surge of claims on the insurers and a long series of poor results in the general insurance business.

One consequence of this development has been the growth of the reinsurance market. Reinsurance companies allow insurance companies to spread large risks (for example, space satellites) and enable smaller companies to take on a larger volume of risks. Volume in the reinsurance market has grown from $6 billion in 1965 to $60 billion in 1985. However, since much reinsurance is provided by insurance companies themselves, there is a limit to the extent that reinsurance can offset risk to the sector as a whole.

Why do insurers not simply increase their premiums to reflect increased risks? Easy as it sounds, it has proved difficult for insurance companies to do so. The industry has been plagued by the large number of firms in the market. It is easy to start an insurance business because there is no machinery to buy or develop and few people to employ. U K insurers have been excluded from many of the fastest-growing overseas markets because the governments in those countries have attempted to develop their own insurance sectors. Customers have also become competitors. Some industries with large insurance needs have tried to bypass the cost of premiums by setting up in-house insurance companies. Only the investment flows have enabled insurance companies to keep going. Booms in both equity markets and interest rates have made investment profitable; there is no guarantee, however, that such conditions will continue.

The insurance industry is a highly cyclical business. If insurance is profitable, firms pile in with the result that premiums drop. Eventually premiums fall to a level below that needed to meet claims. Some firms lose money and drop out of the market. Competition slackens, allowing companies to be profitable again. It may be that the industry is at that point of the cycle when unprofitable firms will be forced out of business.

* Article by W. A. P. Manser in the *Banker*, November 1985.

Export and Credit Insurance

Businesses face not only the risk that their buildings will burn down and their goods will be stolen but also the risk that their debtors will fail to pay. This is a particular problem for exporters who have to deal with clients they may not know too well.

The Export Credits Guarantee Department (ECGD) was set up in 1919 by the Lloyd George coalition with the aim of encouraging exports. The purpose of the ECGD is to guarantee exporters against bad debts by providing credit insurance. Most of the exporters' claims on these policies cite political causes of loss. A revolution or war may prevent exporters from receiving payment for their goods (a good example was the Falklands War in 1982, which disrupted trade with Argentina). Alternatively, an economic crisis in the importing country may cause a government to impose foreign exchange controls and effectively to prevent an importer who genuinely wants to pay from paying for the goods he has received.

The ECGD will cover exporters for 90 per cent of loss if a buyer becomes insolvent or fails to pay within six months. It will cover 95 per cent of all political losses. Most of this cover is provided for consumer goods sold on credit terms of up to 180 days. The ECGD alone offers export-finance facilities for contracts worth more than £1 million and will guarantee loans made to overseas buyers by banks in the UK (that is, if the buyer fails to pay, the ECGD will repay the bank).

In return for this service the ECGD, like any other insurance company, charges a premium. The effect of the world recession has been to increase the number of claims from exporters who find that their clients are unable to pay because of bankruptcy and insolvency. Added to the effects of the debt crisis and the political turmoil of the past few years, the result has been a substantial increase in ECGD premiums.

Credit insurance can also be obtained outside the ECGD. Private insurers have long offered domestic credit insurance. In the export market, however, private insurers have traditionally been unwilling to cover political risk. Consequently, exporters formerly tended to use private insurers only when the ECGD would not cover them because their goods contained too many foreign components. However, the last few years have seen an increase in the private market, with Lloyd's leading the way in covering political risk. Political risk has become a fashionable science, and books and magazines are now devoted to the difficult task of quantifying the effects of possible revolution and disruption.

In the financial markets participants face risks of loss because of movements in interest and exchange rates. The next two chapters will examine the problems caused by such movements and the products developed by financial institutions to help market participants insure against these risks.

[13] Risk Management

Coping with Interest-rate Risk

A problem that faces all borrowers and investors is the possibility that future interest-rate movements will leave them at a disadvantage. A company can choose either to fix its borrowing rate or to let the rate follow the trends in the market. Each decision has its potential disadvantages. A company which borrows at a fixed rate when market rates are 20 per cent will find itself regretting the decision if rates fall to 10 per cent. Similarly, borrowing at a floating rate may ensure that the company's borrowing costs are in line with those in the market, but if rates rise during the lifetime of the loan, the borrower may regret not having fixed the rate.

In each of the above cases investors are exposed to the opposite outcome. If they have lent at a fixed rate, they hope that interest rates will fall rather than rise. If they have lent at a floating rate, their returns will always stay in line with the market. However, if rates fall, they will regret not having fixed the rate on the loan at the prevailing market levels.

Institutions which have borrowed large amounts will try to ensure that they are not over-exposed to interest-rate movements. They will accordingly aim to strike a balance between the proportion of their debt which has a fixed interest rate and the proportion which is floating. Fixed-rate funding is normally available only long-term, and UK companies have been notoriously unwilling to borrow on a long-term basis. As a result they are extremely vulnerable to interest-rate increases – a fact proved by the voluble complaints of the Confederation of British Industry during 1985 when the Chancellor raised interest rates to bolster sterling.

It is important to strike a balance between short- and long-term debt. Too much short-term debt means that the company is very vulnerable to sudden interest-rate rises; too much long-term debt means that the company may find itself with higher than average borrowing costs, both because long-term borrowing is frequently fixed-rate and because, as we saw in Chapter 3, long-term rates are often above short-term. It is also essential for companies to structure the maturity dates of their debt very carefully. If too much debt matures (and is therefore due for repayment) in any one year, the company may find itself short of funds with which to repay the debt. Companies aim, therefore, to structure their debts so that the amounts due to be repaid do not fluctuate violently from one year to the next.

The ideal debt portfolio would have a mixture of fixed-and floating-rate debt and would have as wide a range of maturities as possible. However, such ideals are hard to attain, and most companies find themselves with portfolios that are extremely vulnerable to a rise in interest rates. When that happens the financial markets offer a range of instruments as protection, including the forward-rate agreement, the financial future, the interest-rate option and the swap. They are equally useful to investors who wish to protect the value of their portfolios. Such products have been developed in recent years partly because interest rates in the 1980s have been both high and volatile and partly because banks have been eager to develop new fee-earning products to replace their old loan business (for the reasons, see Chapter 1).

Forward Agreements

A forward/forward, or forward agreement, is simply an arrangement between two institutions to lend or borrow a set amount at a set rate for a set period which will not begin for some months. Suppose, for example, a company knows that it wants to borrow £1 million for a six-month period commencing in six months' time. Rather than wait six months and accept whatever interest rate is then applicable, the company decides to fix the rate in advance and arranges with a bank a forward agreement.

If six-month interest rates are 10 per cent and twelve-month interest rates are 10 per cent, what rate should a bank charge for a six-month loan, beginning six months from now? Surprisingly, the answer is not 10 per cent.

Suppose the amount to be borrowed is £100. If the bank agrees to lend under a forward agreement, it will set aside that £100 for six months until the agreement begins by investing it in a six-month deposit. At the end of six months it will have accumulated £105 (£100 + £5 interest). The bank can now compare its return with the return it would have received had it invested the original deposit for a year, which would have been £110 in total. Under the forward agreement it has £105 after six months and need only charge 9.52 per cent for the second six months to achieve a total return of £110. The rate which the bank will charge for the forward agreement will therefore be slightly over 9.52 per cent (assuming that the bank has no strong view about the direction of future interest-rate movements).

Why does the bank not just avoid all the complex calculations and charge 10 per cent? One answer is competition. Other banks can make all the same calculations and offer a borrower a better rate. The second answer is in the hands of the potential customer. It could effectively create its own six-month forward rate by borrowing £100 for a year and investing the proceeds for six months. At the end of the six months it would have earned £5 interest. It could reinvest that at 10 per cent per annum for six months and earn 25 pence (assuming that interest rates have not changed in the meantime). The effect will be that it pays £10 interest on the year loan but earns £5.25, so paying £4.75 interest net, a rate of 9.5 per cent. Thus the customer need not accept a forward rate much higher than that.

The problem with forward agreements is that they involve the actual borrowing of a sum. If a borrower is seeking to cover existing debt, the effect is to double his credit lines. As a consequence, less cumbersome instruments have been developed which do not involve the principal sums.

Foward-*rate* agreements (FRAs) establish interest rates for borrowers, for lenders or for a set period in advance. When that period is due to begin the parties settle the difference between the prevailing level of interest rates and the rate agreed under the FRA.

Suppose a company has a long-term bank loan on which it pays interest at a floating rate that is reset every six months. At the start of 1987 the company may decide that it does not want to pay more than 10 per cent interest on the loan during the second half of the year. So the company takes out an FRA with a bank (this can, but need not, be the same bank as the one with which the company has the loan). When 1 July arrives the six-month market interest rate is 11 per cent, 1 per cent more than the company has agreed to pay under the FRA. So the bank pays the company 1 per cent to bring its borrowing costs down to 10 per cent. Had interest rates been 9 per cent on 1 July, the company would have paid the bank 1 per cent.

Unlike in the forward/forward market, no principal sum is transferred. notional principal is agreed which matches the size of the loan so that the FRA covers the company's risk. The important part of an FRA, though, is the *rate* at which it is arranged.

Financial Futures

Financial futures are among the biggest growth areas in the world of finance. Their origin lies in the world's commodity markets. In the last century Chicago traders, aware of their vulnerability to sharp swings in agricultural prices, began to quote prices for the delivery of produce many months in advance. Soon trading in wheat, pork belly and coffee 'futures' (as they became known) became as vigorous as trading in the commodity itself. Precious and industrial metals, like gold, silver and copper, soon developed their own futures markets.

Trading on the futures exchanges is conducted by open outcry (the less polite term for it is 'shouting') in floor areas called *pits*. The London International Financial Futures Exchange (see Chapter 14) is a riot of colour as each firm's traders wear different, brightly coloured jackets. If prices are moving fast, a futures exchange can seem like Bedlam as traders desperately seek others who are ready to buy or sell contracts. (A good example of futures trading appears in the film *Trading Places*.) Outside clients can deal with floor traders only through brokers and threfore have to pay their commissions.

With the advent of floating exchange rates (see Chapter 14), it occurred to Chicago traders that there may well be a market for trading in currency futures, since exchange rates seemed to be exhibiting the same volatility as commodity prices. Currency futures quickly became a success; some experts now estimate that 10 per cent of all US foreign-exchange transactions take place on the Chicago futures floor. After the late 1970s and early 1980s had seen equally sharp moves in interest rates the Chicago traders developed interest-rate futures.

How are interest-rate futures used? Essentially, if an institution is worried about the effect of a rise or fall in the level of interest rates, it should buy or sell interest-rate futures to the extent that any movement in interest rates will be cancelled out by a change in the value of the future. The price of an interest-rate future is determined by subtracting the implied interest rate from 100. Thus a futures price of 88 would imply an interest rate of 12 per cent. When interest rates fall, the price of interest-rate futures rises. A cut in rates of 2 per cent will normally push up the price of the future by 2 points; conversely, a rise in interest rates will cause the futures price to fall.

Futures are especially useful as a mechanism for protecting against interest-rate risk because only a small proportion of the nominal value of the future (the margin) is required to be deposited. That margin is adjusted as the price of the future rises or falls. Since both sellers and buyers must deposit margin, it is possible to use futures to cover both the risk of an interest-rate rise and (if you are an investor) of an interest-rate fall.

To see precisely how a future works, suppose that a UK company knows in September that it will need to borrow £1 million for three months in the following December. The company might worry that interest rates could rise in the interim from the September level of 10 per cent. As the company fears an interest-rate rise, it sells futures (remember, a rise in rates leads to a fall in the price of futures).

On LIFFE the nominal size of the sterling interest-rate contract is £250,000. To cover its £1 million risk the company therefore sells four sterling contracts. Each contract carries a margin (set by LIFFE) of £1,500, so both buyer and seller deposits £6,000 with LIFFE's clearing house.

By November interest rates have risen to 12 per cent, the very event that the UK company feared. The futures price has duly fallen from 90 to 88.* This means that the position of the futures buyer has deriorated, since he or she has bought at 90 something which has now fallen to 88. The position of the seller (the company) has improved. The clearing house accordingly credits the account of the seller and debits the account of the buyer. Each full point that a futures price moves is worth £2,500.† So the

* The futures price rarely traces the cash market this neatly. Expectations of future interest-rate movements play an important part, as do supply and demand in the futures market. However, for simplicity the example assumes a close correlation between futures and cash-price movements.

† The size of the contract is £250,000; the base price of the contract is 100; and £250,000 divided by 100 = £2,500.

company's position has improved by £5,000. The futures buyer, however, is £5,000 worse off, and the clearing house accordingly asks the buyer to pay additional margin to bring his or her net position back up to £6,000.

Shortly before the contract is due to expire the buyer and seller agree to close out the futures position without actually exchanging the £1 million. (Most financial futures contracts end without the nominal contract being exchanged.) The clearing house then gives the seller the original £6,000 margin plus the £5,000 payment to reflect the improvement in the company's position. The buyer also receives back the £6,000 margin, but since he or she has paid £11,000, in all the net position is a loss of £5,000.

How has the futures transaction helped the company that was worried about the interest-rate rise? Remember that it was due to borrow £1 million for three months. Had interest rates been 10 per cent, the cost of borrowing £100,000 for three months would have been £25,000. However, interest rates rose to 12 per cent in November, and the company's borrowing cost became £30,000, an increase of £5,000. The profit from the futures transaction therefore met the extra cost of the borrowing exactly. The company was able to protect itself against the rise in interest rates. Had interest rates dropped, the company would have lost on its futures position but had lower borrowing costs.

The most frequent users of interest-rate futures are not companies but banks and institutional fund managers. Many company treasurers have been unwilling to accept the work needed to keep up with the margin payments involved. Banks use futures to cover their open positions when they have failed to match their investments with their liabilities. The fund managers use futures to ensure that a fall in interest rates does not reduce the return on their investments. To do so they *buy* rather than *sell* futures. A fall in interest rates will lead to a rise in the futures price which will offset the losses on investors' portfolios.

In Chicago the vital ingredient that makes the futures markets such a success is a group of speculators, affectionately known as locals. Although futures are useful for those who are concerned about existing loans or assets, they also offer a means of reaping substantial profits from a small initial position, the process known as *leverage*. As we saw in the example above, an initial deposit of £6,000 gave both buyer and seller an interest in £1 million. The company achieved a profit of £5,000 on an initial deposit of £6,000, a promising return for a three months' investment. It is this sort of opportunity for profit that the Chicago locals hope to exploit. Leverage, however, works both ways – the futures buyer in the example lost £5,000 – so locals can as easily be ruined as they can be made millionaires. However, by seeking to take advantage of these speculative opportunities, locals provide the liquidity that helps the banks, fund managers and companies to use the markets effectively.

The taxation climate in the UK is not so favourable to the speculator as it is in the US, and LIFFE, which was launched in 1982, has not been as great a success as its founders hoped. Nevertheless, LIFFE continues to expand its range of futures and options (see Chapter 14). Chicago remains the centre of the world futures markets, although futures exchanges have now been established in New York, Montreal, Toronto, Sydney, Singapore and Hong Kong.

Interest-rate Options

Under the interest-rate option, which is in some ways a refinement of the forward-rate agreement, an option buyer purchases the right (but not the obligation) to lend or borrow at a guaranteed interest rate. In return the option seller receives a payment known as a *premium*, generally paid at the time the option is sold. On the day the option expires it is up to the option buyer to exercise the option and to lend or borrow at the guaranteed rate if it is profitable to do so. However, if the option buyer can achieve a better rate of borrowing or lending in the money markets, he or she will let the option lapse. The maximum loss to the option buyer is therefore the cost of the premium. The size of that premium depends on three factors: the relationship between the interest rate guaranteed under the option and the interest rate in the money markets; the time left before the option is due to expire; and the option seller's assessment of whether interest rates are likely to move quickly.

If, for example, a company wanted to buy an option to *borrow* at 8 per cent at a time when interest rates were 10 per cent, there would be automatic potential for profiting from the option. As a result, the premium for the option would be at least 2 per cent and would be much larger than the premium for an option to borrow at 12 per cent in the same circumstances. An option to *lend* at, say, 12 per cent when interest rates were 10 per cent would carry a large premium, however, since it would have built-in profit potential.

Options which run for longer periods will also carry larger premiums. This is because the probability is greater that, over a long period, rates will move in such a way that the option will become more profitable to exercise. The option seller will charge a larger premium to reflect this extra risk.

How quickly interest rates will move is the hardest of the three elements for the option seller to assess. If the rate has shown a tendency to fluctuate violently in the past, it will obviously carry a higher premium than a rate which has shown a tendency to be stable.

An example will help to clarify the point. A company buys a three-month option to borrow at 10 per cent for three months, based on a nominal principal sum of £1 million. At the time the option is sold, interest rates are 10 per cent and the option seller charges a premium of 1 per cent (£2,500).

Outcome 1 At the end of the three-month period interest rates are 12 per cent. The company exercises the option, thus borrowing at a rate of 2 per cent cheaper than if it had not bought the option (this is equivalent to a saving of £5,000). However, the premium cost 1 per cent (£2,500), and the savings that the company makes (compared with its borrowing costs if it had not bought the option) are £2,500.

Outcome 2 At the end of the three-month period interest rates are 8 per cent. The company lets the option lapse but is free to borrow at the cheaper rate available. Its extra costs are £2,500, the cost of the premium, but its borrowing costs are less than it might have expected at the time when it bought the option.

Swaps

Swaps were once seen as exclusive products which were tailor-made to suit the few sophisticated borrowers who could understand them. By 1985 they had become a $150 billion-a-year industry and a very important source of fee income for some of the world's biggest banks.

The basic concept behind the interest rate swap is that two borrowers raise money separately and then agree to service each other's interest payments. However, many swap deals are much more complicated and can involve several currencies and half a dozen borrowers, with only the bank in the middle aware of all the details.

Why should two borrowers want to pay each other's interest? There are two main reasons. The first concerns the different perceptions of different markets. Investors in one country may be prepared to lend to a US borrower at an advantageous rate but will ask for a higher rate from a UK borrower. In another country it may be the UK borrower which receives the better rate. In those circumstances it can benefit both borrowers to raise funds in the market where their credit is best and then swap the funds.

An example of an early swap deal may help to explain. The World Bank and IBM both wanted to raise funds, the World Bank in Swiss francs and IBM in dollars. Swiss investors had already accepted a good deal of World Bank debt and would accept more only if it were offered at a higher rate. They were keen, however, to invest in a top US corporation like IBM. In the USA the World Bank's credit was perceived as being better than IBM's. So the World Bank borrowed in dollars and IBM in Swiss francs. They then arranged a swap, so that IBM got its dollars and the World Bank its Swiss francs. Each ended up paying less than if both had borrowed separately. Such are the opportunities for borrowing at advantageous rates through swaps that some experts estimate that 80 per cent of Eurobond issues are now swap-linked.

The second reason for arranging swaps concerns the different perceptions of *borrowers* as to the likely direction of future interest-rate movements. As we have seen, borrowers can choose to borrow either at a fixed or at a floating rate. If they think interest rates will rise, they should borrow fixed; if they think interest rates will fall, they should borrow floating. However, they may subsequently decide that they have made the wrong decision. A swap allows borrowers to manage their existing debt. They can choose to swap not only from fixed to floating or vice versa but also from one currency to another.

Now that there is a secondary market in swaps, borrowers can reverse their swap decisions if they wish. Say a borrower had swapped from borrowing fixed to borrowing floating when interest rates were 12 per cent and that rates subsequently dropped to 8 per cent. That swap would now have a value because the borrower is receiving 12 per cent from its counterparty but only paying 8 per cent. The first borrower could sell the swap or arrange another swap by which it would agree to pay a fixed rate of 8 per cent and receive a floating rate. Its floating-rate payment under the first swap would be cancelled out by the second swap. However, it would have cut its fixed-rate payments from 12 to 8 per cent.

How are banks involved in swap deals? Some act as swap principals, agreeing to switch into fixed or floating debt or into another currency as the borrower requires. Normally, such banks have a 'book' of swaps, and they may find that their positions over a number of different swap deals balance each other out. Other banks act purely as swap arrangers, bringing together two different companies with corresponding needs: they earn fees in the process. A third set of banks follow a compromise strategy, acting as principals in a deal until they can find a matching borrower.

Swaps are off-balance-sheet transactions – they are not regarded as assets, and banks are currently not obliged to take precautions against the possibility of default. However, regulatory authorities have shown their concern about the growth of the market. Many poor credits are involved, since swaps give them the opportunity to reduce the cost of borrowing. If swap parties do default, banks may be faced with the payment of above-market interest rates.

What swaps have done is to open up the world's capital markets to a wide range of borrowers. It is now possible for a UK borrower, say, to pick a particular world market where borrowing seems cheap, borrow there and still, through a swap, end up with the sterling debt it really wants.

Special Bond Issues

In addition to the above instruments, borrowers have issued bonds which are designed to be more attractive to investors because they offer protection against adverse interest-rate movements. Many of these bonds are described in Chapter 11.

One recent type of bond issue deserves treatment here because it closely resembles a swap. The *capped floater* offers investors a floating rate set at a margin above LIBOR. However, if LIBOR rates go above a certain level, the bond rates do not follow. A 'cap' is set, which is the maximum rate the issuer will pay. The investor is compensated for the cap because the bond pays a higher than usual margin over LIBOR.

The issuer sells the cap to another borrower which wishes to lock in a maximum cost for its borrowings. The bond issuer can invest the money received from the sale of the cap, so that it receives a stream of payments which it can offset against the higher than usual margin over LIBOR that it is paying on the bond issue. This effectively can bring the cost of the issue to below LIBOR. So the issuer ends up paying less than LIBOR; the investor receives a higher than usual margin *above* LIBOR; and the cap buyer receives protection against a rise in interest rates.

After an initial surge in 1985 the number of capped floaters declined. Instead banks are beginning to sell caps separately from specific bond issues. Such caps are effectively long-term interest-rate options and give the buyer the right to borrow at a specific rate. The bond market is for ever ingenious, however, and it is safe to predict that issues will be designed with a similar clever mix of fixed and floating payments in the future.

All the above instruments deal with interest-rate risk. However, the risk that currencies will move is important to both borrowers and investors and also to businesses which export and import. It is that risk we shall examine in the next chapter.

[14] Foreign Exchange

Look into a foreign-exchange dealing room and you will often see pandemonium. Dealers hang on two or three telephone calls at a time and bellow instructions across the room. Fifteen years ago dealing rooms were much more sedate. Why? The growth in the foreign-exchange markets is due not just to the increased speed of movement of international capital or even to the growth of international trade. It is due to the decline of the old system of fixed exchanges rates and its replacement by floating currencies. Exchange rates now move by amounts which can wipe out profit margins and render investments virtually worthless, and the foreign-exchange markets conduct over $100 billion worth of volume each day as investors and traders try to keep up with market moves. With so much money flowing through the system, exchange rates have become even more volatile. Since 1979 sterling, for example, has risen from $1.80 to $2.40, dropped to $1.03 and risen again to $1.55.

Currency volatility affects everyone, from the biggest multinational to the humblest tourist. Every overseas trade deal involves foreign-exchange decisions. First the people involved must agree which currency should be used to settle the deal. If one party is from West Germany and the other from Switzerland, should the transaction take place in Deutschmarks, Swiss francs or some other currency, like the US dollar? Equally important, when should the currency be delivered? Just as the price of the goods being sold is central to the transaction, so the exchange rate (which is the price of one currency in terms of another) can determine whether the parties make a profit or a loss.

Bretton Woods and After: the Role of Forecasting Today

The post-war system of fixed exchange rates was set up in 1944 at an international conference held in Bretton Woods, New Hampshire. Although not fully operational until 1958, the Bretton Woods system pegged the world's major currencies at fixed rates to the dollar. In turn the dollar was given the strength to act as the linchpin of the world's financial system because of its 'convertibility', at a set rate, into gold.

Gradually the system broke down as the American economy ran into trouble because of President Johnson's attempts to finance the Vietnam war and his 'Great Society' reforms at the same time. By 1971 the dollar lacked the strength to support the system, and President Nixon announced the suspension of the dollar's convertibility into gold. A series of attempts to shore up the system failed; eventually it proved impossible to fix the value of the major currencies against the dollar.

The assumption that lay behind the fixed-rate system was that if one country had an excessive current-account deficit, it would alter its domestic economic policies until balance was restored. The system was capable of surviving the occasional hiccough, such as the sterling devaluation in 1967. However, since the system hinged on the dollar, a US balance-of-payments crisis was a more mortal wound.

Thanks to President Johnson's attempt to pay for both guns and butter, the USA developed enormous current-account deficits which it proved unable to rectify. As a result, the foreign-exchange markets were overloaded with dollars ($1 billion a day flowed into the Bundesbank in May 1971). Speculators had a one-way bet. If they sold dollars and bought a strong currency such as the Deutschmark, they were highly unlikely to lose money, but if the dollar devalued, they would make substantial gains.

The enormous flow of international capital flows today means that no central bank has the reserves to defend its currency against market speculation. As a consequence, a Bretton Woods-type system is unlikely ever to return.

Why have exchange rates been so unstable since the collapse of the Bretton Woods system? Many theories have been developed to explain why exchange rates change, but none has so far explained their movements in such a way that future exchange-rate moves can then be predicted with any degree of accuracy.

Economic theories attempt to explain exchange-rate moves in the long run. Foreign-exchange dealers have to predict exchange rates in the very short run indeed – a day or two at the most. Companies whose profits are hurt or boosted by currency movements often need to know about the medium term – between two months and a year or so. When they turn to currency forecasters they are often disappointed. *Euromoney*'s annual survey of foreign-exchange analysts regularly comes to the conclusion that the forecasters are right in less than half of their predictions – a record worse than might be expected from tossing a coin.

There are two schools of currency forecasters – the economists and the technical analysts – and their methods are radically different. The economists have academic respectability and intellectual recognition. The evidence suggests, however, that the technical analysts have the greater influence in the market.

The Economists

Because the system of fixed exchange rates survived for so long, economic theories about exchange rates have been developed from earlier studies about the way in which the balance of payments changes.

The most important initial distinction to make is that between the current and capital accounts of the balance of payments. The *current account* broadly covers trade payments, although it also includes tourist expenditure and, most important, interest payments and dividends. The *capital account* is concerned largely with purchases of assets – foreign securities such as West German bonds, Japanese shares or physical assets like a factory in the Philippines. Note that purchase of a foreign bond counts as a debit on the capital account, but interest on the bond will be shown as a credit on the current account. The notion of a balance of payments is that a surplus or deficit of a current account will be cancelled by a deficit or surplus on the capital account.

If, under the fixed-rate exchange system, a country was in current-account deficit, then to pay for the excess goods and services that it received from abroad it would have to act to correct the deficit. Trade barriers were ruled out under the General Agreement on Tariffs and Trade (GATT), so the country would be obliged to run down its foreign physical and financial assets or to borrow abroad in order to pay for its imports. In either case the inflow would be recorded as a capital-account surplus that matched the current-account deficit.

In the long term a deficit government was expected to curb demand in the economy, so that domestic consumers cut back their expenditure on both domestic and foreign goods. The price of domestic goods would fall in response to this drop in demand, making them more attractive to foreign consumers and pushing up the country's exports. Since imports would fall (because foreign goods would be more expensive and therefore less attractive to domestic consumers), the net effect would be to restore the balance-of-payments equilibrium. According to this model, devaluation would occur only when a country had run down its reserves so far that it was unable to restore current-account balance at the prevailing exchange rate.

The above example assumes that the capital account is not an independent variable but responds only to changes in the current account. In fact, the international flows of capital mean that the capital account is very much at the mercy of investor demand for foreign and domestic securities. As we saw, this was one of the reasons why the fixed-exchange-rate system did not survive.

In the era of floating rates, economists have attempted to study how the exchange rate affects, and is affected by, both the current and the capital account. Their study has centred on two factors, the level of prices and the level of interest rates.

The study of the effect of prices on exchange rates has focused on the purchasing power parity (PPP) theory. At its simplest the theory argues that exchange rates will tend towards the point at which international purchasing power is equal. In turn that means that differential inflation rates are the most important driving factor behind exchange-rate movements.

The reason why inflation matters is because inflation at too high a level makes a country's goods uncompetitive. If the UK's inflation is 10 per cent per annum while the USA's is zero, British goods will be 10 per cent more expensive than American goods after a year has elapsed. Unless British productivity outpaces that of the USA by 10 per cent, UK sales abroad will fall as customers find it cheaper to buy American or other alternatives, and UK imports will increase as domestic consumers prefer US goods to their own. Hence the current account will deteriorate.

This sorry picture, PPP theorists claim, is redeemed by the exchange rate. If the pound falls by 10 per cent against the dollar in the above example, the cost to the US customer of UK goods (in dollars) stays the same. Similarly, the dollar has risen by 10 per cent, and therefore the cost to the US customer of American goods (in pounds) is the same. So the exchange rate has acted to restore the balance.

Monetarists have adopted and modified this theory. They believe that price increases are caused by an excess money supply. Thus, since the markets know that nations with slack monetary regimes will suffer inflation, they will sell the currency of that country and buy the currency of countries with stricter monetary control. The resulting exchange-rate depreciation will in the long run match the differential in money supply growth between the two countries. Unless money-supply growth is checked, the process of inflation-provoked devaluation will continue.

The concept of an equilibrium level for exchange rates has given PPP theorists a lot of trouble. There is no point of zero inflation and equilibrium currency rates from which subsequent exchange-rate movements can be measured. A base year must therefore be chosen, and the choice of base year often determines whether an exchange rate appears under- or overvalued. The years of rampant Western inflation, 1974–8, are a particular source of problems.

Another major difficulty with the PPP theory is deciding what is defined by inflation. If the price of hairdressing is included in the consumer price index (CPI), will that make the index a reasonable measure of UK competitiveness? How many Americans will cross the Atlantic to get a cheaper perm? More seriously, an important component of any CPI is housing costs, which are irrelevant to consideration of export competitiveness. Even wholesale prices cover items that are not internationally traded. The most popular measure of competitiveness has therefore been unit wage costs – that is, the amount paid per unit of output.

The PPP theory holds out very well for many Third World countries, in particular Latin American, where exchange-rate depreciation against the dollar tends to follow the inflation rate quite closely. When it comes to predicting and explaining the exchange-rate movements of the currencies of the major industrialized countries, however, it has been less successful.

If PPP theory is correct, real exchange rates (nominal exchange rates adjusted for inflation) should stay fairly stable. In fact, research has demonstrated that real rates show considerable volatility and exhibit little sign of returning to any equilibrium level. Some explain this by the concept of 'overshooting', in which because of market inefficiencies, exchange rates over-adjust in response to inflationary differentials. If they do, that makes it all the more difficult to use PPP theory as an exchange-rate predictor.

The level of interest rates is clearly a major factor in the strength or weakness of a currency. This is even more the case after the recent wave of financial deregulation which we noted in Chapter 1. The world is now virtually a single capital market, in which vast quantities of money shift from one country to another in search of short-term gains.

The influence of interest rates is not as easy to assess as might first be thought. To begin with, are investors attracted by the nominal rate or the real rate (the nominal rate adjusted for inflation)? Second, are high interest rates a sign of a healthy or of an ailing economy?

For a long time foreign-exchange speculators perceived currencies in high-interest economies as weak and currencies in low-interest economies as strong. If a currency was weak, the argument went, few people would want to hold it or lend it, since currency depreciation would soon reduce its value. Debtors would want their borrowings denominated in a weak currency, however, since currency depreciation would reduce their debt burden. As a result there would be few lenders and many borrowers in that currency. In other words, demand for borrowings would exceed the supply and thus force the interest rate up.

The converse would apply to strong currencies. Many people would want to hold or lend them, since, added to the interest received would be the extra value gained from the currency's appreciation. On the other hand, few would want their debts denominated in a strong currency, since currency appreciation would keep increasing the effective total of their debt. In a strong currency, therefore, there would be many lenders and few borrowers. The supply of borrowings would exceed demand, forcing the interest rate down. That analysis has been overtaken by the influence of monetarism.

Monetarist economists have argued that high interest rates are often a good sign in an economy, since they restrict demand for credit and therefore reduce the chances of inflation. Low interest rates imply slack control of credit and therefore the possibility of inflationary pressures.

The position has been complicated further by the willingness of governments to push their interest rates up in order to defend their currencies. A notable example of this took place in January 1985, when the UK government was forced to let interest rates rise, as sterling looked like falling to parity with the dollar. Chancellor Lawson's aim was to make the return on sterling investments so appealing to investors that it would attract sufficient sterling buyers to stabilize the pound.

What most economists now think is that the key factor in determining capital inflow is the expected real interest rate – in other words, the return that the investor expects to receive after inflation and exchange rates have been taken into account. Even if nominal interest rates are high, investors will not buy investments in a country if they think that currency depreciation or inflation will wipe out their return. What determines those expectations is hard to define. But the dollar's overwhelming strength in 1983 and 1984 seemed to depend on investors' expectations that the Reagan administration and the Federal Reserve would keep US interest rates high and inflation low.

The latest and most cogent economic theory of exchange-rate movements is the portfolio balance model.* Proponents of this theory argue that exchange rates are effectively the relative prices of international financial assets (e.g. bonds and shares). It is expectations of the likely risk and return of financial assets that determine exchange-rate movements as investors shift their portfolios from one country to another.

The portfolio balance theory is persuasive partly because capital flows are far larger than trade flows. Another reason is that major economic or political events have an effect on the financial markets much more quickly than they do on the prices of goods. Bond prices move almost constantly, thanks to the electronic communications systems: the prices of goods change more slowly and depend on many factors. The combination of trade and capital flows results in the erratic paths of exchange rates as the two factors act sometimes in the same direction and sometimes in opposite directions.

Currency movements thus seem to depend to a large extent on the subjective views of those involved in the international capital markets. This concentration on expectation has given a great boost to the other strand of currency forecasters – the technical analysts.

Technical Analysts

Technical analysts, or 'chartists' as they are often known, believe that all the factors which the economist studies – inflation, the balance of payments, interest rates, etc. – are already known by the market and are

* I am very grateful to David Morrison of Goldman Sachs for his explanation of this theory.

thus reflected in the prices of goods and commodities. This is as true of pork bellies and oil as it is of currencies. The chartists, as their name suggests, study charts which represent the price movements of a particular commodity. Over long periods certain price patterns emerge, which cause the analysts to claim that further developments in the price pattern can be predicted.

Economists have an unfortunate tendency to reject the chartist theories out of hand. However, many traders in the foreign-exchange markets follow the chartists' predictions. To some extent such predictions can become self-fulfilling if enough people believe them. The markets react when a certain point of the chart is reached.

The underlying rationale behind chart analysis is that the key to price movements is human reaction, and that human nature does not change markedly in response to similar events. Among the main patterns that chartists see are the following.

Head and shoulders. This pattern is made up of a major rise in price (the head) separating two smaller rises (the shoulders). If this pattern is established, the price should fall by the same amount as the distance between the head and a line connecting the bottom of the two shoulders.

Broadening top. This pattern has three price peaks at successively higher levels and, between them, two bottoms with the second one lower than the first. If, after the third peak, the price falls below the level of the second bottom, this indicates a major reversal in the price trend.

Double bottoms/tops. A double bottom or top indicates a major reversal in the price trend. Both consist of two troughs (or peaks) separated by a price movement in the opposite direction.

Apart from pattern recognition, technical analysts also study *momentum* and *moving average* models. *Momentum* analysis studies the rate of change of prices rather than merely price levels. If the rate of change is increasing, that indicates that a trend will continue; if the rate of change is decreasing, that indicates that the trend is likely to be reversed. The concept behind the study of *moving averages* is that trends in price movements last long enough to allow shrewd investors to profit and that rules can be discovered which identify the most important of these trends. One of the most significant rules for technical analysts is that a major shift has occurred when a long-term moving average crosses a short-term moving average.

Although technical analysis has very little intellectual respectability in economists' circles, it has had a great impact on the foreign-exchange markets. Many believe it to be a useful forecasting tool in the short term. In the long term, despite some setbacks, economic analysis may yet prove a more successful forecasting technique.

Exchange-rate Blocs

Three major exchange-rate blocs emerged from the wreckage of Bretton Woods; the pound flits unhappily between two of them.

The dollar bloc is the most important, reflecting the pre-eminence of the US dollar in international trade. Not only does Canada closely track the US unit, but the fact that oil is priced in dollars means that the Arab oil-producing countries tie their currencies to the dollar. The Latin American countries, which are heavily dependent on the USA for trade, follow the dollar at one remove. Because their inflation rates are so much higher than the USA's, they allow their currencies to depreciate against the dollar in line with the inflation differential.

The Deutschmark bloc includes nearly all the European currencies. Eight of them are linked by the European Monetary System (EMS), which was formed in 1979. Under the EMS the member currencies can fluctuate within a 2.25 per cent band (4.5 per cent for the lira) either side of their central rate against the European Currency Unit, which is composed of fixed amounts of the EMS member currencies plus sterling and the drachma. When a currency gets out of line with those of other EMS members, the government is obliged to step in and buy or sell it in order to bring it back into line. Sometimes that proves impossible, and the whole system is forced to adjust. Up to the end of 1985 there had been eight such realignments, mainly to accommodate high-inflation currencies like the lira and the French and Belgian franc.

Outside the EMS a number of currencies, such as the Swiss franc and the Austrian schilling, tend to follow the Deutschmark closely because of their trade links with the EMS member states.

The existence of an Asian bloc is disputed by some analysts. Those who believe in it say that it is built round the yen but includes the Malaysian and Singapore dollars and the currencies of other emerging Asian industrial countries. This bloc is less important than it might be, owing to the unwillingness of the Japanese to allow the yen to assume the role in international finance that its economic strength deserves.

Since the UK joined the European Community, the proportion of its trade with Europe has increased sharply, prompting some commentators to argue that sterling should join the EMS. However, in the late 1970s and early 1980s North Sea oil tended to dominate sterling's fortunes, leaving the unit focused more on the dollar than on the Deutschmark. The erratic fortunes of the oil market have caused sterling to fluctuate from $2.40/£1 in early 1981 to near dollar parity in early 1985.

Very few currencies 'float' in the purest sense of the word. When a currency is allowed to float, the government of the country concerned has declared its willingness to let the markets determine the unit's level. As in the January 1985 sterling crisis, the market's view of a currency's correct level can differ sharply from the government's. Many governments are not prepared to give the markets that chance, and they therefore restrict the convertibility of their currencies.

Semi-convertible currencies can usually be bought or sold only through a country's central bank at set exchange rates and then only for documented commercial deals. Some countries have developed elaborately tiered exchange-rate structures, with different rates set for different types of commodity. Semi-convertible currencies are more or less the norm in the Third World, since there countries are very careful to control the flow of imports and capital.

Non-convertible currencies have a restricted circulation and an artificially high exchange rate. Almost all Eastern European countries, whose control over their currencies is an essential part of economic planning, fall into this category. As a result in such currencies there is often a flourishing black market in which exchange rates are priced more realistically.

Basket Currencies

Some governments try to manage their currencies by matching their movements as closely as possible with those of a basket of the currencies of its major trading partners. Norway, Sweden and Finland all do so. In the Scandinavian countries this pegging does not take the form of an officially set rate against the basket. Instead the market is allowed to set the currency's level. Each government has an ideal range within which it would like its currency to fluctuate. If the currency hits the top or bottom of the range, the government will intervene to sell or buy the domestic currency in order to bring it back within the desired range. Occasionally the currency gets so far out of line that devaluation becomes necessary.

The concept of maintaining stability through a basket of currencies has been extended to embrace the creation of two new units for the purpose of international trade and finance, the Special Drawing Right (SDR) and the European Currency Unit (Ecu).

The primary function of the SDR is to serve as a reserve asset of members of the International Monetary Fund (IMF). It was first introduced in 1970, with a value fixed to that of gold, although it was designed to replace gold's function in international finance. In 1974, as a consequence of the break-up of the fixed-exchange-rate system, the SDR's value was fixed as a weighted average of the currencies of sixteen countries, each of whose exports exceeded 1 per cent of the world's total. In 1981 the number of currencies in the basket was reduced to five – the US dollar, the Deutschmark, sterling, the Japanese yen and the French franc, the dollar having by far the biggest weight. The unit is now quite widely used as a peg for Third World currencies, and when countries are forced to borrow from the IMF, loans are usually denominated in SDRs. But the weight of the dollar in the basket has meant that the SDR has been seen merely as a proxy for the US unit, and consequently it has been little used as a medium for international finance.

The Ecu, as has already been mentioned, is the centrepiece of the EMS. As a consequence the European Community institutions have often raised finance in Ecus, which has encouraged the growth of an Ecu-denominated bond market. The French, Belgians and Italians have also been quick to use the Ecu, since it provides funds at lower interest rates than those prevalent in their domestic market and is also much more stable than the dollar against their own currencies. Since it does not involve the dollar as a component, the Ecu is a real alternative to the dollar as a unit of finance for those with currency risk in Europe. However, dreams that it will become the common European currency are unlikely to be fulfilled.

The Role of Governments in a Floating-rate System

Not all the world's currencies float freely. Nevertheless, by far the largest part of the world's trade is conducted in currencies in which market forces play an extremely strong role in setting the rate. That is not to say that governments have renounced the right to intervene in the markets directly.

Governments have to participate in foreign-exchange transactions in the normal course of affairs – for example, to make payments to other nations in the European Community. They can, however, intervene through their central banks in order to influence the markets. They may be prompted by a desire to 'iron out' short-term fluctuations or to add liquidity to a badly disrupted market. Often central banks intervene to try to reverse a market trend, as occurred in 1985 when the Group of Five industrial countries attempted to reduce the value of the dollar.

As has already been mentioned, the size of capital flows is such that it is very difficult for an individual government to defeat the markets. Attempts to talk currencies up or down are rarely successful either. As will be outlined later in this chapter, it is governmental action in other parts of the economy that has most effect on currencies – though the result is not always the one for which governments hope.

The Foreign-exchange Market

Participants in the foreign-exchange market include everyone from the Governor of the Bank of England to you and me when we purchase our foreign currency for a holiday. Tourist purchases are, in fact, among the few foreign-exchange transactions in which note and coins actually change hands. The vast majority of deals take place over the telephone in bank dealing rooms, and funds are transferred telegraphically from one account to another.

At the core of the market are the banks. Most commercial banks have their own foreign-exchange room. Although banks could not deal if they were not providing a service for their corporate clients who need foreign exchange as part of their everyday business, the majority of any bank's deals are done with other banks. One bank has estimated that 95 per cent of its foreign-exchange business is done with other banks and only 5 per cent with outside customers.

There are three major dealing time zones, all of which have more than one centre. London was considered the most important centre, although New York has now probably taken over that role. The market begins each day at 1 a.m. Greenwich Mean Time (GMT), when Tokyo opens.

The Far Eastern time zone holds sway until 9 a.m. GMT, by which time London, Frankfurt, Paris and Zurich have begun the European time-zone trading. By 2 p.m. GMT, New York has opened trading in the American time zone. The market does not close in New York until 10 p.m. GMT. Those dealers who are still awake can trade in San Francisco and Los Angeles until Tokyo opens the next day.

With so many markets to keep track of, the pace of a dealer's life is often frenetic. Most are young, and some are burnt out by their middle thirties. How do they operate?

Suppose a dealer gets a commercial request to buy or sell a large volume of currency. He has several choices. He can satisfy the request himself or ask one of his colleagues to do so. If his colleague cannot, he can ring up a dealer in another bank and hope that he will be able to sell on the currency to his counterpart. But this can be time-consuming. His alternative is to contact a foreign-exchange broker,* whose job is to find a willing counterparty to the deal. In return for this service, the broker charges a commission, which can be as small as one-hundredth of 1 per cent. However, one-hundredth of 1 per cent of deals worth £1 million a time can quickly add up to a lot of money.

The broker will always attempt to cover his position; in other words, he will ensure that he is selling and buying the same amount of currency, so that he is safeguarded against fluctuation. Dealers will usually do the same, although they are allowed, within limits, to leave surplus funds in currencies which they believe will appreciate.

An exchange of currencies for immediate delivery is conducted at the *spot* rate. Dealers will quote two exchange rates for each currency, one at which they will buy the currency and one at which they will sell. The difference between the two is one way in which a bank makes money and is called the *spread.* So if you wanted to buy dollars in exchange for sterling, the bank might offer $1.4850/£1. If you had wanted to buy sterling in exchange for dollars, the rate would have been $1.4870/£1. (For brevity the sterling/dollar rate would be given by a dealer as 50/70.) The 0.2 cent difference between the two rates is the spread. These rates are displayed and continually updated throughout the day in foreign-exchange dealing rooms and on Reuters and Telerate screens, and they appear every day in the *Financial Times.* The faster an exchange rate is

*Often foreign-exchange brokers will be the same people as the money brokers described in Chapter 6.

moving, the wider the spread, since the dealer will not want to be committed to dealing at an unfavourable rate.

Tourists buying foreign currencies will find that the spread is very wide, often several percentage points. Banks can afford to charge each other a narrow spread because the deals are large and frequent and because the competition is intense. The tourist, by comparison, has little bargaining power, and the bank's costs in supplying the small amounts of currencies involved are proportionately higher.

The Forward Rate

Banks will quote a price for a currency which is not wanted for immediate delivery. If a UK company knows that it is going to receive machinery from West Germany in three months' time, for which it will have to pay Deutschmarks, it can fix its exchange rate in advance by locking in a forward rate with a bank. If the spot rate is DM3.718/20 per £1, the bank might offer a three-month forward rate of DM3.680/684 per £1. Once again the bank is taking a spread – notice that the spread for the three-month forward rate is larger than for the spot rate. On screen the bank will in fact show only the differential between the spot and forward rates. So in this case the screen would show:

Rates against the £

	Spot	3-month
Deutschmark	3.7185/95	385/355

Currencies that are more expensive to obtain at the forward rate than at the spot rate are described as being at a *premium*, and those that are cheaper on the forward than on the spot market are at a *discount*. In this case the Deutschmark is at a premium to the pound and the pound is at a discount to the Deutschmark. On a dealer's screen the distinction is shown by the ordering of the forward's spread. As the Deutschmark is at a premium to the pound, the largest figure appears first in the forward column. If the Deutschmark were at a discount, the forward column would read 355/385.

Forward rates are determined largely by interest differentials on the Euromarket. Imagine that West German interest rates were 10 per cent and UK rates were 5 per cent and that the spot and twelve-month forward rates for Deutschmarks against sterling were the same. A UK investor would then be able to buy Deutschmarks at the spot rate and invest the money in West Germany to earn the higher interest rate. At the same time the investor could take out a forward contract with a bank to buy back sterling in exchange for Deutschmarks in a year's time. No money would be lost as a result of currency movements, since the investor has guaranteed the same Deutschmark/sterling rate as when the investment was made. So the investor could benefit from higher West German interest rates without risk. This method of profiting from inconsistencies between markets is known as *arbitrage*.

Attractive though it may seem, the above example could rarely happen in the real world. Every investor would be anxious to profit from the trade. The result would be: (a) increased demand from UK investors for Deutschmarks at the spot rate, driving the Deutschmark up against sterling; (b) increased demand for West German and reduced demand for UK assets, driving West German interest rates down and UK rates up; (c) increased demand for twelve-month sterling, driving the twelve-month Deutschmark rate down and thus opening up a differential with the spot rate, which would be pushed in the opposite direction. All these factors combined would quickly eliminate the investment opportunity described.

Although arbitrage possibilities do sometimes exist and some speculators make a living out of exploiting them, the speed of the markets means that inconsistencies do not last very long. A country which has higher interest rates than those in the UK will have a currency at a discount to the pound on the forward market, so that investors would lose on the currency what they would gain on the interest-rate differential. By contrast, countries with lower interest rates than the UK's will have currencies at a premium to sterling.

The Company's Dilemma

Any company involved in overseas trade has to face the problems described in the introductory paragraphs of this chapter. Which currency should it choose to pay or be paid in, and when should it arrange for that currency to be delivered?

The volatility of the foreign-exchange market is such that currency moves can wipe out profit margins and render companies bankrupt. Suppose a US company had made a five-year investment denominated in sterling in 1981, when the dollar sterling rate was $2.40/£1. By early 1985 the rate had fallen to $1.10/£1. The investment would have had to double in value to eliminate the currency-depreciation effect.

To counter these problems many companies have a set policy for choosing the denominating currency for their transactions. Often this policy will be to trade always in the currency of the country in which the firm is based, in an attempt to eliminate currency risk altogether. This policy works very well until the company attempts to deal with another firm with the same policy but in a different country. It is also very unlikely that a UK company would accept payment in, say, Venezuelan bolivars because of the difficulty of converting the currency when delivered.

For these reasons the majority of international trade is denominated in dollars. Not only is the US unit freely convertible but it is also used by many governments as a reserve currency. Since such a large proportion of their business is done in dollars, companies can match up their payments and receipts to reduce their foreign-exchange risk, using the dollars received from sales to pay for supplies.

If a company cannot arrange to pay or be paid either in dollars or in its native currency, its best option is to ask to be paid in some other strong currency, like the Deutschmark or the Swiss franc. Multinational companies, which usually have to cope with a wide variety of currencies, will attempt to match their payments and receipts in all of the units in which they have transactions in order to keep their total exchange risk to a minimum.

Once a transaction in a particular currency has been arranged, how does a company cope with the foreign-exchange risk involved? Most companies think that their business is trading and not currency speculation, so they will try to avoid risk as much as possible. Suppose a UK company is due to receive dollars three months ahead. It has a number of choices.

First, it could wait for three months, receive the dollars and exchange them for sterling on the spot market. If, in the meantime, the dollar has appreciated against the pound, the company has made money; if the dollar has fallen, the company has lost money.

Second, it could arrange a forward transaction with a bank to sell dollars three months ahead or to buy a dollar-denominated deposit which matures in three months' time. The company's treasurer can sleep at night; the firm is protected against a dollar collapse. But if the dollar rises, the firm will find itself getting a great deal less for its dollars than it might have done.

Third, a middle position: the company could assess which way it thinks the dollar will move. Say it feels there is a 50 per cent chance that it will get a better dollar rate three months ahead than by using the forward market. It therefore sells enough dollars forward to cover 50 per cent of its total position and waits to buy the rest on the spot market. Total disaster has been avoided, and there is the chance of profiting if the dollar rises.

In recent years more and more companies have shown a preference for taking a fourth possible course of action – buying a currency option.

Currency Options

Currency options are similar to the interest-rate options described in Chapter 13. They give the buyer the right, but not the obligation, to buy foreign currency at a specified rate. Thus the buyer is protected against an adverse exchange-rate movement but retains the potential to take advantage of any favourable movement.

Suppose that a UK company is committed to paying US dollars for oil in three months' time. It is worried that sterling will fall during that period, thus forcing up the cost of the oil. Sterling is at that moment $1.20 on the spot market. So the company buys a three-month sterling put option (the right to sell sterling in exchange for dollars) at a strike price of $1.20. If, during the life of the option, sterling falls to $1.10, the company exercises its option and sells sterling at the more favourable rate of $1.20. However, if sterling rises to $1.30, then the company allows the option to lapse and sells sterling (and buys dollars) on the spot market.

The catch is the cost. The option buyer must pay the seller a premium when the option is purchased. That premium is non-returnable and is considerably larger than the cost of using the forward market. The option seller charges more than for forward cover because of the higher risk involved. An option can be exercised at any time before its expiry date, and that means that the seller must be constantly prepared to exchange currency at an unfavourable rate. In the forward market, however, the day and the rate at which currencies will be exchanged are known in advance.

Although the option buyer pays more, it is for a better product than forward cover. If the UK company in the example above had covered its risk by buying a three-month forward contract at $1.21, it would have been unable to benefit from a move in the spot rate to $1.30 and might well have ended up paying more for its oil than its competitors. It is also important to remember that the premium represents the maximum possible cost to the option buyer.

Let us take another example. An American company wishes to buy West German goods. The company negotiates a price of DM1,250,000, which it must pay in three months' time. The spot rate is $0.3950 per DM. The forward rate is $0.4000 per DM. The premium of a $0.4000 DM option is $0.0100 per DM.

Scenario A

The spot rate moves to $0.4200.
If the company does nothing, the cost of goods is:
DM1,250,000 × 0.4200 = $525,000.
If the company buys forward, the cost of goods is:
DM1,250,000 × 0.4000 = $500,000.
If the company buys an option and exercises it, the cost of goods is:
DM1,250,000 × 0.4000,
plus cost of premium:
DM1,250,000 × 0.0100 = $512,500.

Scenario B

The spot price moves to $0.3800.
If the company does nothing, the cost of goods is:
DM1,250,000 × $0.3800 = $475,000.
If the company buys forward, the cost of goods is:
DM1,250,000 × $0.4000 = $500,000.
If the company buys an option and does not exercise it, the cost of goods is:
DM1,250,000 × $0.3800,
plus cost of premium:
DM1,250,000 × $0.0100 = $487,500.

In both scenarios the option outperforms the worst strategy but does not perform as well as the best strategy. This makes options very attractive to many companies, which see them as a form of insurance covering foreign risk rather than fire or theft.

Most companies buy options direct from banks (over-the-counter options – OTCs). However, since December 1982 the Philadelphia Stock Exchange has traded foreign-currency options on its floor, and in 1985 both the London Stock Exchange and the London International Financial Futures Exchange (LIFFE) followed suit. Traded options are for standardized amounts and time periods and are available only in a limited number of currencies. However, their premiums are generally cheaper than those of OTC options.

Currency Futures

Currency futures are priced in dollars per foreign currency unit. (For example, a sterling contract on Chicago might be priced at $1.10 per £1.) Contract sizes are quite small to accommodate the small speculators who give futures exchanges their liquidity.

Those who use currency futures can be divided into two groups: *Speculators* and *hedgers*. *Speculators* act on a hunch that currencies are moving in a particular direction. If they believe that the dollar is going to fall against sterling, then they buy sterling futures in the hope that the value of these will appreciate. *Hedgers* will already be committed to a foreign exchange position and will buy or sell enough futures contracts to ensure that their initial position is cancelled out.

Suppose a US company is due to pay out £100,000 in three months' time. Its worry is that sterling may rise against the dollar over that period. So it buys four sterling futures contracts, each worth £25,000. The prevailing sterling exchange rate is $1.10. If sterling rises to $1.25, the company will find itself paying out $115,000, $5,000 more than it would have paid if the exchange rate had stayed the same. But the futures contracts will have increased in value by the same amount. The company will have covered its losses.

As explained in Chapter 13, the system of margin payments allows users of futures contracts to insure against the risks of currency movements without actually exchanging the nominal amount of the contract.

[15] Personal Finance

Individuals have a wide range of options when considering savings and investments, and the thorough reader should consult professional advice before investing a large sum. There is rarely a perfect answer to an individual's investment requirements. It is wise to remember that professional advisers make investment mistakes, even though they have a great deal of time and considerable resources with which to investigate and analyse the market. All this chapter can do is to indicate the range of investments on offer to the individual and their advantages and disadvantages.

The rules which govern the finances of individuals are not very different from the ones that govern the finance of institutions. There is still a trade-off between liquidity and reward. The deposit account which gives the customer the best interest rate may impose penalities for early withdrawals of money. There is also the same trade-off between risk and reward. Those investments which offer the best return – shares, options, etc. – also involve the possibility of loss. The safest investments offer a steady but unspectacular return.

So before investors sign away their hard-earned savings, they should consider carefully what they expect from their investments. Might they want to withdraw their money early to pay for a car or a holiday? What value do they place on safety? Would they rather forgo the chance of capital gain in order to avoid the possibility of capital loss? Have they a lump sum to invest or a small amount each month? Do they pay income tax and, if so, at what rate? When they have the answer to these questions investors can examine the merits of the various investments on offer more efficiently.

At the risk of sounding banal, there are also some very simple steps which can be as effective as months of analysis of new forms of savings accounts. A wise rule for a credit-card holder, for example, is to pay off the balance at the end of every month. Keeping a credit-card balance of

£200 for a year involves interest payments of £50 or so. Far better to take £200 out of a building society account to pay it off. Although building society interest of, say, 10 per cent (£20) will be lost, there will be an overall gain of £30. A similar principle applies to overdrafts and hire-purchase agreements. There is little point in having both debts and deposits unless you can be sure that the return from an investment will be higher than the cost of debt. Given the costs of overdrafts and credit accounts, there are few investments which can earn more.

Property

Most people make property their main investment. Taking out a mortgage is a different form of investment from the others discussed in this chapter, since it is an investment financed by borrowing. The other schemes discussed involve the use of money saved from income. One of the great advantages of investing in property is that the cost of repaying the *interest* (not the capital) on a mortgage is eligible for income-tax relief at the investor's marginal rate. However, this applies only to the first £30,000 of a mortgage and then only if the house is the main residence of the borrower.

Although the attractions of home ownership seem obvious, it is as well to remember that house buyers are, in fact, making a complex calculation. The alternative to house buying is, of course, renting. Mortgage repayments are at first considerably more expensive than rents, and to the repayments must be added the rates bill. However, mortgage payments go up and down with the rate of interest and not, like rents, with the rate of inflation. After a couple of years the mortgage payment normally becomes compeititive with rents. Most people see the benefits of property investment in terms of the increase in house prices; however, as the market value of one house is increasing, so is the value of others. When the house is sold, the next house may be even more expensive. The costs of moving are also high. Estate agents normally take 1.5 per cent of the price, solicitors a further 1 per cent and stamp duty 1 per cent, making 3.5 per cent in all. On top of those costs are the charges of removal companies and the inconvenience involved.

Just to illustrate the complexities, suppose a young married couple buy a house in London for £40,000 with a deposit of £4,000. Previously they had paid rent of £30 a week each or £3,120 a year. The monthly mortgage payments, after tax relief, are £300 a month, making £3,600 a year, to which rates of £500 are added to make a total of £4,100 in all. There are several extra payments – £400 stamp duty, £400 solicitor's fees and, say, £200 for surveys, making £1,000 in all (first-time buyers pay no estate agent's fees). So in the first year the couple pay out £1,980 more than they would have if they had rented. To that must be added the loss of interest on the £4,000 deposit. At 10 per cent a year, say, that makes an extra £400. So the total income loss is £2,380. Assume that house prices have increased at the end of a year by 10 per cent. The couple have gained £4,000, but if they moved, they would have to pay another £1,000 in moving expenses plus £600 in estate agent's fees. That is an effective capital gain of £2,400, leaving them even in the first year, but it does not allow for costs of repair to the house or of payments on furniture, neither of which are paid by a tenant.

House buying is expensive and can take some time to repay the investment. However, a tenant will pay rent for ever, while most home buyers will have paid off their mortgage by the time they have retired and their earnings have been cut. The worst time for house buyers is soon after their purchase, but, as a salary increases, the burden of a mortgage is reduced.

Whether or not all house buyers have made the sorts of complex calculation described above, investing in property has offered an extremely good hedge against inflation over the last twenty years, thanks particularly to property booms in the early 1970s and 1980s.

Most houses are bought on a mortgage. As has already been described in Chapter 7, the majority of mortgages are provided by building societies. They will normally lend an amount equal to two and a half times an individual's annual income. If a couple are buying a house, the lower of the two incomes will be added to two and a half times the higher (i.e. if one person earns £10,000 and the other £8,000, the possible total will be £25,000 + £8,000 = £33,000).* However, if the buyer cannot provide a deposit of around 5–10 per cent of the house price, most societies will charge a higher interest rate.

For amounts over 80 per cent of the value of the house the building society will demand that the buyer insures against default by paying a one-off premium to an insurance company. Note that the building society

* Some societies will lend up to three times the higher salary and once the lower. All the conditions described can be varied by some societies. It pays to shop around.

will offer a loan, based on its valuation of the house or the agreed sale price, *whichever is the lower*.

If the price of the house is over £30,000, stamp duty of 1 per cent is payable, a particular penalty on house buyers in London, where houses or flats priced below £30,000 are rare.

There are different types of mortgage agreement – the best-known being the *repayment mortgage*, under which the monthly payments are structured over the lifetime of the loan, so that at the end of the period both interest and capital have been repaid. Over the first few years of the mortgage very little of the capital is repaid. This can surprise home buyers who sell their house after a few years.

An alternative to the repayment mortgage is the *endowment mortgage*. At the same time as the borrower takes out the mortgage, he or she takes out a life insurance policy with a monthly premium payment. At the time that the mortgage ends, the insurance policy matures and repays the full amount of the loan. In the meantime the borrower has paid interest but not capital each month to the building society. The tax benefit is thus retained throughout the life of the loan. Some endowment schemes offer a bonus in addition to the amount needed to repay the mortgage, but the premium payments on such a policy are somewhat higher. There are two further advantages of endowment mortgages. One is that if the borrower dies, the loan will be repaid in full. The second is that the policy can be transferred from house to house as the borrower moves.

A *pension mortgage* is similar in principle to an endowment mortgage. In return for extra payments, not only is the house price repaid but also a sizeable income is accumulated. This is a particularly useful scheme for those people who are self-employed and who do not benefit from an occupational pension scheme.

A commonly held belief is that building-society depositors are better placed when it comes to asking for a mortgage. That may have been true in the old days of mortgage rationing, but nowadays the mortgage market is so competitive that, providing the prospective buyer's income is sufficient, he or she should have little problem in finding a mortgage provider. House buyers should be cautious before choosing an institution just because it offers the lowest rate. The lender has no obligation to keep the rates competitive for the full twenty-five-year term of the mortgage. If it decides that it does not like the market, it may no longer undercut its rivals. By contrast, building societies will always have to remain competitive because their main business is mortgage lending.

Pensions

The field of pensions is one of the most difficult topics to survey because of the uncertainty, at the time of writing, over the future of the State Earnings Related Pension Scheme (SERPS). SERPS is the second tier of government-provided pension schemes, the first tier being the old-age pension which is paid for through National Insurance contributions. Most people feel that the basic pension is inadequate as a provision for old age. The SERPS scheme was designed to give a higher benefit to those who wish to make extra payments during their working lives in return for a higher pension. In 1985 the Department of Health and Social Security produced a White Paper proposing that SERPS be abolished: after consultation, the government decided to cut the scheme in half rather than to abolish it altogether.

SERPS provides for companies to 'contract out' of the scheme and to offer employees a private arrangement. Such funds must be approved by the Inland Revenue and are set up as independent trusts. The majority of the 10.5 million members of pension funds in the country are involved in company-run schemes, which provide very good benefits for those who retire after a long period of service for one firm. The maximum benefit generally available is retirement on two-thirds of the final salary, and there are guaranteed benefits for widows (whether the staff member dies in or out of service). The majority of schemes allow employees to take part of the pension as a tax-free lump sum. Contributions from both employers and employees are free of tax, and the fund itself can accumulate tax-free.

Company-run schemes do *not* offer a good deal to those who move jobs frequently. Those who are 26 years old or over, and have worked for five years or more, must have a pension right preserved by law; the amount is determined by dividing the years of service by the years which could have been served if the employee had worked through until retirement. So if an employee joins at 25 and leaves at 30 but could have worked till 65, he or she will receive one-eighth of the entitlement.

Why is that a bad deal? Suppose that you were the employee in the example above and had reached retirement age in 1985. Your eligible service period would be 1945–50, a time when £1,000 per year was a very good wage indeed. One-eighth of that would be £125 a year – not much use in 1985.

If your service is under five years, you can opt to take a lump sum in lieu of the final pension, but if you do, you will be taxed. Your contributions will have been exempt of tax only because they were going towards a final pension. So the lump sum you receive will be less than you expect. It would often have been much more profitable to invest the money in a building society, but few companies allow employees to opt out of making contributions.

There are reasons for the onerous provisions outlined above. If companies had to give a decent pension to all the people who worked for them, no matter how short their period of employment, and if employees could opt out of contributing, pension schemes would never be able to fund themselves. However, the economic effect of pension provisions is surely bad. It encourages workers not to be mobile but to stick with one job. An efficient economy is one in which there are no barriers to labour movement.

All this has led to a call for portable pensions – schemes which workers can carry around from one employer to another. These would be fair to early leavers. If the government's proposal to halve the benefits of SERPS is passed, it seems likely that many companies will reduce the benefits paid under their own schemes. That would encourage banks and insurance companies to offer personal pensions. Such schemes would be related to the amount of the contributions paid and the return on investment achieved by the fund manager rather than to the salary of the employee.

Life Assurance

Life assurance (or insurance) is also one of the biggest forms of personal savings. Until 1984 life-assurance premium payments were tax-free. The combination of tax advantages and small regular payments made the schemes very popular. However, the ethics of insurance salesmen have sometimes been called in question. People approached by a salesman should establish which company he or she works for and should never sign anything at the first meeting. If the policy is good, it will still be good a week later. The interval allows the potential client to find out about the company and to talk to friends or outside experts about the merits of the policy. Many people have agreed to high monthly payments which they have subsequently proved unable to maintain. The penalties for failing to keep up with the payments are normally severe.

However, such policies are a very good idea for young married couples, particularly if they have children. The loss of a partner is shattering enough without the accompaniment of financial loss. If both partners survive, an endowment policy will help, with a lump sum, to pay for the children's education or holidays as they grow older.

There are three basic types of policy. *Term policies* provide insurance against death within a specified period of years. If the insured person lives through the period, no bonus is paid. Premiums are consequently cheap, since insurance companies can rely on the iron laws of probability to determine how likely it is that a given person of a given age will die.

Whole life policies lack a specified term of benefit. Whenever the insured person dies, the insurers must pay. However, the laws of probability still apply. The insurance company will be able to calculate how often it will be required to pay.

The above two forms of policies are both *insurance* policies, since they provide against the risk of death. *Assurance* policies are different because the policy holder is assured of payment. One such is an endowment policy which will be paid at the end of a fixed period – or before if the insured person dies. The premiums are the highest among the various schemes, but the benefits are also normally the highest.

Annuities pay an annual sum from a future date until death (it can be arranged to be paid to either husband or wife until both are deceased). The premium is normally paid in the form of a lump sum. Annuities are particularly popular with couples who are about to retire.

Savings Schemes

Leaving aside the massive investment that many people make in property and pensions, the most common investment for the small investor is in savings schemes of one kind or another. These fall into three main groups: those run by building societies, banks and the government.

Building Societies

The most common building society account is the ordinary share account, which can be started with as little as £1 at any building-society branch. The rate of interest payable is variable and will move up and down with the general level of interest rates in the economy. Although competition sometimes results in different societies offering different rates, they rarely get far out of line. There is little risk involved. The chance of a failure of one of the major building societies, like the Halifax or the Nationwide, is extremely slim, although small building societies have been known to collapse.

With a share account, money can be withdrawn at any time (although for very large amounts you may be required to give a week's notice), and interest is paid twice yearly. In recent years, however, competition between the societies has spurred the development of a whole new range of accounts which offer higher rates for savers. Extra-interest accounts normally require the maintenance of a minimum balance (say, £500) but offer an extra 1.0 or 1.5 per cent a year. Money can still be withdrawn at any time, but if the balance falls below £500, a saver will receive only the ordinary-share rate of interest until the balance is restored. Even higher rates are available when the balance rises above a few thousand pounds.

Other accounts offer a further 0.5 per cent or so if the saver pledges to give ninety days' notice before withdrawals (some societies do not normally pay interest during the ninety-day period). For those who believe they might need to make a withdrawal over the next year or so, this extra 0.5 per cent is unlikely to compensate for the inconvenience or the lost interest. Societies will also offer a slightly higher rate of return if savers promise to save a set amount per month, although there are penalties for withdrawal.

The highest rates of all are available to those who have a very large sum to deposit (£10,000 or more). However, with such a sum there are other opportunities for investment which allow for capital growth as well as interest.

All interest on building-society accounts is paid net of tax, so non-taxpayers should be able to obtain a better rate elsewhere. Since the rate of tax which is deducted is calculated as an average of all the societies' depositors, it is slightly below the basic rate of tax. Higher-rate taxpayers may therefore find building societies competitive.

Banks

Most bank depositors have current accounts which pay no interest at all but provide useful facilities such as chequebooks, cashcards and standing orders. Most of the major banks have now withdrawn the charge they once imposed on cheques if the balance in the current account fell below £100; now they charge only when the customer is in overdraft. The best strategy for the depositor is to keep his current account as close to zero as possible (but always above it). This is difficult to achieve, but it may be worth putting, say, one-third of your salary into a building society or bank deposit account at the start of the month and then transferring it at the end of the month as the current-account balance runs down.

Banks do offer interest-bearing accounts and are trying hard to compete with the building societies. They were helped in doing so by the Budget of 1984, which allowed banks to pay interest net of tax. The simplest interest-bearing account is the deposit account, which pays interest twice yearly. Deposit accounts normally allow customers with a current account at the same bank to switch money smoothly from one account to another. With some accounts the money can be withdrawn only at a few days' notice. Others offer immediate withdrawal from automated teller machines. There are, indeed, few safer places to deposit your money than with one of the country's big four banks. If a major bank were to get into trouble, the government would be forced to rescue it to stabilize the financial system.

Like the building societies, the banks have other accounts which offer more attractive interest rates to those investors who are prepared to deposit a large sum, a regular amount or a moderate sum for a long period. Investors with £2,000–£3,000 of savings should compare the range of accounts offered by the banks and building societies. Remember that all the interest rates are floating and will move up and down with the general level of interest rates. Also bear in mind that the institution which offers the best rate one week may not be the most competitive the next.

National Savings

An even safer investment than either the banks or the building societies is, of course, lending to the government. The main way in which the government borrows from the mass of citizens is through the various national savings schemes, which are operated through post offices. The government offers both taxed and untaxed schemes. The untaxed schemes are mainly in the form of certificates and bonds, which are issued in batches, with each issue setting its own terms. Savings certificates offer a guaranteed (fixed) rate of interest if savers deposit money for a set term, and there are penalties if money is withdrawn before the certificates expire. They are normally sold in £25 units and the maximum holding is £5,000.

To protect the saver against the effects of inflation, the government has introduced index-linked certificates, sometimes called 'granny bonds' because they were designed to appeal to old-age pensioners. The formula for calculating the yield on index-linked certificates is quite complicated. The third issue (made in July 1985), for example, offers not only index-linking but also a bonus interest rate for each successive year that the certificate is held. In the first year the bonus is 2.5 per cent, and the following years offer bonuses of 2.75, 3.25, 4.00 and 5.25 per cent. So if the retail price index rose by a steady 10 per cent a year, £100 invested would become £112.50 after one year (£100 + £10 + £2.50), £126.85 after two years (£112.50 + £11.25 + £3.10) and £190.81 after five years.

It is also possible to save on a regular monthly basis while keeping some protection against inflation, through the index-linked Save As You Earn (SAYE) scheme. Any sum can be saved, from £4 to £50 a month, for five years. Each month the contributions made thus far will receive a supplement to take account of the rise in the retail price index. So the first contribution will be indexed for sixty months, the second for fifty-nine and so on. All gains are free of income tax, capital gains tax and investment-income surcharge. There is also an additional supplement of 0.2 per cent per month (2.5 per cent a year).

After five years investors can opt to leave their money in the scheme for another two years. Despite the fact that they will not make any further contributions, their earnings will continue to be index-linked, and at the end of the two years they will be paid a tax-free bonus equal to two monthly contributions.

Penalties for early withdrawal are not too onerous, although no interest will be paid if money is withdrawn before a year is up. If the scheme is ended between the one- and five-year period, an investor will receive tax-free interest of 6 per cent a year. If he or she should miss a monthly contribution, the contract will be postponed for a month. Six contributions can be missed before the contract is terminated.

The yearly plan, which works on a similar basis of monthly payments, guarantees a fixed rate of return over five years. Investors make contributions only for one year. After that they are sent a certificate, which they must hold for another four years. Further monthly contributions bring more certificates, which will again need to be held for four years. Under the most recent scheme the first year gives a 6 per cent return, and subsequent years give a return of 9.75 per cent. That is an average of 9.28 per cent a year for the full five years. The minimum and maximum monthly investments are £20 and £200 respectively.

Premium bonds are another form of tax-free investment open to the individual investor, but the chances of getting any return at all are fairly small. It has been calculated that a £10 holding of premium bonds held for a year has a one in 100 chance of winning a prize. The probability of hitting the jackpot is one in 12 million. However, despite the poor odds well over £1 billion worth of bonds have been sold since the first were issued by Harold Macmillan.

The government also issues income bonds, which give investors who have deposited a large initial sum a regular monthly income at a higher than average rate of interest. The minimum and maximum investments are £5,000 and £200,000, and the bonds normally have a maximum life of ten years. They may be a particularly good investment for those who have committed a lump sum on retirement. Savers must give three or six months' notice before they can withdraw their funds.

For those who are not able to invest their money for a long period, the National Savings Department offers two rather more conventional accounts. A National Savings ordinary account offers a rather low rate of interest, although the first £70 is tax-free. An investment account is liable to tax but pays a higher rate of interest. A month's notice must be given before withdrawals.

The government, as we saw in Chapters 5 and 8, also issues long-term bonds in large denominations, known as gilts. Most individuals will not have the capital to afford the size of denomination in which gilts are issued, but it is possible to invest in them through the National Savings Stock Register.

The aim of the Stock Register is to allow small investors to invest in the government's gilt-edged securities while paying commissions lower than those charged by stockbrokers. Actual charges are £1 for sums up to £250 and 50 pence for any additional £125. On sales the commission charged is 10 pence for every £10 sold up to £100, with a plateau charge of £1 between £100 and £250. Over £250 there is a further 50 pence charge for every additional £125 sale.

Forms to buy gilts through the Register are available from most post offices. Interest on stock purchased through the Register is paid in full, without deduction of tax, which makes it very attractive to pensioners and other non-taxpayers. Interest may also be paid direct into an investor's bank account. There is no capital gains tax to pay if the gilts increase in value. However, buying and selling through the Register will be rather slower than through a stockbroker, and the price of the gilt on the day the investor decides to sell might not be the price he eventually gets.

Unlike most of the other investments we have so far described, gilts offer the chance of capital gain. As we saw in Chapter 1, the prices of bonds move up and down in inverse proportion to the level of interest rates. So it is possible to buy a gilt at £80 one year, sell it the next at £100 and earn interest in the process. It is also as well to remember that gilts can fall in price as well as rise, so there is a risk which is not involved in holding a building-society deposit. The best time to buy gilts through the Register is when you expect interest rates to fall. Note the distinction between the risk that the borrower will not repay, the *credit risk*, which for gilts is virtually nil, and the risk that the investment will not be profitable, the *market risk*.

Most gilts have a fixed interest rate, which varies according to the general level of rates at the time that they were issued. However, in parallel with the issue of index-linked savings certificates, the government also issues index-linked gilts, which carry a return at a certain level above the rate of inflation. Since the first index-linked gilts were issued inflation has fallen considerably, but as little seems more certain in life than the fact that inflation will rise again, index-linked gilts and savings certificates will no doubt regain their popularity.

Commission must be paid on purchases of gilts through the Register, although the rate of payment will be less than that charged by stockbrokers.

Shares

Ordinary shares are among the traditional investments of the small investor, although, for reasons discussed in Chapter 10, the proportion of shares held by individuals has dwindled since the last war. The British Telecom issue, and other issues like Laura Ashley and Abbey Life, have encouraged hopes that the small investor will return.

One guide published in association with the Stock Exchange* states: 'It is clearly not sensible to spend fifty pounds, a hundred pounds or even a thousand pounds in one company if that is all the capital you have available . . . the expenses involved would make the whole business uneconomic.' Those expenses are the transaction costs involved in buying and selling shares – the broker's commissions and stamp duty. The guide suggests that it is worth investing in shares only if you have £10,000 to £12,000 pounds to spare and the prospect of future surplus income.

Apart from the costs of dealing, there is also the risk – share prices can drop dramatically. Bad news about an individual company may cause its own share price to fall; bad news about a sector of the economy may shake a group of share prices (e.g. those of computer companies); bad news about the economy may cause the prices of *most* shares to tumble. By the time the small investor hears the news, the fall in prices has already occurred.

The best way of dealing with that risk is to spread shareholdings over a wide range of companies. Choosing those companies is really a matter for experts; again, unless the investor has a large amount of capital, dealing in large numbers of shares leads to prohibitive transaction costs.

Which shares should investors buy? It much depends on their attitude to the risk/reward trade-off. If you think the prospect for diamond mining are good, then invest in a mining company. You will be more likely to make your fortune but also more likely to lose your stake than if you had bought shares in ICI. Many investors rashly seize on newspaper reports. A story about booming coffee prices in Brazil will have been known to others long before, and the share price of coffee producers will already reflect the news. The tips given by financial journalists are often useful but not, alas, always right.

One equity trader gave his opinion: 'No one ever went bust by investing

* *Investing in The Stock Exchange*, Professional Publishing Ltd and The Stock Exchange, 1985.

in blue chips.' Blue chips are named after the American gambling convention whereby the most highly valued chips are coloured blue. In share terminology blue chips are big companies with sound records – for example, ICI or BTR. Investing in such companies is relatively safe, although blue-chip companies have been known to fail. Such investments are for those interested in long-term, steady growth rather than a sudden killing.

If there is a hope of a quick killing for the small investor, it lies in new issues. Everyone who bought shares in British Telecom did well. By no means all new issues are so successful, but it may well be that the publicity which surrounds further privatization issues will ensure their success. The investor should read the financial press carefully before such issues. If publicity is generally favourable, it is likely that plenty of other investors will be willing to buy, which will mean that the issue is over-subscribed, and those investors who do not get the shares they want will try to buy the shares on The Stock Exchange, bidding up the price in the process.

Experts have a further rule of thumb: take profits and cut losses. It is luck and not judgement that allows a shareholder to sell at the highest possible price. Better to be sure of a 50 per cent gain than to lose all by trying for 60 per cent. On the loss side, if a share price starts plummeting, the wise investor does not hang on in the Micawberish hope that 'something will turn up'.

How to Follow Share Prices

The *Financial Times* carries each day a host of information about companies and the financial markets. At the back of the paper the previous day's closing share prices are printed. The listings of companies are separated into various groups, which can help the investor to narrow down his or her choice to a particular industry or field.

The columns show the record of the companies. In the two left-hand columns appear the highest and lowest price of the share in the current year. On the right of the company name is the current price (in fact, the average between the buy and sell rate) and its progress, up or down, over the day. The next column, 'Div net', details the amount of dividend paid per share. On the right of 'div net' is the 'C'vr' (cover) column. This figure is calculated by dividing the size of a company's profits by its dividend. If a company has made £100 million in profits and has paid out £40 million in dividends, the 'C'vr' figure will read 2.5, since the company has made enough profit to cover its dividend two and a half times over. In general, the higher the cover figure the better, since it indicates that the company has a strong chance of paying an equivalent, or higher, dividend in future.

Moving further to the right, there is the 'Y'ld Gr's' (Gross Yield) column. This shows the annual return on a shareholding at the current price, assuming the dividend remains unchanged. In the final column the P/E ratio is calculated by dividing the share price by the earnings per share. The latter figure is in itself calculated by dividing the company's after-tax profits by the total number of shares. (A full explanation of the significance of the P/E ratio appears in Chapter 10.)

Making a study of the figures relating to a particular firm, First Leisure, on a random day may help. The company appears in the leisure sector. On Friday, 18 July 1986, its share price was 393 pence. That was 12 pence down on the day and compared with a high and low of 407 and 328 for the year. The last final dividend paid was 6 pence per share, which was covered 3.2 times by its profits (a respectable figure). The yield was only 2.2 per cent, compared with 4.7 per cent for ICI and 4.0 per cent for the leisure sector as a whole, and the P/E ratio of 20 was above the sector average of 16.4.

Those who buy shares will eventually receive a share certificate from the company. Dividends will normally be paid twice a year, at six-monthly intervals. However, it is wise to remember that if a company is in trouble, it will declare only a small dividend, sometimes none at all.

The best way to sell shares is to ring a stockbroker, who will quote an indicative price, which may or may not be the price eventually paid. That will depend on the movement of the share price while the order is being processed. The broker will then send the seller a contract note, stating the terms of a sale. No stamp duty is paid, but sellers do have to pay a further broker's commission.

Capital gains tax of 30 per cent is payable on profits of over £5,900 (as of 1985–6), but share losses can be offset against any profits, and a share loss during the year can be carried forward to offset profits in the following year – though it is a rare private investor who earns enough profits to be subject to capital gains tax.

Unit and Investment Trusts

In Chapter 9 we looked at the importance of the unit and investment trusts. The former have been much the more popular with investors, mainly because it is easier for unit trusts to advertise. Both types of trust are designed to help the small investor by pooling the funds of a whole range of individuals, thereby creating a diversified portfolio of shares. As we have already seen, the small investor on his own is limited to buying shares in two or three companies – a risky business.

Unit trusts create a fund which is divided into units. As the size of the funds increases, so does the price of the unit. There are two prices for each unit (the bid and offer price) depending on whether the trust is buying or selling units. The trust makes money through the spread between the bid and offer prices and also through management charges on the fund. The size of such charges is not always fully explained to potential investors.

It is possible to buy units in trusts which specialize in certain areas of the stock market (e.g. high technology, property or oil). However, as already mentioned, whole areas of the stock market often move together, so the risk-spreading element of investing in such trusts is small. They are designed for the more experienced investor. Unit trusts can also be linked to life assurance in order to allow the investor certain tax advantages. It is possible to invest in such schemes through monthly payments as well as through lump sums.

Over the long term unit trusts have performed very well, earning a return well in excess of the rate of inflation. However, the return on investment trusts can be even higher. This is because, unlike unit trusts, investment trusts can borrow to finance investments (the technique known as *gearing*). Gearing increases the potential return, provided that the trust managers make the right investment decisions. Rather than buy units, an investor buys shares in an investment trust in the same way as he or she would buy shares in any other company.

To market their wares, the investment trusts have increased the range of products on offer. Some schemes automatically reinvest the dividends paid; others allow for regular monthly payments. A new scheme introduced in 1985 by Ivory and Sime and the Tunbridge Wells Equitable Friendly Society links shares in investment trusts with an endowment assurance plan.

This chapter has been able to indicate only the range of potential investments open to the individual. There are many books which explain the schemes in much greater detail, and individual schemes are often described in the financial press. The small investor should consider all the options very carefully before deciding on an investment.

[16] Controlling the City

The previous chapters provide a guide to the variety of financial markets that exist in the UK. This book's intention is to show that the workings of the financial system are not part of some higher system of knowledge but can be understood by the layman. Its aim is not merely to help a few readers to make more money out of their savings accounts or share portfolios; it is also to explain why the financial sector is an important part of the economy, though few profess to understand it. At a time when the City is undergoing many changes it is important that more people should understand their implications.

This last chapter examines the question of whether the City can, and should be, controlled. There are three main schools of thought on this question.

The first, which might be called the 'free market' view, is that financial markets work best when free from regulation. Government regulations, and particularly differential tax treatments, only introduce distortions into the market which prevent it from working efficiently. Free from restrictions, investors will lend where it is most profitable, and borrowers will borrow from the cheapest source. Supply and demand will bring the two sides together.

It is a view which has some evidence to back it. There is little doubt, for example, that mortgage-interest tax relief has diverted the resources of the private sector away from the equity market (and thereby industry) and into property. Stamp tax on share transfers merely makes the London Stock Exchange less competitive than its international neighbours.

The free market view is that the best way to control fraud is to let those in the industry cope with the fraudsters. They are best equipped to spot shady dealing. A statutory system of control will only discourage foreign financial institutions from doing business in London. The result will be that business will go to rival centres, and the UK will lose the foreign-exchange income which the City earns.

Foreign-exchange controls are also a distortion, according to this view. Banks and financial institutions are not involved in a conspiracy to deprive the UK of investment or to weaken sterling. They are merely making rational investment decisions on the basis of the economic information in front of them. The best way to ensure that UK industry receives the investment it needs, and to keep sterling strong, is to make our firms competitive and attractive to investors, not to impose controls and restrictions. If a pension fund is prevented from investing in the areas which it considers most profitable, the people who will suffer will be those who are relying on the funds to give them an adequate pension when they retire.

The opposite viewpoint is held by many on the left. One might call it the 'Trojan horse' view. In essence, the left feels that the City is in a position to frustrate the economic policies and aims of a Labour government. Because of their fear of Labour policies, investors withdraw their money at the hint of a Labour election victory. As a result the FT index falls, sterling plummets and investors divert their funds abroad. On taking office a Labour government is faced with an immediate 'crisis' which makes it difficult for the government to carry out its policies.

According to this argument, investment abroad by pension funds is not in the long-term interests of pension contributors. If UK industry fails to receive the funds it needs, then the standard of living of all UK workers will fall. A higher pension will, in the circumstances, be small compensation. Foreign-exchange controls are essential if investment is to be properly planned.

The problem of regulating the City is simply solved, so proponents of this view maintain. The main City institutions should be nationalized. The argument is well illustrated by Coakley and Harris. They argue that the financial system is 'not just another industry . . . it stands above and over all other economic activities . . . [because] it is the source of the stuff that all industries need, credit and financial capital; it is the means by which all sectors deposit their surplus funds to produce interest and dividends; and within the City are contained the banks, money markets and foreign-exchange markets that handle the cheques, bills of exchange and currency deals that are thrown up by the buying and selling in factory estates and shopping parades throughout the real economy'.*

* Jerry Coakley and Laurence Harris, *The City of Capital* (Basil Blackwell, 1985).

As a result of its importance, the authors argue, the City exerts power, both unconsciously through speculative pressures on exchange and interest rates and consciously through the Governor of the Bank of England and other City spokesmen. The City has used that power time and again in favour of deflation and in order to enhance the City's international role (e.g. in the case of the abolition of exchange controls in 1979).

Although Coakley and Harris recognize that the claim by some commentators that the City has starved UK industry of vital funds does not stand up to rigorous scrutiny,* they still feel that the City's power is too great in a democracy. Nationalization by itself would, they acknowledge, result in few changes in the City's policies. However, if nationalization were accompanied by a positive commitment to invest in British industry and by changes in the ownership of British industry, regeneration of the British economy could occur. The authors accept that such a drastic change would destroy the City's international role. The four hundred or so foreign banks that are now sited in London would gradually drift away. However, they feel that the boost to investment which nationalization would bring would cancel out the lost income from the financial services sector.

Whether such a programme would work is hard to tell. The last French government's programme of nationalization, when it came to power in 1981, was scarcely a roaring success – the administration was forced virtually to reverse its economic policies in 1983. On the other hand, the French economy did not collapse. In the view of Coakley and Harris, however, the French example was not a fair trial, since 'Nothing was done to change the role of finance in the economy, so . . . nationalization had little point to it.'

A programme of banking nationalization in Britain would require a government willing to withstand the inevitable run on sterling, the concerted criticism of the press and perhaps a run on banks by frightened depositors. It seems unlikely that this will ever happen. Certainly, the current Labour leadership is unlikely to pursue such a policy.

There is a third view, held (judging from his public statements) by Sir John Nott, former Conservative Secretary of State for Trade and now

*The Wilson Committee, set up by Prime Minister Callaghan specifically to investigate this question, found little evidence that industry had been denied funds. On the contrary, the problem, in its judgement, was that industry had been uninterested in investment.

chairman of the merchant bank Lazards, and by others. While recognizing that the City is a vital part of the economy, many are dubious that it should pursue its activities untrammelled by regulation. The recent cases of fraud make it clear that the private investor needs protection from the sharper elements in the City. It also seems reasonable to argue that no government should stand back idly and let the City influence the economy as it will.

One particular concern of those who hold this third view is the short-term horizons that obsess today's fund managers. Part of the argument of this book is that financial institutions are required to convert the short-term savings of the private sector into the long-term funds needed by industry. Nowadays, however, fund managers are judged by short-term performance criteria. As a result, they tend to show little patience with companies which have long-term plans. If no short-term results are achieved, the fund managers sell the shares. This in turn leads industrial management to concentrate on short-term results as well. The result is a lack of long-term investment in industry.

Many fund managers may well argue that short-term performance criteria are imposed on them by pension-fund trustees. They in turn are under pressure from the managements of the companies whose pensions they watch over. Whoever is to blame, it seems clear that some way of ensuring that industry receives long-term finance must be found, whether through a free or a government-controlled market.

The free marketeers might argue that any controls on the market will restrict its efficiency. However, there is little evidence that pension-fund managers are particularly efficient at their job. Surveys have found that in many years less than 50 per cent of managers outperformed the FT All-Share index.* A computer programmed to buy only the components of the index would have done better than the majority of professionals. Indeed, there is a growing trend in the USA for so-called 'passive fund management', in which managers merely track a market index.

In the USA financial institutions are controlled by a statutory body, the SEC. Although US banks are inclined to complain about the SEC's regulations, New York has managed to develop as a major financial centre despite the restrictions. Obviously, this is due in part to the dominance of the US economy, but it is hard to argue from the US example

* This may be because there has been a long full market. In their markets, managers tend to outperform indices.

that a statutory system of regulation is inimical to a flourishing financial sector.

The loose regulation system proposed in the Financial Services Bill suits the mid-1980s mood of the free market economy. However, although the tide has turned against more stringent financial regulation, events may conspire to make it popular again. As outlined in Chapter 1, the debt crisis is not yet solved. In the near future it seems likely that at least one debtor nation will find the strain of meeting its repayment requirements intolerable. If a nation defaults, that will hit some British banks hard. The Bank of England may be forced to step in and support them. Such support will be expensive, and it is probable that public pressure to regulate the banks will increase in order to prevent a repeat performance.

Even if the debt crisis fails to explode, the 'Big Bang' may lead to further calls for regulation. The new financial conglomerates will be competing hard for business, and some will undoubtedly lose money. A few may need a Bank of England rescue, in which case the same pressure for more regulation will then occur.

A financial institution's failure may not be the only trigger for a statutory system of regulation. The new system of a Securities and Investment Board with subsidiary self-regulatory organizations may find it impossible to cope with the post-'Big Bang' market. There are many potential conflicts of interest within the new conglomerates. A run of financial scandals would prompt many to argue that only a statutory authority could deal ruthlessly with offenders.

A great deal will, of course, depend on the attitude of the government in power. Mrs Thatcher's administration has long supported the free market. Nevertheless, there has been much disquiet on the Tory backbenches over both the Lloyd's scandals and the Johnson Matthey affair. MPs in marginal seats are unlikely to want the Conservative Party to be tarred with the brush of financial corruption before the next general election. In any case, should the Conservatives lose at the polls, it seems certain that a new Labour government would impose some form of statutory regulation on the City.

The Labour Party also has a policy on overseas investment. It falls far short of the calls for a siege economy of some of its supporters. Nevertheless, it is unlikely to be popular with the City. Shadow Chancellor Roy Hattersley proposes a National Investment Bank which will provide long-term finance for those industries which are likely to promote economic growth. The Bank will be funded by a tax on excessive overseas investment by pension funds.

Will a National Investment Bank work? That will depend on the truth of the proposition that key industries have been deprived of investment. As already noted, the evidence for this view is difficult to assess. However, it is hard to argue that a National Investment Bank would drive away the Eurobond market or the new securities markets established in the wake of the 'Big Bang'.

The City will not be cowed by regulation on the scale currently envisaged. Nor will it be possible for us to do more than keep a check on the way in which the City affects the economy. Nevertheless, the more we understand how the City works, the easier it will be to monitor its excesses and exploit its benefits.

Glossary

ACCEPTANCE HOUSES Institutions which specialize in accepting (guaranteeing) bills of exchange. Sometimes used as a name for the merchant banks, some of whom are members of the Accepting Houses Committee

ADR American Depositary Receipt – mechanism by which foreign shares are traded in the USA

BEARS Investors who believe that share or bond prices are likely to fall

BIG BANG Strictly speaking, the day when minimum commissions were abolished on the Stock Exchange. Also a term used to cover the whole range of changes taking place in the City

BILL A short-term (three months or so) instrument which pays interest to the holder and can be traded. Some bills do not pay interest but are issued at a discount to their face value

BILL MOUNTAIN The bills accumulated by the Bank of England as a result of its over-funding policy

BILL OF EXCHANGE A means of trade payment, used by companies to finance themselves. They pay a fee to an acceptance house, which accepts (guarantees) the bill. They then present the bill to a discount house, which pays them money in advance on the strength of the bill, subject to a discount on its face value. Also known as banker's acceptance and commercial bill

BOND A financial instrument which pays interest to the holder. Most bonds have a set date on which the borrower will repay the holder. Bonds are attractive to investors because they can usually be bought and sold easily

BROKERS Those who link buyers and sellers in return for a commission

BUILDING SOCIETIES Institutions whose primary function is to accept the savings of small depositors and channel them to house buyers in return for the security of a mortgage on the property.

BULLS Investors who believe that share or bond prices are likely to rise

CASH RATIO The proportion of a bank's liabilities which it considers prudent to keep in the form of cash

CERTIFICATE OF DEPOSIT Short-term interest-paying security

CHAPS Clearing House Automated Payment System – an electronic system for settling accounts between the major clearing banks

CHINESE WALL A theoretical barrier within a securities firm which is designed to prevent fraud. One part of the firm may not pass on sensitive information to another if it is against a client's interest

CLEARING BANKS Banks which are part of the clearing system, which significantly reduces the number of interbank payments

COMMERCIAL BANKS Banks which receive a large proportion of their funds from small depositors

COMMITTED SAVINGS Savings made in schemes such as life-assurance policies, whereby the saver guarantees to pay a certain sum each month

COUPON The interest payment on a bond

DEBENTURE A long-term bond issued by a UK company and secured on fixed assets

DEBT CONVERTIBLE Bond which can be converted by an investor into another bond with a different interest rate or maturity

DEBT CRISIS A generic term for the problems which some Third World and Eastern European countries have in repaying loans. If they do default on their loans, many Western banks will be in trouble

DEPRECIATION An accounting term which allows for the run-down in value of a company's assets

DEVALUATION Term, usually applied to currencies, which means simply a one-off loss in value (fall in price) of the currency concerned

DISCOUNT BROKER A broker who offers a no-frills, dealing-only service for a cheap price

DISCOUNT HOUSES Financial institutions which specialize in discounting bills. For years the channel through which the Bank of England operated to influence the financial system

DISCOUNTING The practice of issuing securities at less than their face value. Rather than receiving payment in the form of interest, the holder profits from the difference between the price of the discounted security and its face value

DISINTERMEDIATION Process whereby borrowers bypass banks and borrow directly from investment institutions

DIVIDEND A payment, representing a proportion of profits, that is made to company shareholders

ECGD Export Credit Guarantee Department – government agency which provides trade insurance for exporters

ECU European currency unit – artificial currency composed of the currencies of member states of the European Community

EFTPOS Electronic Funds Transfer at Point of Sale – a scheme which will allow customers to pay retailers with an electronic card. The funds will be automatically debited from a client's account and credited to the retailer's

EMS European Monetary System – under its exchange-rate mechanism Europe's leading currencies (except sterling) are tied together

ENDOWMENT MORTGAGE Mortgage linked to a life-assurance scheme. Only interest is paid during the scheme's life; when the scheme matures, it repays the capital

EQUITY The part of a company owned by its shareholders. Also used as a synonym for share

EQUITY CONVERTIBLE Bond which can be converted into the shares of the issuing company

EUROBOND A bond issued in the Euromarket

EUROCURRENCY Currency traded in the Euromarket (e.g. Eurodollar, Eurosterling)

EUROMARKET The offshore international financial market

EURONOTE A short-term security (under a year) issued in the Euromarket. Under a Euronote facility, a bank agrees to buy or to underwrite a borrower's Euronote programme for a given period of years. The facilities come under various names, like NIFs and RUFs

EXCHANGE EQUALIZATION ACCOUNT Means by which the Bank of England influences exchange rates

EXCHANGE RATE The price at which one currency can be exchanged for another

EXPECTATIONS THEORY The belief that long-term interest rates express investors' views on the likely level of future short-term interest rates. Thus if investors expect short-term interest rates to rise, they will demand a higher interest rate for investing long-term

FACTORING Factors provide both a credit-collection service and short-term finance

FEDERAL RESERVE The US monetary authority which plays a role similar to that of the Bank of England

FINANCE HOUSES Institutions which specialize in funding hire-purchase agreements

FIXED COMMISSIONS Under the old Stock Exchange system, commission paid to brokers was set. This was seen as discouraging competition. Fixed commissions were abolished on 'Big Bang' day – 27 October 1986

FIXED EXCHANGE RATES Currencies with set values against each other which vary only in times of crisis when one or more currencies will revalue or devalue

FLOATING EXCHANGE RATES Currencies whose values against each other are set by market forces

FORFAITING Raising money by selling a company's invoices

FORWARD/FORWARD AGREEMENT Arrangement to lend or borrow a set sum at a set date in the future for a set period at a set rate

FORWARD MARKET Market in which currencies are traded months or years ahead

FRA Forward-Rate Agreement – arrangement to fix a lender's or borrower's interest rate in advance: no capital is exchanged, only the amount by which the agreed rate differs from the eventual market rate

FRN Floating-rate note – a bond which pays an interest rate that varies in line with market rates

FT-30 INDEX Index which tracks the shares prices of thirty leading companies

FUTURES Instruments which give the buyer the right to purchase a commodity at a future date. In the financial markets they are used by those concerned about movements in interest rates, currencies and stock indices

GEARING The ratio between a company's debt and equity. See also leverage

GOLDEN HELLO Payment made to an employee of a rival firm to entice him or her to transfer. One of a whole range of City perks, including golden handcuffs and golden parachutes

GOODWILL An accounting term which describes the intangible assets of a company (e.g. brand names, the skill of the staff)

GOWER REPORT Produced in 1984, its recommendations were the basis of the new regulatory structure in the City

GILTS Bonds issued by the UK government

GROSS YIELD TO REDEMPTION The return which an investor will receive on a bond, allowing for both interest and capital growth, as a percentage of the bond's price

HEDGING The process whereby an institution buys or sells a financial instrument in order to offset the risk that the price of another financial instrument will rise or fall

IDB Inter-dealer broker. An official broker in the government securities (gilts and Treasury Bills) market

IMF International Monetary Fund – supranational organization which has played an important role in the debt crisis

INTEREST A payment made in return for the use of money

INTERNATIONAL EQUITIES Worldwide market in shares. Often traded outside the Stock Exchanges

INVESTMENT TRUST Institution which invests in other firms' shares

ISSUE BY PROSPECTUS Method of selling shares in a company. The prospectus is distributed to potential investors, who are told the price at which shares will be sold

JOBBERS Under the old Stock Exchange system, those who bought and sold shares but could deal with outside investors only through the brokers

JOHNSON MATTHEY BANK Bank which had to be rescued by the Bank of England in 1984 because of its incompetent loan policy

LEASING A kind of rental agreement whereby companies purchase land or equipment and pay for it by instalments

LETTER OF CREDIT A method of financing trade

LEVERAGE In speculative terms, the opportunity for a large profit at a small cost. Also a technical term for the ratio of a firm's debt to its equity

LIBID London Interbank Bid Rate – the rate at which a bank is prepared to borrow from another bank

LIBOR London Interbank Offered Rate – the rate at which a bank is prepared to lend to another bank

LIFE ASSURANCE A form of saving whereby individuals invest a small monthly premium in return for a much larger sum later on. If the saver dies during the scheme, his or her dependants receive a large sum. If the saver does not die, the sum will be paid out at the end of the policy

LIFE COMPANIES Institutions which market life assurance and insurance policies. As a group they are significant investors in British industry

LIFE INSURANCE A scheme whereby individuals pay a premium to a company which guarantees to pay their dependants a lump sum in the event of death. Differs from life assurance in that money is paid only on the death of the saver

LIFFE London International Financial Futures Exchange – exchange for trading futures and options

LIQUIDITY The ease with which a financial asset can be exchanged for goods without the holder incurring financial loss. Thus cash is very liquid, whereas a life assurance policy is not

LIQUIDITY THEORY The principle that investors will demand a greater reward for investing their money for a longer period

LLOYD'S OF LONDON The insurance market

LOAN An agreement whereby one party gives another use of money for a set period in return for the regular payment of interest. Unlike bonds, loans cannot be traded

MAKING A MARKET Buying or selling a financial instrument, no matter what market conditions are like

MARKET SEGMENTATION THEORY The belief that different parts of the debt market are separate and that therefore the yield curve will reflect the different levels of supply and demand for funds within each segment of the market

MATURITY The length of time before a loan or bond will be repaid

MEMBERS' AGENTS People who introduce names to Lloyd's

MERCHANT BANKS Banks that specialize in putting together complicated financial deals. In origin they were closely connected with the financing of trade

MINIMUM LENDING RATE Interest rate which the Bank of England will charge in its role as lender of last resort. Used by the Bank to influence the level of interest rates in the economy

MONEY-AT-CALL Money lent overnight to the discount houses. It can be recalled each morning

MONEY MARKET The market where short-term loans are made and short-term securities traded. 'Short-term' normally means under one year

NAMES Wealthy individuals who provide funds which back Lloyd's insurance policies. If they act as underwriters, they are known as 'working names'

NEW ISSUE The placing of a company's shares on the Stock Exchange

OFFER FOR SALE Method of making a new issue. A bank buys all the shares from the company and sells them to investors at a higher price

OPEC Organization of Petroleum Exporting Countries – which attempts to control the price and production of oil. Had most success in the 1970s

OPTIONS Instruments which give the buyer the right, but not the obligation, to buy or sell a commodity at a certain price. In return the buyer pays a premium. Under this heading are included traded options, currency options and interest-rate options

ORDINARY SHARE The most common, and also the riskiest, type of share. Holders have the right to receive a dividend if one is paid but do not know how much that dividend will be

OVERFUNDING Tactic used by the Bank of England to influence the money supply. It issues more gilts than are needed to finance the budget deficit

OVER-THE-COUNTER MARKET Market where securities are traded outside a regular exchange

PENSION FUNDS The groups that administer pension schemes. They are significant investors in British industry

P/E RATIO Price/earnings ratio – the relationship between a company's share price and its after-tax profit divided by the number of shares

PREFERENCE SHARE Share which guarantees holders a prior claim on dividends. However, the dividend paid will normally be less than that paid to ordinary shareholders

PRINCIPAL The lump sum lent under a loan or bond

PRIVATE PLACEMENT Method of selling securities by distributing them to a few key investors

PSBR Public-sector Borrowing Requirement – the gap between the government's revenue and expenditure

PURCHASING-POWER PARITY The belief that inflationary differentials between countries are the long-run determinants of currency movements

REAL INTEREST RATE The return on an investment once the effect of inflation is taken into account

REPAYMENT MORTGAGE Mortgage on which capital and interest are gradually repaid

REPURCHASE AGREEMENT A deal in which one financial institution sells another a security and agrees to buy it back at a future date

RETAINED EARNINGS Past profits which the company has not distributed to shareholders

RIGHTS ISSUE Sale of additional shares by an existing company

SALE BY TENDER Method of making a new issue in which the price is not set and investors bid for the shares

SAVINGS RATIO The proportion of income which is saved

SCRIP ISSUE The creation of more shares in a company, which are given free to existing shareholders. Also known as a bonus issue

SEAQ Stock Exchange Automated Quotation System – on-screen service for Stock Exchange members which allows them to advertise their share prices

SECURITIES A generic term for tradeable financial assets (bonds, bills, shares)

SECURITIZATION The process whereby untradeable assets become tradeable

SIB Securities and Investment Board – the chief regulatory body under the new financial services system

SINGLE-CAPACITY SYSTEM The old way of dealing on the Stock Exchange. One group (jobbers) bought and sold shares; the other (brokers) linked jobbers with outside investors

SPOT RATE Rate at which currencies are bought and sold today

SPREAD The difference between the price at which a financial institution will buy a security and the price at which it will sell

SRO A body which watches over the practices of a particular part of the financial services industry (e.g. the Stock Exchange). All SROs must in turn answer to the SIB

STAGS Investors who seek to profit from new issues

STOCK EXCHANGE A market where shares and government bonds are exchanged

SWAP An agreement whereby two borrowers agree to pay interest on each other's debt. Under a currency swap they may also repay the capital

SYNDICATED LOAN A loan which several banks have clubbed together to make

TECHNICAL ANALYSTS Those who believe that future price

movements can be predicted by studying the pattern of past movements

TSB Trustee Savings Bank – bank which has traditionally tapped the deposits of small savers

UNDERWRITE To agree, for a fee, to buy securities if they cannot be sold to other investors. In insurance, to agree to accept a risk in return for a premium

UNIT TRUST Institution which invests in shares. Investors buy units whose price falls and rises with the value of the trust's investments

UNLISTED SECURITIES MARKET Market for smaller firms' shares. The regulations are less strict than those of the full Stock Exchange

WARRANTS Instruments which give the buyer the right to purchase a bond or share at a given price. Similar, in principle, to options

WHOLESALE MARKET Another name for the money markets, so called because of the large amounts which are lent and borrowed

YIELD The return on a security expressed as a proportion of its price

YIELD CURVE A diagram which shows the relationship of short-term rates to long-term ones. If long-term rates are above short-term, the curve is said to be positive or upward-sloping: if they are lower, the curve is said to be negative or inverted

ZERO COUPON BOND Bond which pays no interest but is issued at a discount to its face value

Bibliography

Margaret Allen, *A Guide to Insurance* (Pan, 1982)
A. D. Bain, *The Control of the Money Supply*, 3rd edn (Penguin, 1980)
Lloyd Banksen and Michael Lee, *Euronotes* (Euromoney, 1985)
H. Carter and I. Partington, *Applied Economics in Banking and Finance*, 3rd edn (Oxford University Press, 1984)
William Clarke, *Inside the City*, rev. edn (Allen & Unwin, 1983)
C. J. J. Clay and B. S. Wheble, *Modern Merchant Banking*, 2nd edn, rev. by the Hon. L. H. L. Cohen (Woodhead-Faulkner, 1983)
Jerry Coakley and Laurence Harris, *The City of Capital* (Basil Blackwell, 1985)
Brinley Davies, *Business Finance and the City of London*, 2nd edn (Heinemann, 1979)
Peter Donaldson, *Guide to the British Economy*, 4th edn (Penguin, 1976)
Peter Donaldson, *10 × Economics* (Penguin, 1982)
Paul Erdman, *Paul Erdman's Money Guide* (Sphere, 1985)
Paul Ferris, *Gentlemen of Fortune* (Weidenfeld & Nicolson, 1984)
Frederick G. Fisher III, *The Eurodollar Bond Market* (Euromoney, 1979)
Frederick G. Fisher III, *International Bonds* (Euromoney, 1981)
J. K. Galbraith, *Money: Whence it Came, Where it Went* (Penguin, 1977)
Tim Hindle, *The Pocket Banker* (Basil Blackwell/*Economist*, 1985)
Geoffrey Hodgson, *Lloyd's of London: A Reputation at Risk* (Penguin, 1986)
Daniel Hodson (ed.), *Corporate Finance and Treasury Management* (Gee & Co., 1984)
Ken Hoyle and Geoffrey Whitehead, *Money and Banking Made Simple* (Heinemann, 1982)
Investing in the Stock Exchange (Professional Publishing, 1985)
R. B. Johnston, *The Economics of the Euromarket* (Macmillan, 1983)
Geoffrey Knott, *Understanding Financial Management* (Pan, 1985)
Anne O. Krueger, *Exchange-Rate Determination* (Cambridge University Press, 1983)
Harold Lever and Christopher Huhne, *Debt and Danger* (Penguin, 1985)
Robert P. McDonald, *International Syndicated Loans* (Euromoney, 1982)
Hamish McRae and Frances Cairncross, *Capital City* (Methuen, 1985)

J. Maratko and D. Stratford, *Key Developments in Personal Finance* (Basil Blackwell, 1985)

Alex Murray, *101 Ways of Investing and Saving Money*, 3rd edn (Telegraph Publications, 1985)

R. H. Parker, *Understanding Company Financial Statements*, 2nd edn (Penguin 1982)

K. V. Peasnall and C. W. R. Ward, *British Financial Markets and Institutions* (Prentice-Hall, 1985)

F. E. Perry, *The Elements of Banking*, 4th edn (Methuen, 1984)

Brian Phillips, *Building Society Finance* (Van Nostrand Reinhold, 1983)

John Plender and Paul Wallace, *The Square Mile* (Century, 1985)

James Rowlatt, *A Guide to Saving and Investment* (Pan, 1984)

Anthony Sampson, *The Money Lenders* (Coronet, 1981)

Felicity Taylor, *How to Invest Successfully* (Kogan Page, 1983)

Georges Ugeux, *Floating Rate Notes* (Euromoney, 1981)

Rudi Weisweiller, *Introduction to Foreign Exchange* (Woodhead-Faulkner, 1983)

Index

MORE ABOUT PENGUINS, PELICANS, PEREGRINES AND PUFFINS

For further information about books available from Penguins please write to Dept EP, Penguin Books Ltd, Harmondsworth, Middlesex UB7 0DA.

In the U.S.A.: For a complete list of books available from Penguins in the United States write to Dept DG, Penguin Books, 299 Murray Hill Parkway, East Rutherford, New Jersey 07073.

In Canada: For a complete list of books available from Penguins in Canada write to Penguin Books Canada Limited, 2801 John Street, Markham, Ontario L3R 1B4.

In Australia: For a complete list of books available from Penguins in Australia write to the Marketing Department, Penguin Books Australia Ltd, P.O. Box 257, Ringwood, Victoria 3134.

In New Zealand: For a complete list of books available from Penguins in New Zealand write to the Marketing Department, Penguin Books (N.Z.) Ltd, Private Bag, Takapuna, Auckland 9.

In India: For a complete list of books available from Penguins in India write to Penguin Overseas Ltd, 706 Eros Apartments, 56 Nehru Place, New Delhi 110019.

A CHOICE OF PENGUINS

☐ ***Man and the Natural World*** **Keith Thomas**

Changing attitudes in England, 1500–1800. 'An encyclopedic study of man's relationship to animals and plants . . . a book to read again and again' – Paul Theroux, *Sunday Times* Books of the Year

☐ ***Jean Rhys: Letters 1931–66***
Edited by Francis Wyndham and Diana Melly

'Eloquent and invaluable . . . her life emerges, and with it a portrait of an unexpectedly indomitable figure' – Marina Warner in the *Sunday Times*

☐ ***The French Revolution*** **Christopher Hibbert**

'One of the best accounts of the Revolution that I know . . . Mr Hibbert is outstanding' – J. H. Plumb in the *Sunday Telegraph*

☐ ***Isak Dinesen*** **Judith Thurman**

The acclaimed life of Karen Blixen, 'beautiful bride, disappointed wife, radiant lover, bereft and widowed woman, writer, sibyl, Scheherazade, child of Lucifer, Baroness; always a unique human being . . . an assiduously researched and finely narrated biography' – *Books & Bookmen*

☐ ***The Amateur Naturalist***
Gerald Durrell with Lee Durrell

'Delight . . . on every page . . . packed with authoritative writing, learning without pomposity . . . it represents a real bargain' – *The Times Educational Supplement.* 'What treats are in store for the average British household' – *Daily Express*

☐ ***When the Wind Blows*** **Raymond Briggs**

'A visual parable against nuclear war: all the more chilling for being in the form of a strip cartoon' – *Sunday Times*. 'The most eloquent anti-Bomb statement you are likely to read' – *Daily Mail*

A CHOICE OF PELICANS AND PEREGRINES

☐ ***The Knight, the Lady and the Priest***
Georges Duby

The acclaimed study of the making of modern marriage in medieval France. 'He has traced this story – sometimes amusing, often horrifying, always startling – in a series of brilliant vignettes' – *Observer*

☐ ***The Limits of Soviet Power*** **Jonathan Steele**

The Kremlin's foreign policy – Brezhnev to Chernenko, is discussed in this informed, informative 'wholly invaluable and extraordinarily timely study' – *Guardian*

☐ ***Understanding Organizations*** **Charles B. Handy**

Third Edition. Designed as a practical source-book for managers, this Pelican looks at the concepts, key issues and current fashions in tackling organizational problems.

☐ ***The Pelican Freud Library: Volume 12***

Containing the major essays: *Civilization, Society and Religion, Group Psychology* and *Civilization and Its Discontents*, plus other works.

☐ ***Windows on the Mind*** **Erich Harth**

Is there a physical explanation for the various phenomena that we call 'mind'? Professor Harth takes in age-old philosophers as well as the latest neuroscientific theories in his masterly study of memory, perception, free will, selfhood, sensation and other richly controversial fields.

☐ ***The Pelican History of the World***
J. M. Roberts

'A stupendous achievement . . . This is the unrivalled World History for our day' – A. J. P. Taylor

A CHOICE OF PELICANS AND PEREGRINES

☐ ***A Question of Economics*** **Peter Donaldson**

Twenty key issues – from the City and big business to trades unions – clarified and discussed by Peter Donaldson, author of *10 × Economics* and one of our greatest popularizers of economics.

☐ ***Inside the Inner City*** **Paul Harrison**

A report on urban poverty and conflict by the author of *Inside the Third World*. 'A major piece of evidence' – *Sunday Times*. 'A classic: it tells us what it is really like to be poor, and why' – *Time Out*

☐ ***What Philosophy Is*** **Anthony O'Hear**

What are human beings? How should people act? How do our thoughts and words relate to reality? Contemporary attitudes to these age-old questions are discussed in this new study, an eloquent and brilliant introduction to philosophy today.

☐ ***The Arabs*** **Peter Mansfield**

New Edition. 'Should be studied by anyone who wants to know about the Arab world and how the Arabs have become what they are today' – *Sunday Times*

☐ ***Religion and the Rise of Capitalism***
R. H. Tawney

The classic study of religious thought of social and economic issues from the later middle ages to the early eighteenth century.

☐ ***The Mathematical Experience***
Philip J. Davis and Reuben Hersh

Not since *Gödel, Escher, Bach* has such an entertaining book been written on the relationship of mathematics to the arts and sciences. 'It deserves to be read by everyone . . . an instant classic' – *New Scientist*

PENGUIN REFERENCE BOOKS

☐ ***The Penguin Map of the World***

Clear, colourful, crammed with information and fully up-to-date, this is a useful map to stick on your wall at home, at school or in the office.

☐ ***The Penguin Map of Europe***

Covers all land eastwards to the Urals, southwards to North Africa and up to Syria, Iraq and Iran * Scale = 1:5,500,000 * 4-colour artwork * Features main roads, railways, oil and gas pipelines, plus extra information including national flags, currencies and populations.

☐ ***The Penguin Map of the British Isles***

Including the Orkneys, the Shetlands, the Channel Islands and much of Normandy, this excellent map is ideal for planning routes and touring holidays, or as a study aid.

☐ ***The Penguin Dictionary of Quotations***

A treasure-trove of over 12,000 new gems and old favourites, from Aesop and Matthew Arnold to Xenophon and Zola.

☐ ***The Penguin Dictionary of Art and Artists***

Fifth Edition. 'A vast amount of information intelligently presented, carefully detailed, abreast of current thought and scholarship and easy to read' – *The Times Literary Supplement*

☐ ***The Penguin Pocket Thesaurus***

A pocket-sized version of Roget's classic, and an essential companion for all commuters, crossword addicts, students, journalists and the stuck-for-words.

PENGUIN REFERENCE BOOKS

☐ ***The Penguin Dictionary of Troublesome Words***

A witty, straightforward guide to the pitfalls and hotly disputed issues in standard written English, illustrated with examples and including a glossary of grammatical terms and an appendix on punctuation.

☐ ***The Penguin Guide to the Law***

This acclaimed reference book is designed for everyday use, and forms the most comprehensive handbook ever published on the law as it affects the individual.

☐ ***The Penguin Dictionary of Religions***

The rites, beliefs, gods and holy books of all the major religions throughout the world are covered in this book, which is illustrated with charts, maps and line drawings.

☐ ***The Penguin Medical Encyclopedia***

Covers the body and mind in sickness and in health, including drugs, surgery, history, institutions, medical vocabulary and many other aspects. Second Edition. 'Highly commendable' – *Journal of the Institute of Health Education*

☐ ***The Penguin Dictionary of Physical Geography***

This book discusses all the main terms used, in over 5,000 entries illustrated with diagrams and meticulously cross-referenced.

☐ ***Roget's Thesaurus***

Specially adapted for Penguins, Sue Lloyd's acclaimed new version of Roget's original will help you find the right words for your purposes. 'As normal a part of an intelligent household's library as the Bible, Shakespeare or a dictionary' – *Daily Telegraph*